Deliberative Mini-Publics

Involving Citizens in the Democratic Process

Edited by
Kimmo Grönlund, André Bächtiger
and Maija Setälä

First published by the ECPR Press in 2014

The ECPR Press is the publishing imprint of the European Consortium for Political Research (ECPR), a scholarly association, which supports and encourages the training, research and cross-national cooperation of political scientists in institutions throughout Europe and beyond.

ECPR Press
University of Essex
Wivenhoe Park
Colchester
CO4 3SQ
UK

Typeset by ECPR Press

Printed and bound by Lightning Source

British Library Cataloguing in Publication Data

A catalogue record for this book is available from the British Library

Hardback ISBN: 978-1-907301-32-2
Paperback ISBN: 978-1-785521-59-1
PDF ISBN: 978-1-785520-41-9
EPUB ISBN: 978-1-785520-42-6
Kindle ISBN: 978-1-785520-43-3

www.ecpr.eu/ecprpress

ECPR – *Studies in European Political Science* is a series of high-quality edited volumes on topics at the cutting edge of current political science and political thought. All volumes are research-based offering new perspectives in the study of politics with contributions from leading scholars working in the relevant fields. Most of the volumes originate from ECPR events including the Joint Sessions of Workshops, the Research Sessions, and the General Conferences.
Books in this series:

Personal Representation: The Neglected Dimension of Electoral Systems
ISBN: 9781907301162
Edited by Josep Colomer

Political Participation in France and Germany
ISBN: 9781907301315
Oscar Gabriel, Silke Keil, and Eric Kerrouche

Political Trust: Why Context Matters
ISBN: 9781907301230
Edited by Sonja Zmerli and Marc Hooghe

**Practices of Interparliamentary Coordination in International Politics:
The European Union and Beyond**
ISBN: 9781907301308
Edited by Ben Crum and John Erik Fossum

The Political Ecology of the Metropolis
ISBN: 9781907301377
*Edited by Jefferey M Sellers, Daniel Kübler, R. Alan Walks
and Melanie Walter-Rogg*

**Please visit www.ecpr.eu/ecprpress for up-to-date information about new
publications.**

Contents

List of Figures and Tables

List of Abbreviations

BCCA	British Columbia Citizens' Assembly
DP	Deliberative Poll®
DQI	Discourse Quality Index
EPP	European People's Party
ODP	Online Deliberative Polling®
PUC	Public Utility Commission

Contributors

ANDRÉ BÄCHTIGER is a Research Professor of the Swiss National Science Foundation at the University of Lucerne. His research focuses on the challenges of mapping and measuring deliberation and political communication as well as understanding the preconditions and outcomes of high-quality deliberation in the contexts of both representative institutions and mini-publics. His research has been published by Cambridge University Press and in the *Journal of Political Philosophy, Political Studies, Journal of Conflict Resolution, European Political Science Review* and *Acta Politica.* He is currently co-writing a book on *Mapping and Measuring Deliberation* (with John Parkinson), forthcoming from Oxford University Press in 2014.

DIDIER CALUWAERTS is a Democracy Fellow at the Ash Center for Democratic Governance and Innovation at Harvard University and a post-doctoral Fellow of the Research Foundation – Flanders (FWO) at the Vrije Universiteit Brussels. His research deals with deliberative and participatory democracy, ethnic conflict, political psychology and experimental methods.

AUBIN CALVERT holds a PhD in Political Science from the University of British Columbia. Her major research interests include democratic theory and political communication. In particular, her work has focused on the nature, effects and implications of strategic uses of language in democratic politics. Her dissertation also identifies new ways in which democratic institutions might promote good political judgements, despite the fact that the ways people use language in politics are almost always strategic.

JAMES S. FISHKIN holds the Janet M. Peck Chair in International Communication at Stanford University, where he is Professor of Communication and Professor of Political Science. He is also Director of Stanford's Center for Deliberative Democracy and Chair of the Department of Communication. He is the author of a number of books including *Democracy and Deliberation: New directions for democratic reform* (1991), *The Dialogue of Justice* (1992), *The Voice of the People: Public opinion and democracy* (1995), *Deliberation Day* (2004, with Bruce Ackerman) and *When the People Speak: Deliberative democracy and public consultation* (2009).

MARLÈNE GERBER holds a PhD in political science from the University of Bern, Switzerland. Currently, she is Assistant Director of the *Année Politique Suisse*, the Annual Yearbook of Swiss Politics, located at the Institute of Political Science, University of Bern. Her principal research interests include deliberation, political communication and political participation.

KIMMO GRÖNLUND is a Professor of Political Science and the Director of the Social Science Research Institute at Åbo Akademi University. Currently, he is the Principal Investigator of the Finnish National Election Study and Convenor (together with Prof. Brigitte Geißel) of the ECPR Standing Group on Democratic Innovations. His major research interests include political behaviour in general and electoral behaviour in particular; the role of social and institutional trust in democracy, as well as experimental research, especially on citizen deliberation. He has published on these topics in journals such as the *European Political Science Review*, *Political Studies*, *Scandinavian Political Studies*, *Electoral Studies* and the *American Review of Public Administration*.

KAISA HERNE is a Professor of Political Science at the University of Tampere. Her research focuses on questions of justice and fairness, the notion of impartiality, deliberative democracy and voting rules. She uses the experimental method widely in her research. Her articles have been published, for example, in *Inquiry, Political Behavior* and *Political Studies*.

DIMOKRITOS KAVADIAS is an Assistant Professor in the Political Science department of the Free University of Brussels. He also teaches at the social work department at the University of Antwerp. His teaching is mainly on methodology courses. His research interests include social work research, educational sociology, educational policy, political psychology, civic education, political socialisation and political behaviour.

CLAUDIA LANDWEHR is a Professor of Public Policy at Johannes Gutenberg-Universität, Mainz. Her research focuses on theories of deliberative democracy, institutional design and public policy, in particular health politics and policy. She is the author of *Political Conflict and Political Preferences* (ECPR Press 2009) and has published articles in the *Journal of Political Philosophy*, *Contemporary Political Theory*, *European Political Science Review*, *Governance* and *Public Administration*.

MICHAEL E. MORRELL is an Associate Professor of Political Science at the University of Connecticut. Currently, he is working on various current projects related to deliberation, emotions in politics and political participation, including research on the New England Town Meeting in Connecticut and the Oregon Citizens' Initiative Review. Trained as a political theorist who appreciates grounded research, he seeks to bridge the gap between normative theory and empirical political science. He is the author of *Empathy and Democracy: Feeling, thinking and deliberation* (Penn State University Press, 2010), which was recently released in paperback. His research has also appeared in journals such as *Political Research Quarterly*, *Political Behavior*, *Public Opinion Quarterly* and *Public Affairs Quarterly*.

SIMON NIEMEYER is an Australian Research Council (ARC) Future Fellow based at the University of Canberra. He is currently a visiting fellow at the Department of Government at the University of Uppsala. His main research interests cover deliberative democracy and environmental governance, particularly with respect to climate change. In recent years, his specific focus has been on the role of deliberation in the transformation of preferences and the implications of empirical findings for normative democratic theory and the institutionalisation of deliberative democracy. As well as holding his Future Fellowship, he is the lead investigator on an ARC project concerning the possibilities of achieving mass public deliberation and a co-CI on a project on deliberative democracy and achieving just outcomes when adapting to climate change (with David Schlosberg).

IAN O'FLYNN is Senior Lecturer in Political Theory in the School of Geography, Politics and Sociology, Newcastle University, UK. He has held visiting positions at Harvard University, the University of Pennsylvania and the Australian National University. His main research interest is in exploring the implications of deliberative democracy for multicultural and multinational societies. He is the author of *Deliberative Democracy and Divided Societies* (2006) and his articles have appeared in journals such as the *British Journal of Political Science, Government and Opposition, Political Studies* and *Politics, Philosophy and Economics*.

MATT RYAN is a Senior Research Assistant at the Centre for Citizenship, Globalisation and Governance (C2G2) at the University of Southampton, where he collaborates on the design and implementation of field experiments that assess the impact of social information on citizen contributions to public services. He is also a project collaborator on www.participedia.net. His research focuses on political and civic participation, contemporary democratic theory, innovations in social science research methodology and its pedagogy. His doctoral research applies fuzzy-set qualitative comparative analysis to cumulate knowledge on democratic innovations.

MAIJA SETÄLÄ is a Professor in Political Science at the University of Turku, Finland. Setälä received her PhD at the London School of Economics in 1997. She specialises in democratic theory, political trust, direct democracy and democratic innovation and has published a number of articles and books on these topics. Setälä has also applied experimental methods as she collaborates with a group of researchers organising experiments on citizen deliberation. Her articles have been published in, for example, the *European Journal of Political Research, Political Studies* and *European Political Science Review.*

GRAHAM SMITH is a Professor of Politics at the Centre for the Study of Democracy (CSD), University of Westminster. He has written a number of books and essays on aspects of democratic theory and practice, including *Democratic Innovations: Designing institutions for citizen participation* (Cambridge

University Press, 2009). He is on the Executive Committee for *Participedia*, an open-knowledge global platform for researchers and practitioners in the field of democratic innovation and public engagement.

GAURAV SOOD is a National Fellow at the Hoover Institution at Stanford University. Gaurav is currently exploring antecedents and consequences of group-based affect, focusing mainly on political groups. In previous work on the topic, he found that in the US, in recent times, many of those who identify with a political party hold negative stereotypes about supporters of the main opposing party. In his recent work, he has explored the impact of group-based affect (and reasoning) on ideological accountability. He finds that elites of the respondent's own party are only modestly penalised for taking extreme positions. His other research interests include exploring how people learn from data and documenting biases in the data accessible to people.

KIM STRANDBERG holds a PhD in Political Science and is a Senior Researcher and Adjunct Professor at the Social Science Research Institute at the Department of Politics and Administration of Åbo Akademi University (Finland). His primary areas of research are political communication, citizen deliberation and political uses of the Internet. He has published on these topics in journals such as *Party Politics*, *New Media & Society*, *Information Polity*, *Scandinavian Political Studies* and *Journal of Information Technology and Politics*.

MARK E. WARREN holds the Harold and Dorrie Merilees Chair for the Study of Democracy at the University of British Columbia. He is especially interested in democratic innovations, civil society and democratic governance, and political corruption. Warren is author of *Democracy and Association* (Princeton University Press), editor of *Democracy and Trust* (Cambridge University Press) and co-editor of *Designing Deliberative Democracy: The British Columbia Citizens' Assembly* (Cambridge University Press 2008). His work has appeared in journals such as the *American Political Science Review*, *American Journal of Political Science* and *Political Theory*. He is currently working with an international team on a project called *Participedia*, which uses a web-based platform to document democratic innovations around the world.

Foreword

Kimmo Grönlund, André Bächtiger and Maija Setälä are three of the major players in a remarkable global network of scholars working at the interface of democratic theory, political practice, and empirical inquiry. Other key members of this network make important contributions to this collection. Together, they consider how democratic ideals can be put into practice, and how we might need to re-think those ideals in light of the lessons of experience, focusing on the key institution of the mini-public. Mini-publics might seem to be a relatively recent invention, but they embody some democratic ideals and hopes of very long standing, promising cures for at least some of the ills that afflict contemporary democracies – though they might also find application in weakly democratic or even non-democratic contexts, such as the international system.

Deliberative mini-publics are being implemented to an ever-increasing degree in many different parts of the world – also at international, even global levels – and have firmly established themselves as an essential part of any agenda to deepen democracy. Be it in contemplating the risks of new technologies, the merits of alternative electoral systems, how different sides in deeply divided societies might co-exist more productively, what global actions should be taken on issues like climate change, how city plans should be developed, how budgets should be allocated, it seems there are no limits to the range of topics to which mini-publics might be applied. Of course, getting governments, international organizations, and others to attend to what mini-publics recommend is another matter entirely, and contributors to this collection do indeed address tough questions about how deliberative mini-publics might have more of an impact. Equally tough questions arise when it comes to the recruitment of participants and design details of mini-publics, and how they might measure up to democratic ideals in different sorts of contexts; these questions too are addressed here. Though deliberative mini-publics have received plenty of attention, this is the first book to bring together a range of key authors to generate a synoptic view of the democratic prospects and problems of this crucial kind of deliberative innovation.

Critics might point out that they there is more to democracy than deliberation, and more to deliberation than the mini-public, and that is true enough. But mini-publics show that given the chance, ordinary people can be effective and competent participants in politics on complex and divisive issues, that innovative institutional designs can contribute to more reflective public opinion formation and representation, and help us understand how authentic deliberation might be possible in larger settings. For these reasons and many others, deliberative mini-publics merit our attention, and there is no better place for the interested reader to start than with this book.

John Dryzek
Centenary Professor, ANZSOG Institute for Governance,
University of Canberra

Preface

The first ideas of putting together a volume on deliberative mini-publics emerged in a panel with the same theme at the ECPR General Conference in Potsdam (2009). After that, we started thinking both about the content and the contributors of such a volume. We felt that the time had come to reflect upon the practice of deliberative mini-publics in a systematic manner as well as to generate some ideas for how mini-publics could be designed and used in even more effective and policy-relevant ways, given the fact that their impact on public policy is frequently meagre or absent. We drafted an outline for the book and then contacted potential authors. These consist of both established scholars who have studied deliberative mini-publics in-depth and younger colleagues having conducted innovative research on that topic. The initial responses were positive throughout and we are very pleased with the final outcome.

We would first like to thank the ECPR Press and especially Dario Castiglione for their interest in and support of this volume. The two anonymous referees have made valuable comments on the individual chapters and the structure of the volume, helping to enhance its coherence. Many of the individual chapters have been presented at various conferences and workshops, especially at the Conference Deliberative Democracy in Action in Turku/Åbo (Finland) in May 2012. We would like to thank participants at these venues for stimulating and encouraging comments on the chapters. We also would like to thank Maija Karjalainen for editorial assistance; she has been an essential helping hand in technical matters and also an excellent interlocutor on substantial issues. Finally, we acknowledge the generous financial support by Academy of Finland (Decision no. 251222), the Swiss National Science Foundation (PP00P1_128576 and 100017_140265, and the Centre of Excellence 'Democracy – A Citizen Perspective' at Åbo Akademi University.

Kimmo Grönlund, André Bächtiger and Maija Setälä
July 2014

Chapter One

Introduction

Kimmo Grönlund, André Bächtiger and Maija Setälä

Democratic innovations that engage citizens in political decision-making processes are increasingly popular and various participatory practices have been implemented across the world (Smith 2009: 1). This book is about one particular type of democratic innovation, namely *deliberative mini-publics*. The term deliberative mini-public is used to refer to forums, usually organised by policy-makers, where citizens representing different viewpoints are gathered together to deliberate on a particular issue in small-N groups (Fung 2003; Goodin and Dryzek 2006).

To some extent, the growing interest in mini-publics and other democratic innovations can be explained by concern about the declining trend in partisan forms of political participation. Established democracies have witnessed a clear decrease in traditional forms of political participation, such as voting and party membership, and a simultaneous expansion of new issue-based forms of political action (Manin 1997; Norris 2002; Dalton 2006; Dalton 2008). In this situation, deliberative mini-publics and other democratic innovations can be seen as a means to increase the responsiveness of policy-making to public opinion.

Even though some scholars, most notably Schumpeter (1994[1943]), have supported a minimalist form of democracy in which political elites compete against each other at elections and the *vox populi* is restricted to the act of voting, most students of democracy value citizen participation as a key to democratic government. In his seminal work *Democracy and its Critics*, Dahl (1989) argued that there is a need for mechanisms that allow citizens to participate in the process of making collective decisions. His suggestion was to establish a citizen forum called *mini-demos* (or *mini-populus*), where one thousand randomly selected citizens would deliberate and form opinions on actual political issues. One mini-demos could decide on the agenda of issues, whereas each major issue would have its own mini-demos. The judgement of a mini-demos would be the verdict of the demos itself (Dahl 1989: 340). At the same time, the mini-demos would help to address the pressing problems of contemporary democracies, such as the increased complexity and the scale of political issues.

Since the 1960s, the goal of participatory democrats has been to promote political engagement among citizenry (Pateman 1970). According to this view, liberal democracies guarantee the right to vote but they do not guarantee equal opportunities for citizens to take part in democratic discourse and decision-making. For example, people who have scarce economic resources are not as likely to take part in collective decisions as their wealthier fellow citizens and, if they do, their voices may not be heard (Dahl 1989: 114–8). More recently, Pateman (2012) has called the task of creating a participatory society a struggle for democratising democracy. She compares it with the long fight for universal suffrage and expects it to be a similarly drawn-out process.

Participatory democrats emphasise the educative effects of civic activity. People learn by doing – taking part politically educates them to think publicly as citizens. For example, Barber (1984: 152) promotes the goal of universal participation where 'every citizen is his own politician, without the intermediary of expertise'. As an element of his programme of reforming democracy, Barber (1984: 267–81) suggests the institutionalisation of 'strong democratic talk', for example, through deliberative 'town meetings' for which representatives are chosen by lot among citizens. Town meetings would also be organised to deliberate issues of regional and national scale; interactive telecommunications technologies would be used to facilitate deliberations.

The earliest designs that would nowadays be regarded as deliberative mini-publics, planning cells and citizens' juries, date from the 1970s. The development of these formats was motivated by the need to bridge the observed gap between citizens and elected representatives and other policy-makers (Crosby 1995). The Danish model of consensus conferences, developed in the 1980s by the Danish Board of Technology, was more specifically designed to help policy-making on technically complex issues (Joss 1998). Although the basic ideas and formats of deliberative mini-publics were elaborated by democratic theorists and practitioners before the 'deliberative turn' in the 1990s, scholarly interest in mini-publics has certainly been boosted by developments in democratic theory. The deliberative turn in democratic theory shifted the focus to democratic discourses in various contexts, such as parliaments and the public spheres of civil society.

As Chambers (2012: 53) puts it, 'deliberative democracy as a theoretical perspective invites scholars to shift the study of democratic regimes from a voting-centric research agenda to a deliberative- or talk-centric research agenda'. Moreover, theoretical debate on deliberative democracy has certainly influenced the practices of deliberative mini-publics. Some deliberative democrats have been particularly interested in developing methods of engaging citizens in reasoned and balanced deliberations (Fishkin 1991). Deliberative Polling®, developed by James Fishkin and Robert Luskin in the early 1990s, was designed to address the problems of measuring public opinion through raw opinion polls. The aim of deliberative polling is to provide a method of measuring enlightened and reflected public opinion, by allowing people to gain information and deliberate on a political issue in small-n groups.

Deliberative Polls® have become a 'gold standard' in organising deliberative mini-publics (Mansbridge 2010). In fact, Fishkin's (2009: 81) idea of creating a 'microcosm' of the people through random sampling reflects the original idea of Dahl's mini-demos. Examples of recent deliberative mini-publics aimed at engaging a representative sample of the demos include the famous British Columbia Citizen Assembly, concerned with working out a new electoral system (Warren and Pearse 2008; Fournier *et al.* 2010); the Australian Citizens' Parliament, dealing with future of Australian democracy (Carson *et al.* 2013); and the Belgian 'G1000', trying to set a citizen-based political agenda in times of deadlocked politics (Derenne 2012).

Despite widespread scholarly and public interest in deliberative mini-publics, their overall political impact has been relatively modest so far (*see*, for example, Papadopoulos and Warin 2007). Mini-publics have typically been initiated by policy-makers as *ad hoc* consultative bodies. Unlike some other democratic innovations, such as different forms of direct democracy and certain practices of participatory budgeting, deliberative mini-publics do not usually involve the authorisation of participating citizens to make public decisions. There have been doubts whether these kinds of consultative, top-down forums can actually empower citizens or whether they are just forms of token participation, expected to provide legitimation for the government. For example, Carole Pateman (2012) has recently criticised deliberative mini-publics on these grounds. The question of the 'uptake' of deliberative mini-publics in decision-making seems crucial, therefore. More generally, it must be asked whether the processes and outcomes of mini-publics can be 'scaled up' in ways that would actually improve the overall quality of democracy.

These criticisms notwithstanding, there is still much hope among theorists – and practitioners as well – that deliberative mini-publics contribute to the renewal of representative democracy (for example, Ferejohn 2008). Therefore, it is essential to make them the object of in-depth scientific inquiry. Only then can we judge whether and how much deliberative mini-publics live up to the hopes of theorists and practitioners. This volume attempts to shed light on this crucial question.

The aim and scope of the book

The book offers a panoply of insights into deliberative mini-publics, ranging from definitional issues, design features, processes and outcomes, to impacts. Given the sheer quantity of (deliberative) mini-publics in contemporary policy-making, we do not attempt to provide an exhaustive overview of them. In particular, we do not address the manifold experiences with mini-publics in the administrative realm, such as healthcare provisioning. Following Goodin and Dryzek (2006), we focus on more idealised notions of deliberative mini-publics, including representativeness of participant selection and the quality of deliberative interactions among participants. As such, our book is guided by theories of democracy, mostly but not exclusively by theories of deliberative democracy. Our book is also motivated by the specific feature of mini-publics that they provide opportunities to study central claims of democratic theory and certain hypotheses in political science.

The individual chapters deal with the basic ideas of mini-publics and issues related to their design, as well as the evaluation of processes and outcomes of deliberation. Ultimately, the book aims to answer the questions of how mini-publics *should* be designed and how they *should* be used in order to achieve their potential to improve the quality of democracy. The book consists of four parts.

Part One deals with conceptual issues and normative ideas related to mini-publics. Part Two addresses questions pertaining to the design and modalities of mini-publics. Deliberative processes in mini-publics and their outcomes are analysed in Part Three. Part Four discusses the possible roles of mini-publics in democratic systems.

Part One of the book tackles the questions of how deliberative mini-publics should be defined and what kinds of normative ideas they are based upon. In Chapter Two, Matthew Ryan and Graham Smith discuss which different endeavours involving citizens in political talk can be defined as deliberative mini-publics. Smith and Ryan emphasise recruitment and find that the most restrictive definition is used in the Deliberative Poll®, which, similarly to Dahl's idea, recruits its participants through random selection. A broader definition of mini-publics does not require pure random selection of participants but still attributes importance to 'employing quasi-random sampling techniques'. These mini-publics include citizens' juries, consensus conferences, planning cells and the British Columbia Citizens' Assembly as well as 21st Century Town Meetings®. Smith and Ryan also discuss a third, even broader definition of mini-publics that moves beyond Dahl's original idea in that these citizen forums recruit people on the basis of self-selection only.

In Chapter Three, James S. Fishkin provides a presentation and arguments in favour of his application of the mini-public, the Deliberative Poll®. He discusses the rationale behind four models of democracy: competitive; elite-based, participatory and deliberative. These models are compared with each other according to normative criteria of political equality, participation, deliberation and non-tyranny. Fishkin considers various ways in which deliberative polls could be used in the context of different models of democracy.

In Chapter Four, Ian O'Flynn and Gaurav Sood provide a constructive critique of deliberative polls and other mini-publics. They also turn to Dahl and his requirement of political equality as the most basic democratic standard. Five criteria are discussed in relation to deliberative mini-publics: inclusion, effective participation, enlightened understanding, voting equality at the decisive stage and control of the agenda. These criteria are used to point out certain problems in the current design and use of mini-publics.

Part Two addresses specific issues related to the design and implementation of deliberative mini-publics. In Chapter Five, Maija Setälä and Kaisa Herne discuss the prospects of the use of deliberative mini-publics as 'laboratories' of democratic deliberation and clarify the relationship between normative theory and empirical research. They identify a need for controlled experiments in addition to the commonly used quasi-experimental designs. Also, the importance of increased validity by repeating the test of the hypothesis is emphasised.

Claudia Landwehr deals with a specific feature of mini-publics in Chapter Six. Her focus is on the role of facilitation in small-N groups. She presents a typology of how a facilitator in group deliberation can act and analyses how these different roles may affect deliberation and its outcomes. She identifies four different roles – the chair, the moderator, the mediator and the facilitator – and calls for controlled studies in which the role is altered in order to see how this intermediary influences deliberation in practice.

Chapter Seven, authored by Kim Strandberg and Kimmo Grönlund, deals with online deliberation. Already Barber (1984) and Dahl (1989) mentioned the possibility of using 'telecommunications' in order to make deliberation easier in large-scale societies but their books were written before the internet was universal. Strandberg and Grönlund present both general ideas of online discussion for democratic purposes and specific experiments on online deliberation. They compare designs and outcomes in order to summarise the knowledge so far and conclude that an intensive dialogue between scientists and policy-makers is still needed before online deliberation can be made an integral part of the decision-making process.

Part Three turns to the deliberative process and its outcomes. In Chapter Eight André Bächtiger and Marlène Gerber provide an exploratory analysis of deliberation in Europolis, a transnational Deliberative Poll®. Their starting point is the potential 'damage' of being too polite in deliberation. Too 'gentlemanly' conversations might in some cases be less epistemically fruitful than more contestatory modes of communication. Bächtiger and Gerber find that opinion diversity among the participants in the beginning did not guarantee vigorous contestation and a 'clash of conflicting arguments'. This is an important finding when the design of deliberative mini-publics is thought of.

In Chapter Nine, Didier Caluwaerts and Dimokritos Kavadias provide evidence from a Belgian bilingual deliberative mini-public. Their starting point is the generally held belief that democracy in divided societies can only be stable if it is left to elites and citizens remain rather passive subjects. Caluwaerts and Kavadias find that citizens in divided groups are able to act in a deliberative manner and even generate high-quality deliberation. They conclude: 'Rather than undermining rational and inclusive decision making, division seems to create openness towards others by confronting people with the radically different views of the other side'.

In Chapter Ten, Michael Morrell discusses how three types of biases can pose threats to 'deliberative success' in mini-publics. First, attribution bias refers to the way in which individuals evaluate their own behaviour and the behaviours of others. Second, in-group versus out-group bias concerns the fact that people are usually positively disposed toward people with whom they identify, whereas they have more negative views of those unlike them. Third, there is a risk of information-processing biases. Morrell discusses confirmation bias, in which people tend to confirm their prior beliefs and disconfirm competing beliefs, and the common-knowledge effect, which means people tend to focus on information shared by all participants prior to discussion. Morrell encourages researchers to acknowledge these biases when designing mini-publics.

Part Four of the book looks at the possible impacts of deliberative mini-publics. Rather than reviewing earlier experiences of mini-publics, the aim is to envision innovative ways of using mini-publics in order to improve the quality of public debate and decision-making. Simon Niemeyer ponders the possibility that the deliberative processes of mini-publics could be replicated among the public at large. His view seems to run counter to those deliberative democrats who emphasise the 'division of deliberative labour' (such as Richardson 2002).

In Chapter Twelve, Aubin Calvert and Mark E. Warren address framing as a problem for democratic deliberation. To date, the framing literature has not been connected with the theory and practice of deliberation. Calvert and Warren make a first attempt in this direction. They point out different kinds of framing effects that are harmful and suggest that deliberative mini-publics could be used as a remedy for these.

In Chapter Thirteen, André Bächtiger, Maija Setälä and Kimmo Grönlund analyse the extent to which different designs of mini-publics can enhance two central normative goals of deliberative democracy, that is, inclusion and epistemic fruitfulness. The chapter argues that there is scope for improvement both in terms of the (micro) design of mini-publics and their macro-political role in public decision-making. Concrete suggestions are made on how mini-public deliberations could be organised in order to make them more consequential in the policy-making process and among the public at large.

References

Barber, B. (1984) *Strong Democracy: Participatory democracy for a new age*, Berkeley: University of California Press.

Carson, L., Gastil, J., Hartz-Karp, J. and Lubensky, R. (eds) (2013) *The Australian Citizens' Parliament and the Future of Deliberative Democracy*, PSU Press.

Chambers, S. (2012) 'Deliberation and mass democracy', in J. Parkinson and J. Mansbridge (eds) *Deliberative Systems: Deliberative democracy at the large scale*, Cambridge: Cambridge University Press, pp. 52–71.

Crosby, N. (1995) 'Citizens juries: one solution for difficult environmental questions', in O. Renn, T. Webles and P. Wiedemann (eds) *Fairness and Competence in Citizen Participation*, Kluwer: Dordrecht, pp. 157–74.

Dahl, R. A. (1989) *Democracy and its Critics*, New Haven, CT and London: Yale University Press.

Dalton, R. J. (2006) *Citizen Politics: Public opinion and political parties in advanced industrial democracies*, 4th edition, Washington, DC: CQ Press.

— (2008) *The Good Citizen: How a younger generation is reshaping American politics*, Washington, DC: CQ Press.

Derenne, B. (2012) *G1000 Final Report: Democratic innovation in practice*, Legal deposit D-2012–8490–09, Brussels: G1000.

Dryzek, J. S. (2000) *Deliberative Democracy and Beyond: Liberals, critics, contestations*, Oxford: Oxford University Press.

Ferejohn, J. (2008) 'Conclusion: The Citizens' Assembly model' in M. E. Warren and H. Pearse (eds) *Designing Deliberative Democracy: The British Columbia Citizens' Assembly*, Cambridge: Cambridge University Press, pp. 192–213.

Fishkin, J. S. (1991) *Democracy and Deliberation: New directions for democratic reform*, New Haven, CT: Yale University Press.

— (2009) *When the People Speak*, Oxford: Oxford University Press.

Fournier, P., van der Kolk, H. Kenneth Carty, R. Blais, A. and Rose, J. (2010) *When Citizens Decide: Lessons from Citizens' assemblies on electoral reform*, Oxford: Oxford University Press.

Fung, A. (2003) 'Survey article: recipes for public spheres: eight institutional design choices and their consequences', *Journal of Political Philosophy* 11 (3): 338–67.

Goodin, R. E. and Dryzek, J. S.(2006) 'Deliberative impacts: the macro-political uptake of mini-publics', *Politics and Society* 34: 219–44.

Joss, S. (1998) 'Danish consensus conferences as a model of participatory technology assessment: an impact study of consensus conference on Danish Parliament and Danish public debate', *Science and Public Policy* 25 (1): 2–22.

Manin, B. (1997) *The Principles of Representative Government*, Cambridge: Cambridge University Press.

Mansbridge, J. (2010) 'Deliberative Polling as the gold standard', *The Good Society*, 19 (1): 55–62.

Norris, P. (2002) *Democratic Phoenix: Reinventing political activism*, Cambridge: Cambridge University Press.

Papadopoulos, Y. and Warin, P. (2007) 'Are innovative, participatory and deliberative procedures in policy making democratic and effective?', *European Journal of Political Research* 46: 445–72.

Pateman, C. (1970) *Participation and Democratic Theory*, Cambridge: Cambridge University Press.

— (2012) 'Participatory democracy revisited', *Perspectives on Politics*, 10 (1): 7–19.

Richardson, H. S. (2002) *Democratic Autonomy: Public reasoning about the ends of policy*, Oxford: Oxford University Press.

Smith, G. (2009) *Democratic Innovations: Designing institutions for citizen participation*, Cambridge: Cambridge University Press.

Schumpeter, J. (1943/1994) *Capitalism, Socialism and Democracy*, London: Routledge.

Warren, M. and Pearse, H. (eds) (2008) *Designing Deliberative Democracy: The British Columbia Citizens' Assembly*, Cambridge: Cambridge University Press.

Chapter Two

Defining Mini-Publics

Matthew Ryan and Graham Smith

Contemporary democratic theory and, in particular, work on deliberative democracy, is notable for the degree to which it has taken both an 'institutional' and 'institutionalised' turn. The institutional turn implies an increased focus on the ways in which citizen engagement is shaped by its context, with particular attention to the extent to which different rules and norms enable (or otherwise) participation and deliberation on the part of citizens. The institutionalised turn refers to a focus on a set of innovative institutions that enable citizens to play a more or less formal role in the political decision-making process. It is in this context that the term 'mini-public' has emerged: a class of institutions that directly engage citizens, promote democratic deliberation and have, at times, been institutionalised into contemporary decision-making processes.

But the range of institutional forms captured by the term mini-publics is contested: there is no consistent usage of the concept. Ensuring a degree of clarity (without necessarily expecting complete agreement) in how the term is used is important for concerted scientific investigation within the research community and for the communication of findings to those engaged in the (re-)design of decision-making institutions. It is with this ambiguity in definition that this chapter engages. Initially, we locate the interest in mini-publics in relation to recent attempts to define an organising principle that represents the broad set of institutional and institutionalised practices of citizen engagement that have caught the interest of democratic theorists. We then turn our attention to the literature on mini-publics, highlighting the differences in the range of institutions that theorists have included under the term and what is at stake in relation to these competing definitions. The chapter then offers some reflections on why these particular institutions have been of interest to deliberative democrats and concludes with thoughts on how research on mini-publics might be taken forward.

Searching for an organising principle

The traditional democratic institutional concerns of political science have been broadly electoral and constitutional in nature. This has been complemented by an interest in novel, radical and autonomous forms of protest activity: the politics and practices of new social movements. The attention given by democratic theorists to these two very different forms of political engagement and institutions meant that a wide range of democratic institutions was typically overlooked: institutions that had been specifically crafted to provide an occasion for citizens to engage directly in the political process beyond electoral or protest activities. As democratic theorists' attention turned to questions of participation and deliberation in democratic decision-making on the part of citizens, the variety of institutional forms and experiments that have been organised around the world came into focus, offering new empirical cases to explore in light of theoretical developments. This naturally led to attempts to define an organising principle to distinguish the characteristics of these practices (Fung 2003;[1] Smith 2009; Warren 2009). Mark Warren has offered the category of 'governance-driven democratization':

> It is within this domain that we are seeing a rapid development of what are often called 'citizen engagement' and 'public engagement' processes – that is, everything from the public hearings and mandatory public comment periods that emerged after World War II, to the stakeholder meetings that began to spread in the 1980s, and to newer consensus conferences, town hall meetings, citizen juries, citizen assemblies, deliberative polling, online dialogues, deliberative planning, participatory budgeting, study circles, planning cells, collaborative learning, and even participatory theatre […] There are, most probably, nearly one hundred named processes. Typically, these processes use the languages of participation and deliberation; they are designed for particular policy problems; they bypass the formal institutions of democracy, and they do not involve protest, lobbying, or obstruction (Warren 2009: 5–6).

For Warren, governance-driven democratisation has a number of characteristics: it emerges as a 'response to democratic deficits'; 'tends to be elite-driven'; its 'evolution is often de-linked from electoral democracy'; and it has 'an important capacity to bring into existence dynamic, serial, and overlapping peoples and constituencies based on the 'all affected' principle in contrast to pre-defined and relatively static territorial constituencies' (*Ibid.*: 5).

Warren makes the links with deliberative democracy explicit within his analysis: governance-driven democratisation enables deliberation in a way that is not possible in the electoral arena or the broader public sphere.

> governance-driven democratization provides some specific kinds of deliberative opportunities that exist neither in the electoral arena nor in the public sphere. In electoral democracy, deliberation is often undercut by the strategic features of campaigns, elections, and party politics. Public sphere deliberation runs the gamut of possibilities, and is essential to public opinion formation. But public discussion is often poorly linked to the learning, problem solving, and sustained attention necessary for policy decisions (*Ibid.*: 10).

---

1. Fung's early approach to classifying this range of practices will be discussed later in the chapter, since he used the term 'mini-public' as his organising principle.

Graham Smith offers another attempt at defining the broad field of study, namely 'democratic innovations': institutions that have been 'specifically designed to increase and deepen citizen participation in the political decision-making process' (Smith 2009: 1). Again, Smith points to the problems associated with democratic deficits as a driver for the emergence of democratic innovations. The term 'innovations' reflects the 'departure from the traditional institutional architecture that we normally attribute to advanced industrial democracies' (*Ibid.*). For Smith, there are two defining characteristics of such democratic innovations: they engage citizens (rather than representatives of organised interests) and they play a role in the political decision-making process (*Ibid.*: 2).

Warren and Smith's attempts to define a field of practice share many similarities. There are, however, some differences in scope and emphasis. For example, Smith extends the reach of institutions under his conception of democratic innovations to include direct legislation. While direct democracy in the form of citizens' initiatives, popular referendums and the like is commonplace in some polities, it is taken to be an innovation when it diffuses beyond these jurisdictions. The exclusion of direct legislation within Warren's account of governance-driven democratisation is indicative of the priority he places on institutions that embody deliberation: the practice of direct legislation bears more resemblance to electoral politics, where 'deliberation is often undercut by the strategic features of campaigns, elections, and party politics' (Warren 2009: 10). In comparison, for Smith, deliberation is only one of a number of democratic goods that democratic institutions might realise: other democratic goods may well take priority in designing forms of citizen engagement that can still be designated democratic innovations.

Mini-publics: A contested field

The organising principles 'governance-driven democratisation' and 'democratic innovations' capture a wide range of institutions designed to engage citizens. Within this range we find the contested class of institutions termed 'mini-publics'. Within the literature on mini-publics, we distinguish a range of definitions that can be understood along a continuum. These range from the most expansive definition offered by Archon Fung (2003) through to the most restrictive account defended by James Fishkin (2009); contrasting intermediate definitions are offered by Goodin and Dryzek (2006) and Smith (2009). These four authors/essays have been selected because they engage explicitly with the definitional question and because they are increasingly referenced within the literature. While many other writers have used the term mini-public, it is not with the same degree of accuracy or reflection on the field.

Text box 2.1: Definitions of mini-publics

Mini-publics – what's in and out?

Restrictive definition includes:

- *Deliberative Poll$^\circledR$ (DP):* Random selection of 250–500 citizens brought together for one or two days to hear evidence from experts and deliberate in small groups. Pre- and post-event opinion polls allow measurement of changes in opinion and knowledge and a honorarium incentivises participation.

Intermediate definition also includes:

- *British Columbia Citizens' Assembly (BCCA):* Stratified random sample of 160 BC voters, who met regularly over a year (in 2004) to learn about and deliberate over changes to the electoral system. Their recommendation was put to a binding public referendum.
- *Planning cells:* A number of cells of 25 randomly-selected citizens meet over a few days and are provided with information on a policy issue. They deliberate and prioritise potential courses of action. Moderators prepare a final report for the commissioning body.
- *Citizens' juries:* Similar to a single planning cell, 12–24 citizens, typically selected using quotas or stratified sampling, deliberate over two to four days and produce a report of recommendations.
- *Consensus conferences:* Typically focused on a controversial scientific or technological development, a stratified sample of interested volunteers participates in an extensive learning phase before deliberating and making recommendations.
- *21st Century Town Meetings:* Targeted mobilisation of up to 5,000 citizens, who meet for one day. Facilitated small-group discussions are integrated using networked computers and electronic voting pads to relay themes and votes almost instantaneously.

Expansive definition also includes:

- *Participatory budgeting:* In the Porto Alegre model, citizens participate in a series of open assembly meetings to raise neighbourhood concerns; these are prioritised at regional budget forums and decisions on budget priorities are decided at a municipal budget council dominated by elected citizen delegates.
- *Chicago community policing:* Monthly open meetings in local communities where citizens and beat officers discuss priorities, collaborate on solutions and review progress.
- *Oregon Health Plan:* A series of 47 community meetings across the state with presentations, facilitated small-group discussion and prioritisation of options.

The expansive definition: Fung

In 2003 Fung published a seminal survey article, 'Recipes for public spheres: eight institutional design choices and their consequences'. In that essay, Fung aimed to raise awareness of the development of mini-publics: 'deliberately constructed' institutions that 'lie in the neighbourhood of administrative agencies and secondary associations rather than constitutions and basic structures' (Fung 2003: 339). Instead of the continual focus on the 'large institutions, trends and potential responses' that make up the extensive public sphere, political theorists and scientists would do well to learn from the emerging practice of mini-publics that are 'creating instances of more perfect public spheres' (*Ibid.*: 338).

In the survey article, Fung focuses on five different 'mini-public' designs that have subsequently become the subject of much academic scrutiny: deliberative polls, American Speaks citizen summits (also commonly referred to as 21st Century Town Meetings®), Oregon Health Plan, Chicago community policing and participatory budgeting in Porto Alegre (*see* Text Box 2.1 for details of designs).

The diversity of designs that Fung includes within his expansive definition of mini-publics is confirmed when he turns to an evaluation of the extent to which different institutional forms contribute to the quality of democratic governance: different types of mini-publics realise different combinations of democratic qualities. For Fung, a range of democratic qualities can be grouped within four broad categories: the character of participation and deliberation; information-pooling and individual transformation; popular control and state capacity; and political effects (Fung 2003: 347–52).

Using the five examples of mini-publics, Fung offers evidence of the different democratic consequences of their design choices and makes clear the way in which creative design requires trade-offs in realising democratic qualities. For example, deliberative polling is taken to be particularly effective in overcoming bias through the use of random selection and the promotion of informed and high-quality deliberation through balanced briefing materials, facilitated small-group discussions and the availability of experts. However, for Fung, it is less impressive in affecting popular control and broader mobilisation. But where one design is recognised as being weak, another can be particularly strong: take, for example, the capacity of participatory budgeting to realise popular control and mobilisation alongside other democratic qualities. While in his essay and in other work Fung focuses attention on the importance of deliberation, this is still seen as only one of a number of democratic qualities: different designs are better at promoting deliberation than others.[2]

Because of the variety of designs that fall under the expansive definition, in particular the way in which they realise very different combinations of democratic qualities, it is difficult for Fung to say much about the shared characteristics of

---

2. Fung's approach to analysing mini-publics prefigures Smith's analysis of democratic innovations, although Smith focuses on the realisation of a smaller number of democratic and institutional goods (Smith 2009).

mini-publics. To bring order to the variety of democratic practices, Fung offers a four-part categorisation of mini-publics according to their primary objective:

educative forum that aims to create nearly ideal conditions for citizens to form, articulate, and refine opinions about particular public issues through conversations with one another (*Ibid.*: 340).

participatory advisory panel [...] aims not only to improve the quality of opinion, but also to align public policies with considered preferences (*Ibid.*: 341).

participatory problem-solving collaboration [...] envisions a continuous and symbiotic relationship between the state and public sphere aimed at solving particular collective problems (*Ibid.*: 341).

participatory democratic governance, is more ambitious than the other three. This flavour of mini-public seeks to incorporate direct citizen voices into the determination of policy agendas (*Ibid.*: 342).

In a different publication of the same year, *Deepening Democracy: Institutional innovations in empowered participatory governance*, edited by Fung and Erik Olin Wright, only two of the five mini-public designs in the survey article are discussed in any depth: Chicago Community Policing and Participatory Budgeting in Porto Alegre.[3] For Fung and Wright, empowered participatory governance abides by three general principles: '(1) a focus on specific, tangible problems, (2) involvement of ordinary people affected by these problems and officials close to them, and (3) the deliberative development of solutions to these problems' (Fung and Wright 2003: 15). Such institutions map on to the last two sub-categories of mini-publics: participatory problem-solving collaboration and the more ambitious participatory democratic governance.

Fung's expansive definition of mini-publics means that, in his hands, the term encompasses the broad scope of institutional design between the electoral arena and the public sphere, in much the same way as Warren and Smith are using the terms 'governance-driven democratization' and 'democratic innovations' respectively. Fung's sub-categorisation indicates the way that, as he uses it, the term mini-public captures an array of very different designs with very different democratic qualities and functions: mini-public is used to describe a broad field of participatory and deliberative activity. The question that we shall return to as the chapter progresses is whether it is more helpful to be more restrictive than Fung in the use of mini-public as a particular category or class of governance-driven democratisation or democratic innovation. It is to more restrictive definitions that we now turn.

---

3. Two other designs are also analysed in this collection: decentralised planning in Kerala and Habitat Conservation Planning in the United States.

The most restrictive definition: Fishkin

One of the institutions that Fung analyses in his work on mini-publics is the Deliberative Poll®, the creation of the political theorist and policy entrepreneur James Fishkin. For most academics, it is enough to critique: to find fault with existing institutional arrangements, while offering token (often idealistic) suggestions for rearranging the institutional furniture. But Fishkin has done what no other democratic theorist has attempted; namely design his own democratic institution – the Deliberative Poll® (DP) – and has spent over fifteen years promoting its adoption and analysing the results of its implementation. Fishkin has ventured across continents, political systems, levels of governance and issues: implementing DPs in the US and Europe (East, West and the EU itself), Australia, China and Thailand; on topics including candidate selection, social and education policy, urban budgeting and energy choices. Fishkin has become synonymous with the DP and the form of deliberative democracy that he believes it embodies (*see*, for example, Chapter Three in this volume; Fishkin 1997; 2009) and has done more than most in promoting alternative forms of citizen engagement and deliberation to a wider academic and practitioner audience. But, at the same time, Fishkin can be (and has been) accused of over-emphasising the virtues of DPs against all other designs: for him, the DP is the only existing institution that fully warrants the designation mini-public, or his preferred term 'deliberative microcosm': 'a modest and practical strategy for realising deliberative democracy' (Fishkin 2009: 81).

In his most recent book, *When the People Speak: Deliberative democracy and public consultation*, Fishkin convincingly makes the case for 'the need for a social science research program assessing the merits and limitations of various institutional designs that might realize deliberative democracy' (*Ibid.*: 98), where '[t]he idea is to assess the designs that best stand up to critical scrutiny so as to capture the promise of deliberation and avoid potential objections to it' (*Ibid.*: 157). His particular approach to deliberative democracy means that only certain designs warrant sustained attention.

Fishkin holds that deliberative democracy is to be distinguished from other theories of democracy (competitive, elite and participatory) by its capacity to realise both political equality and deliberation (*Ibid.*: 65–94). While the principle of deliberative democracy suggests face-to-face deliberation between all citizens, this is not practical for a number of reasons, most significantly for Fishkin because some citizens will engage more than others. Political equality will be undermined. Thus the most practical strategy for realising deliberative democracy is the deliberative microcosm, where statistical representation of the relevant population is achieved and the mini-public is constructed such that all participants have the opportunity to participate in deliberations on an equal standing (*Ibid.*: 54–60).

For Fishkin, this combination of the democratic values of political equality and deliberation is only fully realised in deliberative polls: other designs (as we shall discuss below) fail to realise these values. It is through the realisation of political equality and deliberation that Fishkin makes the strong counterfactual claim about the considered preferences of participants in a DP.

The Deliberative Poll® is unlike any poll or survey ever conducted. Ordinary polls model what the public is thinking, even though the public may not be thinking very much or paying much attention. A Deliberative Poll® attempts to model what the public would think, had it a better opportunity to consider the question at issue (Fishkin 1997: 162).

The combination of political equality achieved through random selection and deliberation legitimises the considered preferences of participants as worthy of consideration by decision-makers and the wider public.

On this basis, Fishkin distinguishes DPs from other designs within the field of governance-driven democratisation and/or democratic innovations. First, it differentiates mini-publics from the designs Fung highlights in his sub-category of empowered participatory governance. For Fishkin, the self-selection/popular element of such designs – where forums are open to all citizens who wish to engage – undermines political equality as he understands it.[4] Twenty-first Century Town Meetings, participatory budgeting and Oregon Health Plan receive short shrift for not using randomised selection techniques. On 21st Century Town Meetings, Fishkin states that 'this design gives no confidence in any claims to representativeness [...] when the response rate is miniscule and there are no incentives, an initial effort at random sampling can easily transform into virtually pure self-selection' (2009: 112; see also Fishkin 2011: 172). Again, the oft-praised design of participatory budgeting in Porto Alegre is criticised for being 'unrepresentative' because of its reliance on popular assemblies and consequent failure to institutionalise 'scientific samples' (Fishkin 2009: 218). Fishkin is quick to highlight the invitation he received from the state of Rio Grande du Sol to sponsor a Deliberative Poll® in 2007 in Porto Alegre, 'precisely to represent everyone in the state' (Fishkin 2011: 172). For Fishkin, mini-publics (deliberative microcosms) are very different from empowered participatory governance.

Second, other designs that appear to share a strong family resemblance – including citizens' juries, consensus conferences, planning cells and the citizens' assemblies held in BC and Ontario (see Text Box 2.1 for brief details of designs) – are taken to have at least one of two design faults that mean that they do not fully warrant the designation deliberative microcosm or mini-public. First, they tend to have an element of self-selection (for example, citizens put themselves forward and then a sample is drawn from that group), or use quasi-random sampling techniques, such as stratification or quota sampling, to ensure the presence of particular social groups for political reasons. For example, on consensus conferences Fishkin argues: 'They begin with self-selection and then employ such small numbers that any claims to representativeness cannot be credibly established' (2009: 24). BCCA is seen as a more 'creditable effort' but falls down on similar grounds (Ibid.: 113). For Fishkin, the failure to use standard random sampling means that strong

---

4. In principle, it is possible for an institutional design that uses (quasi-)random selection to be categorised as empowered participatory governance. For example, the combination of the BCCA and the binding referendum that follows appears to fulfil the necessary criteria.

inferences about the judgement of the wider population cannot be made and thus the legitimacy of the design is undermined. Second, he is critical of designs that end with a collective recommendation rather than individual judgements. Here Fishkin is concerned that such processes undermine political equality as social pressure can be put on individuals to bend to the collective will (*Ibid.*: 132–3).

Is this restrictive definition of mini-publics plausible and useful in distinguishing different types of democratic design? There are reasons to be sceptical of Fishkin's desire to delineate DP from all other designs, in particular those that use quasi-random sampling techniques to generate a broadly (although not statistically) representative sample. First, we can question his emphasis on ensuring statistical representation and the use of pre- and post-deliberation attitudinal surveys. For Fishkin, this is important in order to draw inferences to the wider population. At the level of social-science experiment he is entirely correct. But this seems too high a threshold for all mini-publics. It is not always possible to attract the resources that random sampling and the other design features of DPs require. And designs will differ because political purposes vary. There may be good reasons for over-sampling certain social groups to ensure their presence, sometimes in higher numbers than their proportion in the broader population: for example, a critical mass of participants from minority social groups may be needed to ensure their voice is recognised and heard (James 2008). Similarly, the BCCA's political legitimacy rested in part on establishing quotas: ensuring that there was equal gender and constituency representation; and that aboriginal members were added when none emerged from the sampling process. Further, comparing aggregated pre-and post-deliberation opinions may not always be enough for decision-makers and the wider public, who may be interested in receiving a recommendation on how to proceed where participants have had to collectively weigh up and come to a decision about competing options.

Relatedly, in actual practice, DPs achieve 'near-random selection' (Warren and Pearse 2008: 6) and thus its difference from other designs that use quasi-random sampling techniques is one of degree rather than type. Amongst democratic designs, DPs are generally the closest to achieving random samples but it is well known that no sampling technique achieves a purely random selection. The main sampling error of DPs, which also affects traditional surveys, relates to the incomplete nature of any database from which the sample of citizens is taken. While in some polities we find fairly extensive population registries (such as in Finland and Sweden), DPs often have to rely on random-digit dialling, which, as Fishkin himself recognises, tends to 'skew towards older populations, who have land lines and are more likely to be at home, and towards the better educated, who are more likely to be willing to talk with the pollster' (Fishkin and Farrar 2005: 74; *see also* Traugott 2003). Further, experience from deliberative polls suggests that '[t]hose who decide to attend are usually somewhat more politically active and better educated than the initial sample' (Fishkin and Farrar 2005: 74). Finally, Fishkin has not entirely shied away from stratification himself: for example in the European DP, Europolis, 'the overall sample was stratified according to the size of the population of the respective countries on the overall European population' (Isernia *et al.* 2012).

Given his desire for a systematic research programme assessing the merits and limitations of various institutional designs, Fishkin's exclusion of citizens' juries, consensus conferences, BCCA and the like is too swift and his criticisms of these and other designs too scathing. There is error and bias in sampling for DPs and he fails to recognise the important role that stratification or quotas, as well as the crafting of recommendations, can play in legitimising designs. While the social scientist may desire probability sampling for good academic reasons, its virtues will not always be recognised in politically sensitive situations.

Reflecting back on the distinction that Fishkin offers between deliberative microcosms (or mini-publics) and designs that he believes are more influenced by participatory democracy (such as participatory budgeting) may help us in drawing more effective distinctions. Echoing somewhat Fung's approach to analysing institutions (Fung 2003), Fishkin argues that we cannot realise three democratic values in a single design: political equality, deliberation and participation, where the latter is defined as mass participation (Fishkin 2009: 32–64).[5] Fishkin makes it clear that he is interested in a specific form of deliberative democracy and therefore the self-selection that (mass) participation implies undermines the other two values. But if we follow Fishkin in making a strong distinction between participatory and deliberative forms of democracy (a theme we return to below), then the designs that he criticises for only using quasi-random selection would appear to be much closer to his definition of deliberative microcosm than they are to Fung's empowered participatory governance. It is this family resemblance that is the basis of intermediate definitions.

Intermediate definitions: Goodin and Dryzek/Smith

Somewhere between Fung's expansive definition and Fishkin's highly restrictive approach, we find definitions of mini-publics used by most contributors to this volume and more broadly within democratic theory and practice. But even then there are some minor differences between intermediate definitions as represented by Goodin and Dryzek (2006) and Smith (2009), which hang primarily on the importance given to employing quasi-random sampling techniques.

In many ways, both Goodin and Dryzek and Smith follow Fishkin in highlighting the importance of the combination of representativeness and deliberation. However, they do not insist on 'pure' randomness (which, as we have already argued, DPs come closest to but do not actually achieve). Goodin and Dryzek (2006: 220) argue that mini-publics are 'designed to be groups small enough to be genuinely deliberative, and representative enough to be genuinely democratic (though rarely will they meet standards of statistical representativeness, and they are never representative in the electoral sense)'.

---

5. For a critique of Fishkin's proposal to use these three democratic values as the basis of analysing institutional designs, *see* Smith 2010.

They explicitly distinguish their approach from the more expansive notion: 'Our definition of mini-public is narrower than that of Fung, who would include under the mini-public heading exercises that rely completely on self-selection' (*Ibid.*: 221). While they recognise that there is some self-selection in the institutions they include, the degree is much less, and of a different form, than in the case of participatory budgeting or community policing. They thus include designs that use quasi-random sampling techniques – DPs as well as citizens' assemblies, citizens' juries, planning cells and consensus conferences – but also 21st Century Town Meetings, which employ mobilisation strategies aimed at engaging traditionally excluded communities. While participants in such Town Meetings are not as representative as other mini-publics, they are also typically not as skewed as forms of empowered participatory governance.

Smith (2009) finds himself somewhere between Fishkin and Goodin and Dryzek. He limits the class of institutions to those which employ some element of quasi-randomisation – or aim to achieve 'near-random selection' (Warren and Pearse 2008) – alongside structured (or facilitated) deliberation between participants. He highlights a series of institutional characteristics on which family resemblance is based: quasi-random sampling; citizens paid an honorarium for participating; independent facilitation to ensure fairness of proceedings; evidence from and cross-examination of expert witnesses; deliberation amongst citizens in small groups and plenary sessions (Smith 2009: 76). Mini-publics can be distinguished from two other main categories of democratic innovation: those institutions that rely on popular assemblies (for example, traditional town meetings and participatory budgeting), which maps on to Fung's empowered participatory governance; and direct legislation that gives all citizens decision-making and, at times, agenda-setting powers (for example, citizens' initiatives and popular referendums). For Smith, a fourth category, 'e-democracy', is residual, highlighting the lack of attention given to ICT-enabled designs amongst democratic theorists.

The point of contention and ambiguity between Goodin and Dryzek and Smith is then represented by designs such as 21st Century Town Meetings. It is likely that Goodin and Dryzek were willing to extend their definition beyond quasi-random sampling because of their particular interest in reviewing different aspects of policy impact: without including 21st Century Town Meetings, the record of mini-publics (BCCA aside) is rather poor. Or it could be that other analysts – represented in this chapter by Fishkin and Smith – are too wedded to particular sampling strategies. For Smith, this case generates significant ambiguities: the reliance on self-selection (albeit it with targeted mobilisation strategies) places it closer to popular assembly-based innovations; but in relation to the other institutional criteria it resembles mini-publics. Additionally, its use of networked computer technologies means it also has a place within the e-democracy category. All in all, a salutary lesson in trying to place order on a complex reality.

Mini-publics and deliberative democracy

Whether the 21st Century Town Meeting is 'in' or 'out', the distinctions at work in these intermediate definitions is useful. We can draw out two common primary defining characteristics of mini-publics: an institution in which (1) a broadly inclusive and representative sub-group of an affected population engage in (2) structured deliberation enabled by independent facilitation. A third defining characteristic is implied by the examples quoted by analysts, namely the institution is organised with the aim of aligning political decision-making with the considered views of citizens. The stress here is on the aim of affecting public policy: there is relatively little evidence to suggest that most mini-publics have had any impact in that sense (Goodin and Dryzek 2006). Particular designs will embody these three design characteristics to greater or lesser extent; for those for which these are the principal design features, the definition 'mini-public' is most appropriate.

These defining characteristics provide a clear insight into why such institutions have captured the attention of deliberative democrats. Quasi-random selection techniques resonate with the original democratic device of Athenian democracy and offer a mechanism that averts the danger of participation being dominated by organised interests and those who desire political power. Whether some commentators (such as Fishkin and Smith) are fetishising such techniques in the definition of mini-publics is another matter: the primary aim is clearly to engage an inclusive group of participants from the affected population, from which no social group or perspective, particularly those who are traditionally politically marginalised, is excluded. And here we can see why particular designs might aim to oversample or use targeted mobilisation strategies to ensure the presence of social groups that are typically absent from political decision-making processes. Inclusiveness may be better served by over-representing those social groups and perspectives not normally present and/or heard.

This stress on inclusive participation across social groups chimes strongly with the form of political equality promoted by deliberative democrats. And the second defining characteristic further reinforces this connection between institutional design and democratic theory: the focus on the manner in which engagement between participating citizens is enabled. Through careful design, in particular facilitation, provision of balanced information and small-group work, a 'safe space' is created in which an inclusive group of participants is enabled to contribute to deliberations on public issues (Moore 2012). The institutional conditions are in place for the emergence and sustenance of deliberative virtues such as respect and reciprocity and for considered opinion-formation.

The way in which these characteristics are articulated is then to reject Fishkin's overly restrictive definition of mini-publics. It also differs significantly from Fung's more extensive use of the term (although his sub-category 'participatory advisory panels' has similar characteristics). Fung's own differentiation between democratic designs and a more extended focus on empowered participatory governance indicates that there are significant differences in both the way and extent to which they enable deliberation and participation; differences that are masked through the generic use of the term mini-public.

Distinguishing mini-publics from empowered participatory governance highlights different ways in which deliberative democracy is understood. The intermediate definition of mini-publics focuses on a 'protected' space for deliberation between a broadly inclusive and representative group of citizens, away from the pressures of everyday politics, in particular, the undue influence of special interests. In comparison, those institutions that Fung classifies as empowered participatory governance – and which Smith categorises under popular-assembly-based designs – are much more embedded in everyday politics. According to Fung, this leads to different forms of deliberation: more reasoned and dispassionate 'cool' deliberation in mini-publics (using the intermediate definition) compared to 'hot' deliberation driven by high stakes for participants in empowered participatory governance (Fung 2003: 345). While this claim certainly requires more systematic empirical verification, his point is that design will affect both the quality of deliberation and the priority afforded to realising that good against other goods. PB meetings in Porto Alegre may have strict time-limits for speakers (Baiocchi 2005) and trained facilitators at Chicago beat meetings may have been able to promote the voices of marginalised groups, leading to drastic changes in decision-making (Fung 2003); but in these cases of empowered participatory governance, the realisation of democratic goods other than deliberation is equally or more prominent in the designs. While democratic theorists are interested in the extent to which cases of empowered participatory governance are sites of democratic deliberation, it is a broader understanding of participation and empowerment that are critical drivers for these institutions. For some, this highlights a more profound distinction between different types of democracy and between their different ambitions, namely deliberative and participatory. For example, Carole Pateman has claimed that mini-publics

> are not integrated into the overall system of representative government or democratic institutions, nor do they become part of the regular political cycle in the life of a community. More generally, a problem with deliberative democracy – a problem of particular concern for supporters of participatory democracy – is that the primary interest of its advocates lies in the process of deliberation inside deliberative forums. They are not usually concerned with structural features of the wider society (Pateman 2012: 11).

There is a danger of over-simplifying the connections between particular designs and particular democratic theories: mini-publics as an expression of deliberative democracy; participatory budgeting as an expression of participatory democracy. Equally, many deliberative theorists will not accept Pateman's characterisation of the field. That said, mini-publics remain of particular interest to theorists of a deliberative persuasion, simply because their institutional characteristics offer an opportunity to explore empirically some of the familiar claims of deliberative democracy.

Concluding thoughts: Taking research on mini-publics forward

It is an important task to clarify what we mean by the term mini-public. We are still at a relatively early stage of phenomenological development; sub-fields of political science have always benefited from early conceptual work in organising their scope and principles (Lijphart 1971). What is particularly striking and indeed promising about this area of inquiry is the way in which it is informed by combinations of theoretical and empirical insights, as many of the other chapters in this volume attest. One way that such phenomenological development will move forward is both the case analysis of new institutional designs and comparative analysis across cases. Currently though, much of the work in this area rests on the analysis of a relatively small number of familiar cases; as new institutional designs emerge, they often force a reappraisal of what are deemed core characteristics of classes of phenomena. This certainly happened when the 21st Century Town Meeting model emerged, forcing analysts to reconsider the stress that was being placed on quasi-random selection techniques. One of the challenges in work on mini-publics and other forms of citizen engagement is the difficulty of keeping up-to-date with developments in the field: as ever, practice is outstripping analysis. Here initiatives such as *Participedia* – an open-access platform providing details of democratic innovations around the world – are likely to play a central role in raising awareness of new designs within the research and practitioner community and thus destabilising existing definitions and opening up new ways of seeing the world.[6]

Beyond this ongoing process of making sense of the broad field of activity, we highlight three areas where research on mini-publics (and more generally democratic innovations / governance-driven democratisation) is pressing. The first is more systematic investigation of the extent to which democratic deliberation is enabled within different mini-public designs. This may seem counter-intuitive, given that structured deliberation is one key element of our definition. But much of the research on mini-publics remains primarily suggestive, focusing on the institutional conditions most likely to promote deliberation. There is a need for evidence that deliberation actually emerges in practice. Let us return to Fishkin who, like other writers on mini-publics, makes strong claims about the extent to which democratic deliberation is promoted within DPs. The impressive evidence he marshals in his various publications focuses primarily on opinion- and knowledge-change on the part of participants. These are extremely interesting findings and the basis of a significant research programme. A focus on preference- and opinion-change alone, however, tells us little about the deliberative quality of interactions within the mini-public. We should not take for granted that random sampling, balanced background information, facilitated small-group discussion and plenary sessions in which experts are interrogated promote deliberation. Sophisticated analysis of facilitated small-group sessions is beginning to appear

---

6.   www.participedia.net

in both DPs and other mini-public designs.[7] For example, Marlene Gerber has applied network analysis to offer early evidence of how different facilitation styles affect the experience of participants (Gerber 2011); and there is a promise of the further application of the discourse quality index (DQI) on the deliberations of participants in the same Europe-wide DP (Isernia *et al.* 2012). Taking a different approach, Simon Niemeyer employs evidence from a range of citizens' juries to analyse the degree to which participants achieve meta-consensus through inter-subjective reasoning (*see*, for example, Niemeyer and Dryzek 2007). Such analysis will provide much needed substantive evidence on the conditions under which deliberation is – or is not – realised in such institutions.

If this first challenge relates to the internal workings of mini-publics, the second focuses on their broader effects. There is still much to understand about the conditions under which mini-publics have an impact on the political process. There are at least two agendas for research here. The first and most obvious is a better understanding of the conditions under which mini-publics affect political decision-making. This is particularly pressing given the extent to which there is an increasing normative commitment within the theoretical literature to embedding mini-publics. One of the most ambitious examples is James Bohman's (2012) call for the embedding of mini-demoi – mini-publics with decisional authority – to increase the representativeness and democratic qualities of transnational forms of governance. But Goodin and Dryzek's (2006) influential paper suggests that actual practice is a long way from such normative ambition, with an impact on decision-making that is relatively limited. The tendency of analysts to focus on exemplary cases (for example, Smith 2009) leads to an overestimate of the impact of mini-publics as a class of institutions. But if we are to go beyond highlighting specific cases and better understand the conditions that lead to impact, we need a programme of comparative analysis across cases that have had different degrees of success in affecting decision-making. Here again, initiatives such as *Participedia* may provide valuable evidence: not just of further cases, but also because the embedded data on each case may enable more systematic comparison, perhaps utilising new developments in qualitative comparative analysis.[8]

A second promising agenda on the impact of mini-publics has also emerged drawing on research on BCCA. Not only did this mini-public have a significant impact on the decision-making process, but evidence from opinion polls suggests it shaped the opinions of the broader public: those who were aware of the BCCA were more likely to support its recommendations in the referendum that followed. They deemed it trustworthy, either because they were impressed by its expertise or because it was a representative group of ordinary citizens who had come to an

---

7.   Analysis of DPs has arguably been held back by the fact that data on DPs are not necessarily available to the broader research community in a timely fashion. There is often no opportunity for the broader social-science community to interrogate the raw data, leaving the findings based on DPs open to often unnecessary suspicion and criticism.

8.   For an application of fuzzy-set qualitative comparative analysis on participatory budgeting, *see* Ryan and Smith 2012.

agreement (Cutler *et al.* 2008; Mackenzie and Warren 2012). Better understanding the connection between mini-publics and the broader public sphere is a pressing issue, particularly the potentially sensitive relationship between such protected democratic spaces and the actions and intentions of the media.

A third area where a significant research agenda is beginning to emerge is on online mini-publics (*see also* Strandberg and Grönlund in Chapter Seven of this volume). Much of the theorising and empirical analysis – and arguably much of the democratic practice of mini-publics themselves – rests on face-to-face interactions between citizens, although 21st Century Town Meetings combine both offline and online engagement. Given the promise of information and communication technology (ICT) to overcome barriers of space and time, there is real potential for extending the reach of mini-publics. This is certainly the view of Fishkin and his colleagues, who have developed and tested online deliberative polling (ODP), utilising voice-operated software to reduce the impact of digital capital such as ICT competence. Experimental work suggests that shifts in preference and knowledge do occur in this online context but not to the same degree as in traditional face-to-face DPs (Iyengar *et al.* 2005; Luskin *et al.* 2006). The major challenge for online mini-publics is the design question. As Scott Wright and John Street argue, 'the democratic possibilities opened up (or closed off) by websites are not a product of the technology as such, but of the ways in which it is constructed, by the way it is designed' (Wright and Street 2007: 850). The way in which different online media are constructed has a profound impact on the extent to which democratic deliberation is realised (Price 2006; Coleman and Blumler 2009). In analysing developments in online forums, Davy Janssen and Raphaël Kies highlight two characteristics that have a significant impact on the form of interaction between citizens. The first is the 'technical architecture', in particular whether the online discussion space is real-time (chat-rooms) or asynchronous (e-mail list; newsgroups; bulletin boards; forums); the latter being more conducive to deliberation (Janssen and Kies 2005: 321). The second characteristic is the manner in which online discussion spaces are organised. They offer a non-exhaustive list of variables that are likely to have an effect on the quality of engagement: whether or not participants are required to identify themselves; limits to openness and freedom of speech; the existence and form of moderation; and the extent to which participants are able to set the agenda for debate (*Ibid.*: 321–2). There are significant design challenges to be overcome to ensure that online institutions engage both an inclusive and representative sample of affected populations and realise democratic deliberation (Smith *et al.* 2013).

Let us conclude by returning to Fishkin and his argument of 'the need for a social science research program assessing the merits and limitations of various institutional designs that might realize deliberative democracy' (2009: 98). Mini-publics are one such set of institutional designs – although not the only one. This chapter has engaged in a process of ground-clearing: attempting to make sense of what is at stake in different conceptions of mini-publics. Conceptual ground-clearing is only one element of a social-science research programme. Other contributors to this volume take such a research programme in more substantive directions.

References

Baiocchi, G. (2005) *Militants and Citizens: The politics of participatory democracy in Porto Alegre*, Stanford, CA: Stanford University Press.

Bohman, J. (2012) 'Representation in the deliberative system', in J. Mansbridge and J. Parkinson (eds) *Deliberative Systems: Deliberative democracy at large scale*, Cambridge: Cambridge University Press.

Coleman, S. and Blumler, J. (2009) *The Internet and Democratic Citizenship: Theory, practice, policy*, Cambridge: Cambridge University Press.

Cutler, F., Johnston, R., Carty, R. K., Blais, A. and Fournier, P. (2008) 'Deliberation, information and trust: the BC citizens' assembly as agenda-setter', in M. E. Warren and H. Pearse (eds) *Designing Deliberative Democracy: The British Columbia citizens' assembly*, Cambridge: Cambridge University Press.

Fishkin, J. S. (1997) *The Voice of the People*, New Haven, CT: Yale University Press.

— (2009) *When the People Speak: Deliberative democracy and public consultation*, Oxford: Oxford University Press.

— (2011) 'Review of Democratic Innovations: Designing Institutions for Citizen Participation by Graham Smith', Perspectives on Politics 9 (1): 171–3.

Fishkin, J. S., Camarano, E., Luskin, R. C. and Siu, A. (2010) 'Deliberative participatory consultation: the first Deliberative Poll in Porto Alegre', paper presented at the American Political Science Association Annual Meeting, Washington, DC.

Fishkin, J. S. and Farrar, C. (2005) 'Deliberative polling', in J. Gastil and P. Levine (eds) *The Deliberative Democracy Handbook: Strategies for effective civic engagement in the 21st century*, San Francisco, CA: Jossey Bass.

Fung, A. (2003), 'Survey article: recipes for public spheres: eight institutional design choices and their consequences', *Journal of Political Philosophy*, II (3): 338–67.

Fung, A. and Wright, E. O. (eds) (2003) *Deepening Democracy: Institutional innovations in empowered participatory governance*, London: Verso.

Gerber, M. (2011) 'Who are the voices of Europe? Evidence from a pan-European Deliberative Poll', paper presented at the ECPR General Conference, Reykjavik.

Goodin, R. E. and Dryzek, J. S. (2006) 'Deliberative impacts: the macro-political uptake of mini-publics', *Politics & Society* 34 (2): 219–44.

Isernia, P., Fishkin, J., Steiner, J. and Di Mauro, D. (2012) 'Toward a European public sphere – The Europolis project, in R. Kies and P. Nanz (eds) *Is Europe Listening to Us? Successes and failures in EU citizen consultations*, London: Ashgate.

Iyengar, S., Luskin, R. C. and Fishkin, J. S. (2005) 'Deliberative preferences in the presidential nomination campaign: Evidence from an online Deliberative Poll', working paper, The Center for Deliberative Democracy, Stanford University. Online. Available http://cdd.stanford.edu/research/papers/2005/presidential-nomination.pdf (accessed 1 October 2013).

James, M. R. (2008) 'Descriptive representation in citizen assemblies', in M. E. Warren and H. Pearse (eds) *Designing Deliberative Democracy: The British Columbia citizens' assembly*, Cambridge: Cambridge University Press.

Janssen, D. and Kies, R. (2005) 'Online forums and deliberative democracy', *Acta Politica* 40: 317–35.

Lijphart, A. (1971) 'Comparative politics and the comparative method', *American Political Science Review* 65: 682–93.

Luskin, R. C., Fishkin, J. S. and Iyengar, S. (2006) 'Considered opinions on U.S. foreign policy: Face-to-face versus online deliberative polling', working paper, The Center for Deliberative Democracy, Stanford University. Online. Available http://cdd.stanford.edu/research/papers/2006/foreign-policy.pdf (accessed 1 October 2013).

Mackenzie, M. K. and Warren, M. E. (2012) 'Two trust-based uses of minipublics in democratic systems', in J. Mansbridge and J. Parkinson (eds) *Deliberative Systems: Deliberative democracy at large scale*, Cambridge: Cambridge University Press.

Moore, A. (2012) 'Following from the front: theorizing deliberative facilitation', *Critical Policy Studies* 6 (2): 146–62.

Niemeyer, S. and Dryzek, J. (2007) 'The ends of deliberation: metaconsensus and intersubjective rationality as ideal outcomes', *Swiss Political Science Review* 13 (4): 497–526.

Pateman, C. (2012) 'Participatory democracy revisited', *Perspectives on Politics* (10)1: 7–19.

Price, V. (2006) 'Citizens deliberating online: Theory and some evidence,' in T. Davies (ed.) *Online Deliberation: Design, research, and practice*, Stanford, CA: CLSI Publications.

Ryan, M. and Smith, G. (2012) 'Towards a comparative analysis of democratic innovations: lessons from a small-N fs-QCA of participatory budgeting', *Revista Internacional de Sociología* 70 (extra 2): 89–120.

Smith, G. (2009) *Democratic Innovations: Designing institutions for citizen participation*, Cambridge: Cambridge University Press.

Smith, G. (2010) 'Review of *When the People Speak: Deliberative democracy and public consultation*, by James S. Fishkin', *Perspectives on Politics* (8) 3: 908–9.

Smith, G., John, P. and Sturgis, P. (2013) 'Taking political engagement online: an experimental analysis of asynchronous discussion forums', *Political Studies* 61 (4): 709–30.

Traugott, M. W. (2003) 'Can we trust the polls? It all depends', *The Brookings Review* 21: 8–11.

Warren, M. E. (2009) 'Governance-driven democratization', *Critical Policy Studies* (3) 1: 3–13.

Warren, M. E. and Pearse, H. (eds) (2008) *Introduction Designing Deliberative Democracy: the British Columbia Citizens' Assembly*, Cambridge: Cambridge University Press, pp. 1–19.

Wright, S. and Street. J. (2007) 'Democracy, deliberation and design: the case of online discussion forums', *New Media and Society* 9: 849–69.

Chapter Three

Deliberative Democracy in Context: Reflections on Theory and Practice

James S. Fishkin

The world is full of established institutions that claim to be democratic. Proponents of deliberative democracy need to confront two questions: First, why do we need yet another sort of institution: what does deliberative democracy *add*? Second, how might such designs fruitfully relate to current institutions that embody one notion or another of democracy – how does deliberative democracy *connect*?[1]

In this paper, I will first distinguish four competing theories of democracy and identify the sorts of institutions that embody them. Three are familiar and well established while the fourth, deliberative democracy, is largely aspirational. As an effort to embody deliberative democracy, I will focus on the Deliberative Poll[®2] (DP) and discuss cases in which it has been employed. I will illustrate how those cases supplement or enrich decisions made in accordance with one or another of the other three theories – competitive democracy, mass participation, or elite deliberation (which I distinguish from deliberative democracy by the people themselves). In the case of competitive democracy, I will focus on how the DP can be used for candidate selection (a case from Greece) and in advising the public before elections (the recent use of the DP in European parliamentary elections). In the case of elite deliberation, I will focus on how the DP can advise expert decision about the public's values and priorities. The electric utility cases in Texas offer an illustration here. In the case of participatory democracy, I will focus on the DP's connection to initiatives and referenda. The recent California project in which the DP was used to set an agenda for possible initiative propositions will be discussed.

Four democratic theories

There is not one democratic theory, but many. In order to get a handle on the range of different possible positions, I think it is useful to think of some core component principles – political equality, (mass) participation, deliberation, and

1. A version of this paper was presented at the Yale-Oslo conference on Epistemic Democracy, October 2011. My thanks to Helene Landemore for hosting that conference and for her comments. I would also like to thank Kimmo Grönlund and Maija Setälä for their helpful reactions to this draft.

2. Deliberative Polling[®] is a trademark of James S. Fishkin. The trademark is for quality control and supports the research of the Center for Deliberative Democracy at Stanford.

avoiding tyranny of the majority (which I will call 'non-tyranny'). Three of these principles are internal to the design of democratic institutions and one (non-tyranny) is about the effects of democratic decision, effects that have long worried critics of democracy. If we consider these four principles essential components of a democratic theory, then the variations in commitment to them provide a kind of rudimentary grammar that allows us to specify the range of alternative theories. In other words, we can get a handle on different democratic theories according to whether or not they accept these component principles.

By political equality I mean, roughly, the equal consideration of one's views in the design of institutions. Does the design of a decision process give each person a theoretically equal chance of being the decisive voter? Or, to take an obvious example, do voters in Rhode Island have far more voting power than voters in New York in selecting members of the Senate? By participation I mean actions by voters or ordinary citizens intended to influence politics or policy or to influence the dialogue about them. By deliberation, I mean the weighing of reasons under good conditions in shared discussion about what should be done. The good conditions specify access to reasonably good information and to balanced discussion with others who are willing to participate conscientiously. This summary is a simplification but should do for now. By non-tyranny, I mean the avoidance of a policy that would impose severe deprivations when an alternative policy could have been chosen that would not have imposed severe deprivations on anyone (Fishkin 1979). Obviously there are many interesting complexities about the definition of severe deprivations, but the basic idea is that a democratic decision should not impose very severe losses on some when an alternative policy would not have imposed such losses on anyone. The idea is to rule out only some of the most egregious policy choices and leave the rest for democratic decision.[3]

Table 3.1: Four democratic theories

	Competitive democracy	Elite deliberation	Participatory democracy	Deliberative democracy
Political equality	+	?	+	+
Participation	?	?	+	?
Deliberation	?	+	?	+
Non-tyranny	+	+	?	?

Each of these four positions embraces a commitment to two of the principles just mentioned. The position is usually agnostic about the other two. While there are obviously sixteen possible positions defined by acceptance or rejection of the four principles, I have argued elsewhere that the useful positions reduce to these

---

3. This scheme and its implications are developed in more detail in Fishkin (2009). This paper draws on those arguments.

four.[4] Variations that aspire to more than the four are either unworkable or merely utopian or empty (such as the rejection of all four principles). Those that aspire to fewer include elements of one of these but are less ambitious than necessary.

The four positions have all been influential. In some cases, I modify a familiar position to make it more defensible, in order to get the strongest version of each position.

By competitive democracy I mean the notion of democracy championed by Joseph Schumpeter (1942) and more recently by Richard Posner (2003). Democracy is not about collective will-formation but just a 'competitive struggle for the people's vote', to use Schumpeter's famous phrase. Legal guarantees, particularly constitutional ones, are designed to protect against tyranny of the majority. Within that constraint, all we need are competitive elections. While Schumpeter did not even specify political equality in competitive elections, I have included it here, on the grounds that it makes the position more defensible than would a position that embraced competitive elections in rotten boroughs. The question marks signal agnosticism about the other two principles. Some variants of this position avoid prizing participation, viewing it as a threat to stability or to elite decision-making. Better not to arouse the masses as their passions might be dangerous and motivate factions adverse to the rights of others, threatening the position's commitment to protect against tyranny of the majority. Because of collective-action problems and incentives for 'rational ignorance' (to use Anthony Downs' well known fomulation) little can be expected of ordinary citizens. This position makes that minimalism a virtue (Posner 2003: 172–3).

By elite deliberation I mean the notion of indirect filtration championed by Madison in his design for the US Constitution. The constitutional convention, the ratifying conventions, the US Senate were supposed to be small, elite bodies that would consider the competing arguments. They would 'refine and enlarge the public views by passing them through the medium of a chosen body of citizens' as Madison said in Federalist 10 when discussing the role of representatives. Madison held that the public views of such a deliberative body 'might better serve justice and the public good than would the views of the people themselves if convened for the purpose'. A similar position of elite deliberation was given further development in J. S. Mill's *Considerations on Representative Government* (Mill 1991: 116) particularly in his account of the 'Congress of Opinions' which was supposed to embody a microcosm of the nation's views 'where those whose opinion is over-ruled feel satisfied that it is heard, and set aside not by a mere act of will, but for what are thought superior reasons' (prefiguring Jürgen Habermas's famous notion about being convinced only by the 'forceless force of the better argument' (Habermas 1996: chapter seven)). This position, like the last one, avoids embracing mass participation as a value. The passions or interests that might motivate factions are best left un-aroused. The Founders after all, had lived through Shays' rebellion and had an image of unfiltered mass opinion as

---

4.   *See* Fishkin (2009), Appendix: Why We Only Need Four Democratic Theories.

dangerous. If only the Athenians had had a senate, they might not have killed Socrates.[5]

By participatory democracy, I mean an emphasis on mass participation combined with equal counting. While many proponents of participatory democracy would also embrace deliberation, the essential components of the position require participation, perhaps prized partly for its educative function (Pateman 1976) and equality in considering the views offered or expressed in that participation (even if that expression is by secret ballot). The two positions, participatory and deliberative democracy are distinct.[6] Advocates of participatory democracy might also advocate voter handbooks and new technology for voter information, as did the Progressives, but the foremost priority is that people should participate, whether or not they become informed or discuss the issues.[7] Part of the problem with this position is that it is sometimes advocated based on a picture of small-scale decision-making, such as the New England town meeting, in which discussion is facilitated; but then implemented in the social context of mass democracy – the California process of ballot initiatives, for example, where essentially plebiscitary processes are employed for constitutional change.

A fourth position, which I call deliberative democracy, attempts to combine deliberation by the people themselves with an equal consideration of the views that result. One method for implementing this two-fold aspiration is the deliberative microcosm chosen by lot, a model whose essential idea goes back to Ancient Athens for institutions such as the Council of 500, the *nomethetai* (legislative commissions), the *graphe paranomon* and the citizens' jury. Modern instances of something like this idea include the citizens' assemblies in British Columbia and Ontario and the research programme in which I am involved (Deliberative Polling® or DP). A second approach to implementing deliberative democracy would be the kind of institution Bruce Ackerman and I outline in *Deliberation Day*. Here the idea would be to get everyone deliberating in a balanced process of reason-giving with good information, much like the conditions in the DP. One could either get the whole population or a representative sample of the population deliberating. In one case, equal participation by everyone before an election embodies political equality in the selection process. In the other case, political equality in the selection process is achieved by giving everyone an equal chance of being chosen.

Why should we care about deliberative democracy when we have established institutions of one sort or another that embody the other three theories? What would it add? As indicated by the chart, what it adds is reason-based public-will

---

5. *See* Madison (1788) if the Athenians had only had a senate: 'Popular liberty might then have escaped the indelible reproach of decreeing to the same citizens the hemlock on one day and statues on the next.'

6. For a discussion of how the focus on participation has changed to a focus on deliberation, *see* Pateman 2012.

7. For an overview, *see* Magleby (1984: 137–9) on the relative ineffectiveness of voter handbooks and other efforts to get voters more informed.

formation by the people themselves. Competitive democracy, as formulated most famously by Schumpeter, was dismissive of this possibility, focusing instead on just 'the competitive struggle for the people's vote'. It does not matter, on this view, how misled the people may be, how ill informed, how lacking in reasons. Most anything goes in the competition. Just count the votes. Elite deliberation is clearly a theory that prizes deliberation but deliberation on behalf of the people by representatives, not by the people themselves. Participatory democrats mostly embrace deliberation.[8] Progressive reformers have long distributed voter handbooks and other information. But the essential elements of the position involve participation and political equality. And as I have argued in the trilemma of democratic reform (Fishkin 2009: chapter two), at the large scale, this puts individual voters in the position of participating in plebiscitary democracy with incentives for rational ignorance. If I have one vote in millions, I am unlikely to pay a lot of attention to voter handbooks or well intentioned public-affairs programming. Would that it were otherwise: that we could effectively motivate large-scale participation and deliberation at the same time. But, for the most part, we have been notably unsuccessful in creating social contexts that would scale up the kind of balanced deliberation we find in mini-publics to large populations.

Deliberation and public-will formation

By *deliberation* we mean the process by which individuals sincerely weigh the merits of competing arguments in discussions together. Elsewhere, I have argued that we can talk about the *quality* of a deliberative process in terms of five conditions:

a. Information: the extent to which participants are given access to reasonably accurate information that they believe to be relevant to the issue.

b. Substantive balance: the extent to which arguments offered by one side or from one perspective are answered by considerations offered by those who hold other perspectives.

c. Diversity: the extent to which the major positions in the public are represented by participants in the discussion.

d. Conscientiousness: the extent to which participants sincerely weigh the merits of the arguments.

---

8. *See*, for example, Pateman 2012. But the embrace is incidental. Where possible, it is good to have both but there is no recognition that, as scale increases, there is likely to be a trade-off between more deliberation and more participation.

  e. Equal consideration: the extent to which arguments offered by all participants are considered on the merits regardless of which participants offer them (Fishkin 2009: 33–4).

The DP design aspires to realise these five conditions to a high degree, at least compared with public opinion as we ordinarily find it. The projects always include an initial briefing document, whose balance and accuracy is certified by an advisory group that represents the competing points of view. The random sample is randomly assigned to small groups, each with a trained moderator. Those moderators are trained to cover the agenda in the briefing document and to ensure that no one dominates the discussion. Participants come up with key questions that are addressed to panellists in plenary sessions, with balanced panels of experts answering them and with more than one expert answering each question, so that opposing points of view are aired by the experts. At the end of the process, participants take a confidential questionnaire with similar questions to those they took before deliberation.

This simple design serves information gains since the participants learn from the vetted briefing materials, the competing expert panellists and from each other. We always measure information and the projects routinely show large information gains.

The second criterion, substantive balance, is served by the vetted materials and by the balanced panels. In addition, we know from Alice Siu's work examining transcripts of the small-group deliberations that it is balanced argumentation that tends to move opinion (Siu 2008). The third criterion, diversity of viewpoints, is served by the random sample itself, to the extent that it is a good sample reproducing the diversity in the population. A good random sample will provide a microcosm of the population's attitudes as well as demographics. The DP design provides data for evaluating whether this has been achieved, since the initial attitudes of participants can be compared to those from non-participants. In addition, if the advisory group is properly constructed, its diversity should also be reflected in the briefing materials and in the choice of panellists. The fourth criterion, conscientiousness, rests with the participants. But remember that they are not running for re-election. They are there to discuss public issues because the design of the process attempts to give them a sense that their voice matters. Under these conditions, they have every reason to behave sincerely. The fifth condition, equal consideration, is fostered by an atmosphere of group discussion in which everyone's voice is valued. Its success in showing non-domination by the more privileged has been demonstrated by our analyses of whether or not the opinion changes systematically move in the direction of the initial positions of the more privileged. They do not. It is also apparent from the evaluation questions that participants perceive an equal process in which all viewpoints are valued.

Of course the DP design is but one possible design for facilitating deliberation by the mass public. There may well be other successful designs. The importance of the relatively good news thus far is not that it makes the case that public consultations should only be conducted with DPs. Rather it makes the case that fulfilling these criteria for deliberation can be achieved to a high degree. The basic idea is to take a random, representative sample and engage it in good conditions for thinking about the issues. This is our account of good conditions. With changing technology, someone else may well come up with an alternative account. But this account works well and thus shows that it is possible to achieve public deliberation with samples that are highly representative.

Adding the DP to competitive democracy

As noted, we have many established institutions of Schumpeterian competitive democracy around the world. Of course with different electoral systems, different levels of development and different media systems, the terms of competition may differ from one polity to another. But the basic point is that, from this perspective, parties and candidates do whatever is necessary within the rules to win and maintain office. They have little need to foster a value such as deliberation on the part of the mass public, unless particular circumstances make that advantageous. As a result, competitive democracy without deliberation lacks meaningful public-will formation. Of course, this is no surprise. Schumpeter ridiculed 'classical' theories of democracy for presuming some account of meaningful public-will formation. He then offered a modern alternative that dispensed with it. In his recent restatement of the theory, Posner did much the same (Posner 2003).

If we prize the public will as the very point of democracy, are there points of connection for deliberative democracy within the on-going mechanisms of competition? Generations of reform since the Progressives have focused on giving the public more of a role, with the hope that, as a side benefit, people would be motivated to become informed. Australian Progressives, for example, pushed compulsory voting with something like this rationale. The idea was that if people *had* to vote, they would go to the trouble to become informed and really think about the power they had to exercise. But Australian experience (or Brazilian for that matter) has not borne that out. People may be compelled to vote but they do *not* feel as a result an effective motivation to spend significantly more time becoming well informed or discussing the issues with diverse others. There is no effective individual motivation to become informed if your individual vote is trivial in its effect. American Progressives pushed direct democracy, a subject we will return to, including mass primaries that would change candidate selection. But the primary has turned out to be a low-information environment, heavy on television spending, in which voters need to distinguish between candidates without the one key heuristic of party. The Progressives also pushed voter handbooks, which we still have, but often have not read.

The end result has been a lack of information and deliberation both in candidate selection and in the general election. This pattern holds true in most places most of the time.

First, it is worth noting that if people deliberated in an election, it could well make a significant difference to the outcome. For example, a DP in the 1997 British General Election showed very large opinion changes in the sample, including a 22-point increase in support for the Lib Dems (Fishkin *et al.* 2010).

Perhaps an even better demonstration is the European Parliament, where it is fairly obvious that elections are currently 'second order' and there is little or no substantive deliberation by voters. In fact there is little communication across political boundaries. The unitary version of the European-wide public sphere, where arguments would be shared and elections would hold people accountable across the boundaries of language and nationality, is an aspiration of European scholars, most forcefully presented by Habermas. But it has come to seem utopian or even impossible. It was, however, piloted with the mass public in a recent DP before the European Parliamentary Elections. There was not only substantive deliberation across all the boundaries of language and nationality but a coherent connection after deliberation between policy positions and voting intention, voting intentions – at least in the case of the Greens. Support for the Greens went up three-fold and that support was coherently connected after deliberation with support for concerted action on climate change and with more welcoming policies on immigration (both positions of the Greens). The other parties had more ambiguous positions on climate change and immigration and the voters did not make coherent connections between these issues and support for those parties. Hence the European wide public sphere experiment was only partly successful in connecting policy positions with voting intentions, but this only shows the limitations of a field experiment with a real election. If the parties are ambiguous, the voters, even if more informed, may not know how to connect policy preferences with voting (Fishkin *et al.* forthcoming).

The difficulty with connecting this kind of microcosmic deliberation to actual elections in competitive democratic systems is that the microcosm has no clear effect on everyone else. Even media broadcasts, which have been common with Deliberative Polls®, have limited effects in the height of an election season where there is so much coverage from every possible angle.

Note, first, that the experiments show that if people deliberated it would make a difference (Farrar *et al.* 2010). Advocates of heuristics who try to conclude that deliberation would make little difference to voting intention are sometimes, perhaps often, proved wrong. And in any case, when people deliberate and weigh the reasons, their votes have a different meaning. They become an expression of considered judgements rather than 'off the top of the head' impressions.

Bruce Ackerman and I have a scheme for spreading an experience like a Deliberative Poll® to the entire electorate. We call it Deliberation Day and we think it would offer the most authentic and consequential point of entry for deliberation into competitive democracy. It would be the most authentic because then the entire public would weigh competing arguments (rather than listening to cues from the microcosm). It would be the most consequential because a transformation in public opinion would have big effects on voting intentions. Lacking Deliberation Day, a second best would be to adapt John Gastil's proposal to put the recommendations of a deliberating microcosm on the ballot or on the voter handbook. That would clearly give them impact. However, it would not really get the wider public to participate in deliberation. Rather it would amplify the effect of the microcosm's conclusions.

A quite different point of entry would be candidate selection. The Deliberative Poll® was originally conceived as a new way of starting off the presidential primary season. Instead of Iowa and New Hampshire (or even the Iowa straw poll), it would represent voters in the entire country and it would represent their considered judgements, rather than their off the top of the head impressions of candidates' soundbites. The 1996 National Issues Convention successfully piloted this notion on the issues and with the participation of the candidates; but it did not include candidate evaluations (it just focused on the issues) so it did not have the desired effect.

However, in 2006, a more daring application took place in Greece. One of the country's two major parties, PASOK, led by George Papandreou, used the DP to officially select its candidate for a major office. Faced with the idea of possibly democratising candidate selection, Papandreou thought the deliberative microcosm chosen by lot or random sampling offered a method that would take the choice out of the hands of party elites while at the same time allowing for a deliberative choice –one based on extensive discussion and information. A random sample of all registered voters was convened in Maroussi, the large suburb of Athens which hosted the Olympics, to choose PASOK's candidate for a mayor. The least well known of the six finalists was eventually selected after an entire day of dialogue in small groups and questioning of the candidates on the issues in two long plenary sessions. Papandreou proposed this as a new mode of candidate selection that should have wider application in Greece and elsewhere in Europe (Fishkin *et al.* 2008; Papandreou 2006).

Primaries were originally proposed as a means of empowering the public to determine candidate selection. But they have become tests of fund-raising, organisation and the ability to communicate via soundbite campaigns. A deliberative process of candidate selection that also was representative of the people rather than of party elites would add a significant dimension of public-will formation to the processes of competitive democracy.

Adding the DP to elite deliberation

The American Republic was born in a vision of elite deliberation, not competitive democracy. Madison famously engaged in the 'strategy of successive filtrations' of public opinion for the constitutional convention, the ratifying conventions, the Senate and even the Electoral College. Representatives were supposed to 'refine and enlarge the public views by passing them through the medium of a chosen body of citizens.' But this vision was either innocent of political parties or hostile to it. In the modern republic one must look in unexpected places for elite deliberation independent of calculations of partisan advantage. One such place turned out to be the Texas Public Utility Commission (PUC) in 1996 and the years immediately following.

The PUC was given the option by the legislature to require the state's eight regulated public utilities to consult the populations in their service territories before submitting 'Integrated Resource Plans' about how they proposed to meet the future energy needs in their areas. Were they going to use coal, natural gas, wind power or other renewable sources? Were they going to engage in demand-side management (conservation, so cutting the need for power) or were they going to pipe in the power from outside (requiring investment in transmission lines)?

Hundreds of millions of dollars turned on these decisions. The companies, when faced with the requirement to consult the public, quickly realised that if they did conventional polls, the public would be unlikely to have the kind of detailed information that would make the consultations meaningful. If they did focus groups, they could never demonstrate that they were representative. If they had open meetings, they were likely to be dominated by lobbyists and special interests. So all eight utilities conducted DPs.

The DPs began with briefing materials vetted by advisory groups involving all the relevant stakeholders that might comment on the results in a regulatory proceeding – environmental groups, consumer groups, advocates of alternative energy, the large industrial customers, advocates of the different forms of energy. With difficulty they would all eventually be led to agree on materials that posed the different options with pros and cons that were vetted for balance and accuracy. These materials provided the basis for discussion and for the questionnaires given before and after deliberation.

Averaged over the eight projects, the percentage of the public willing to pay more on its monthly utility bill for wind power went from 54 per cent to 84 per cent. A similar rise in support took place for conservation or demand-side management. Generally, the public went for mixtures of natural gas (which was clean and relatively inexpensive) over coal (which was even cheaper but much dirtier). It supported wind power and conservation and was willing to pay for it. Each project produced an integrated resource plan based on the results yielding larger and larger investments in wind power. The accumulated data from all eight projects provided the legislature with a basis for including a 'renewable energy portfolio' in new legislation strongly supported by the PUC. The end result of these consultations was that Texas went from being last among the fifty states in wind power in 1996, when the projects started, to surpassing California in 2007 as the number-one state in wind power (Fishkin 2009: 152–4).

Adding the DP to participatory democracy

As with competitive democracy, the DP can be added before a public vote. In both Australia and Denmark, the DPs were nationally broadcast before referenda, in Australia before the Republic referendum and in Denmark before the euro referendum. In both cases, there were significant opinion changes, significant coverage and some clear media effects on the issues in the dialogue and perhaps on voting intention. The effect on voting intention was clearer in Australia since the results were much sharper. But the effect on the dialogue was dramatic in Denmark since serious issues were raised in the DP about possible effects of euro membership on the pension system and the government did not succeed in responding to those concerns either on the broadcast or later in the campaign. The policy elites had not thought of the issues in terms close to the voters and there is nothing more precious to voters who are heavily taxed in a welfare state than the security of their pensions. So in the Danish case, the deliberating public ended up changing the agenda of discussion (or at least priming a key issue) before the national vote.

A more recent project, *What's Next California* gave the public even more of a role by formally determining an agenda for public vote. California, like 23 other states, does not just have referendums, it has initiatives – in which the people rather than the legislature can put a proposition on the ballot. As it happens, October 2011 marked the 100th anniversary of the initiative in California. Born in hopes of genuine self-government, it has only occasionally lived up to those aspirations. The agenda is often set by special interests, who spend immense sums to persuade, manipulate or confuse the public.

California's first state-wide DP shows how the people can take hold of the agenda for direct democracy. It will likely lead to a number of proposals being put on the ballot. If it succeeds, it will, in itself, be a deliberative reform. Six of the proposals became Proposition 31 which went on the ballot in 2012. However, those six proposals were combined with other elements which were not part of the citizens' deliberations and those added proposals attracted opposition. Hence this first effort at deliberative agenda setting in the California initiative was only partly successful.

How can the people actually deliberate about complex reforms in a state the size of California? The DP, based on an ancient form of democracy, provides a solution theory to the defects of mass participatory democracy. A deliberating microcosm chosen by random sample can seriously engage with the issues and come to a considered judgement based on good information. A mini-version of the population can engage in extensive face-to-face discussion and weigh the reasons for any proposal being important enough to bring to a public vote. In ancient Athens, the Council of 500, chosen by lot, set the agenda for everyone's votes in the Assembly. In this case, a representative group of 412 Californians, chosen by random sampling, attempted to set the agenda for everyone's votes in ballot propositions. From the standpoint of statistics, one does not need a larger sample to represent a larger population. And the sample gathered for the California project was demonstrably representative in all the key demographics as well as in party and political ideology.

What's Next California is the first state-wide Deliberative Poll® in California. It showed dramatic changes in opinion once people thought about the issues. To the surprise of many reform advocates the people did not support getting the legislature involved in the initiative. But they did support requirements for transparency and citizen-review of initiative propositions. To the surprise of many observers, the people did not support a part time-legislature with part-time pay, at least, once they thought about it in the weekend deliberations. But they did support dramatic changes in the structure of the legislature itself – increasing the number of legislators and increasing the length of terms in the Assembly and State Senate so that people were not running for re-election from the moment they took office. Despite an initial 14 per cent approval rating for the legislature, the support for increasing the terms of the legislature went from 33 per cent on first contact to 80 per cent at the end of the weekend. There was also strong support, after deliberation, for realignment of government service delivery, moving it more to the local level provided that guarantees were in place for accountability. And there was even support for certain tax proposals, including a lowering of the two-thirds threshold for new taxes required by Proposition 13 (CDD 2011).

The basic insight of the Progressives was correct – the people are capable of self-government. It is just a question of adjusting the institutional design so that individual voters, each with one vote in millions, can feel it is worth their time and effort to pay attention. In this case, as with competitive democracy, it seems that the most consequential route to real influence for deliberative democracy is in setting the agenda for public voting. If the people deliberatively select candidates, then there is an element of public-will formation in the competitive democracy process. If the people deliberatively select the alternatives that are worth a public vote, then there is an element of public-will formation in direct democracy, even on the scale of California.

These entry points for deliberative democracy are far from exhausting the possibilities. But they offer glimpses of what is possible. We are in a period of dramatic mass disaffection from the political process in many countries around the globe. Such disaffection can be channelled into populism or it can be channelled into thoughtful redesign. Rethinking the prospects for deliberative democracy should be part of that dialogue.

References

CDD (Center for Deliberative Democracy) (2011) *What's Next California: Overview and Results.* Online. Available http://cdd.stanford.edu/polls/california/2011/nextca-results.pdf (accessed 17 October 2013).

Farrar, C. *et al.* (2010) 'Disaggregating deliberation's effects: an experiment within a Deliberative Poll', *British Journal of Political Science* 40: 333–47.

Fishkin, J. (1979) *Tyranny and Legitimacy: A critique of political theories*, Baltimore: Johns Hopkins University Press.

—— (2009) *When the People Speak: Deliberative democracy and public consultation*, Oxford: Oxford University Press.

Fishkin, J. S. *et al.* (2008) 'Returning deliberative democracy to Athens: Deliberative Polling for candidate selection', working paper, The Center for Deliberative Democracy, Stanford University. Online. Available http://cdd.stanford.edu/research/papers/2008/candidate-selection.pdf (accessed 17 October 2013).

Fishkin, J. S., He, B., Luskin, R. C. and Siu, A. (2010) 'Deliberative democracy in an unlikely place: deliberative polling in China', *British Journal of Political Science* 40 (1): 435–48.

Fishkin, J. S., Luskin, R. C. and Jowell, R. (2000) 'Deliberative polling and public consultation', *Parliamentary Affairs* 53: 657–660.

Fishkin, J. Luskin, R. C. and Siu, A. (forthcoming) 'Europolis and the European wide public sphere: Empirical explorations of a counter-factual ideal', *European Union Politics.*

Habermas, J. (1996) *Between Facts and Norms: Contributions to a discourse theory of law and democracy*, Cambridge, MA: MIT Press.

Madison, J. (1788) 'The senate continued', Federalist No. 63, *Federalist Papers.*

Magleby, D. (1984) *Direct Legislation: Voting on ballot propositions*, Baltimore, MD: John Hopkins University Press.

Mill, J. S. (1991 [1862]) *Considerations on Representative Government*, New York: Prometheus Books.

Papandreou, G. (2006) 'Picking candidates by the numbers', *International Herald Tribune*. Online. Available http://www.nytimes.com/2006/06/07/opinion/07iht-edpapa.1914443.html (accessed 17 October 2013).

Pateman, C. (1976) *Participation and Democratic Theory*, Cambridge: Cambridge University Press.

—— (2012) 'Participatory democracy revisited', *Perspectives on Politics*, 10 (1): 7–19.

Posner, R. (2003) *Law, Pragmatism and Democracy*, Cambridge, MA: Harvard University Press.

Schumpeter, J. A. (1942) *Capitalism, Socialism and Democracy*, New York: Harper & Row.

Siu, A. (2008) *Look Who's Talking*, PhD dissertation, Stanford University, Department of Communication.

Chapter Four

What Would Dahl Say?: An Appraisal of the Democratic Credentials of Deliberative Polls® and Other Mini-Publics

Ian O'Flynn and Gaurav Sood

Introduction

The concept of deliberation is both rich and complex. Without attempting too precise a definition, we take it to be a form of reasoned, open-minded discussion. Those who engage in it may have very different views but they must still be willing to listen to and reflect upon opposing arguments and to respond to them seriously. Of course, deliberation is practised in many different spheres and to a variety of ends. In this chapter, we focus on deliberation that contributes to democracy. In a democracy, important decisions of law and policy depend on the views and opinions of those who will be bound by them. Insofar as deliberation helps those bound by the decisions to refine their views and opinions, more thoughtful and informed policy decisions will result.

That, at least, is the claim. In practice, however, much will depend on the conditions under which deliberation occurs. As democrats, we want people to deliberate under conditions that can themselves be described as 'democratic'. But there is plenty of disagreement about precisely which conditions (embodied in an institution, procedure, practice, etc.) ought to apply (Weale 1999: 40–2). In this chapter, we take our lead from Robert Dahl, and in particular from his *Democracy and Its Critics* (1989). As he argues in that book, the most basic democratic standard of all is the principle of political equality. That principle supposes not just that each person is to have his interests treated with equal consideration but also that each person is to have an equal right to say what his interests are. That is, of course, a relatively abstract formulation. Yet, according to Dahl, the extent to which a political institution satisfies this principle can be assessed by judgeing its adherence to five more specific procedural criteria, namely inclusion, effective participation, enlightened understanding, voting equality at the decisive stage, and control of the agenda (Dahl 1989: chapters 8–9).

While other criteria can be invoked, we think that these five offer a fairly objective set of standards by which to assess the democratic credentials of mini-publics in general and deliberative polls in particular.[1] Before proceeding with our analysis, however, a number of provisos need to be entered. Dahl claims that we could not call a political process democratic unless it satisfied the five criteria. Yet that claim needs to be appropriately understood. Since these are criteria of an ideal political order, we might, in practice, allow some deviation from them and still call that order democratic. Nor would we necessarily expect every democratic institution to satisfy all five – for example, participants in deliberative polls do not vote, let alone vote at the decisive stage (more on which below). However, the fact that a particular institution does not satisfy one or other of the criteria can still be telling. It can remind us that a certain 'sequencing' of the democratic process is probably inevitable (Goodin 2005).

Inclusion

> The demos should include all adults subject to the binding collective decisions of the demos (Dahl 1989: 120).

One of the most fundamental questions in democratic theory is who to include in the 'demos' (see, for example, Goodin 2007; Miller 2009). The answer, according to Dahl, lies in a form of inclusive egalitarianism: if one is to be bound by a decision, one should be included on equal terms in the process by which that decision is made. So, to what extent do deliberative polls and other mini-publics conceptualise the demos as one that includes all who are potentially bound by its decisions; and to what extent do they succeed in turning concept into reality?

The answer to the first part of this question is complicated by difficulties in identifying who is bound by the decision. Take, for example, the Northern Ireland Deliberative Poll® on education reform (Luskin et al. 2014), which limited participation to parents of school-aged children. On the one hand, this restriction seems appropriate since parents of school-aged children constitute the current pool of adults who would be the bound by the reforms (if there were to be any). Yet, on the other hand, one might think it odd to exclude adults who plan to have children in the future and who may therefore find themselves bound by decisions in which they had no part. Time therefore complicates assessments of who is bound by a decision.

Such assessments are also complicated by the fact that a decision might affect some people directly while affecting others only indirectly. For example, since decisions about education policy inevitably have implications for the public purse, one might reasonably argue that all adults should be included, whether or not they have children in school. Indeed, even if it were the case that some people were

---

1.   It might be thought that the standards of assessment that need to be applied in the case of an analysis such as ours are those that derive from deliberative theory itself. Yet that would plainly bias our analysis from the start. By contrast, Dahl's five criteria strike us as appropriately 'neutral' with respect to the content of different democratic models, deliberative or otherwise.

in no way bound by the decision, one might want to include them anyway. For instance, even if the effects of the policy were limited to parents of school-aged children, one might still want to include those adults whose children have already gone through the education system so as to learn from their experiences. Those experiences may suggest different ways of 'framing' education policy and hence very different categories of assessment. In this vein, some deliberative theorists have suggested focusing on the representation of 'discursive frames' as well as persons or groups (Dryzek and Niemeyer 2008). Implementing this suggestion, however, poses novel challenges. How, for example, could we be sure that all of the relevant discourses were expressed or included in the course of a Deliberative Poll®? Since discourses are not person-centred, conventional sampling, focused on people, may not do the trick.

Besides questions about who to include are questions about how to include. By definition, literally including all is not an option for mini-publics. However, not including all comes at a cost. The cost depends on the diversity of interests, opinions, private knowledge, social or demographic groups, or some combination thereof in the population. For instance, a single person can 'represent' all if everyone is the same. But if everyone is different, then nothing less than including all will do. More generally, more diversity means that we lose more when a few hundred speak for a few million. Yet while mini-publics do not include all (or even attempt to recruit larger samples commensurate with greater diversity of opinion on certain issues), their designers continue to claim that that they are inclusive (Goodin and Dryzek 2006: 221). Typically, they justify such claims by arguing either (1) that the mini-public does not restrict access to anyone or (2) that the mini-public gives everyone an equal chance to be included.

For example, in the United States, executive agencies such as the Food and Drug Administration and the Environmental Protection Agency are required to hold public hearings before adopting any major regulation (Fung 2003: 342). Since public hearings are technically open to all, it also allows these agencies to claim that they are inclusive. Yet, while taking an open-to-all approach is certainly a convenient way of 'recruiting' a sample, such samples of convenience often pose inconvenient questions. Who exactly attends public hearings? Are they mainly drawn from the ranks of those who feel strongly about an issue, the more educated, or the representatives of well organised and richly resourced interest groups?[2] If there were any doubt, data amply confirm such distortions (Golden 1998).

The second justification has been used by the various Citizens' Assemblies, deliberative polls and, more recently, by the Australian Citizens' Parliament (Dryzek 2009: 2). However, claims about giving everyone an equal chance can falter because of weaknesses in the theory underlying recruitment procedures (sampling) and due to failures in implementation. For instance, the British

---

2. Can institutions that rely on a participant pool mostly composed of 'stakeholders' be classed as 'democratic'? From our perspective, the violation of the principle of political equality is too great for them to be classed as such.

Columbia (BC) Citizens' Assembly on Electoral Reform used quota sampling. Quota sampling can be understood as stratified random sampling without (or weakened adherence to) randomisation: instead of randomisation, quota samples rely on interviewer discretion. However, reliance on interviewer discretion tends to yield samples that have significant biases in who is included in the sample (*see* Moser and Stuart 1953; Jowell *et al.* 1993).[3]

By contrast, deliberative polls typically rely on 'random' sampling.[4] While in theory random sampling stands on firmer ground than quota sampling (*see*, for example, Lynn and Jowell 1996), it can still yield samples from which entire groups (or segments of the population) are missing. In practice, this caveat rarely needs to be applied and can be solved by stratified random sampling (as practised by the Australian Citizens' Parliament). Doing so, however, requires prior knowledge of the relevant groups and their proportions in the population at large.

The far more important and vexing issue with respect to random sampling is the slippage between theory and practice. In practice, random sampling often reduces to Random Digit Dialling (RDD).[5] RDD frequently fails to ensure that each member of the relevant population has an equal chance to be part of the participant pool. Such failures are a consequence of either non-coverage or non-response.

Non-coverage is the failure to include all in the sampling frame (*see also* Ryan and Smith in Chapter Two of this volume). For example, the homeless, prisoners, those in hospital, and active-duty soldiers often have an exactly zero chance of being a participant. More generally, sub-populations with lower rates of ownership of fixed landline phones are liable to be under-represented. To be sure, the sub-populations that lack access to fixed landlines may vary over time. Whereas in the past household income was an important variable (Groves 1989: 117–19), the problem today is mostly due to the rise of cell-phone-only households: in some countries, cell phone directories do not exist while in other countries the auto-dialling of cell phones is not allowed. Omission of cell-phone-only households means that certain subgroups, especially the young, are under-represented in RDD surveys (*see* Keeter *et al.* 2007).

By contrast, non-response is the failure to contact certain (kinds of) people. It is usually due to a lack of resources. Lack of time, money and interviewer training can all exacerbate non-response bias. For instance, notable gender asymmetries in the Northern Ireland Deliberative Poll® were attributed to a 'compressed field period', which did not leave enough time to contact enough men (Luskin *et al.*

---

3. Quota sampling has over the years attracted such opprobrium in academic circles that even studies comparing it to random sampling have all but gone out of fashion.

4. In some deliberative polls, the initial sample is recruited via non-probability marketing panels – for example, the sample for the 'Power 2010' Deliberative Poll® was recruited by YouGov from its online panel. Samples from these online panels often fare badly compared to probability samples (see Yeager et al. 2011; cf. Ansolabehere and Schaffner 2011).

5. In some countries (e.g. Finland and Sweden) random samples are drawn from population registries and hence are much less susceptible to non-coverage issues.

2014); the fact that many Northern Irish women stay at home to rear their children while their husbands go out to work meant that men were harder to reach. In general, the net effect of such failures may be such that, in practice, not a lot may separate poorly done surveys based on probability sampling from survey samples recruited via vastly inferior techniques.

Recruitment of the initial sample is but one half of the process that determines who participates in a Deliberative Poll[®]. The surveyed respondents (or a random subset) are invited to participate, and often enough a great many of the invited – roughly seventy-five per cent on average – do not.[6] However, the proportion of the invitees who eventually participate varies widely across polls, and across sub-populations. For instance, while nearly 92 per cent of those invited participated in a local Deliberative Poll[®] in China (Fishkin *et al.* 2010) only about 12 per cent did so in a Deliberative Poll[®] in Greece (Fishkin *et al.* 2008), and only 4.1 per cent did so in a Deliberative Poll[®] in Argentina.[7] More troublingly, in the Greek Deliberative Poll[®], the percentage of women in the participant sample was 23 per cent lower than their percentage in the recruitment sample.

Little is known of why participation rates differ so widely across polls. However we have some knowledge of the biases in who turns up. For instance, participants are typically significantly more knowledgeable than the non-participants (Westwood and Sood 2010). That suggests that political interest plays a role in the decision (not) to attend deliberative polls. Regularly failing to include those not interested in politics along with the chasmic differences that sometimes appear on socio-demographic variables undercut claims to a reliable process that guarantees inclusion. In fact, a variety of inducements (such as honorariums) that can potentially reduce asymmetries in participation are applied patchily and, from what we gather, offered when resources are available and not when researchers think it necessary. If practitioners are serious about turning concepts into reality, they will need to be frank about acknowledging failures,[8] serious about studying them, and punctilious about implementing lessons learned from analyses.

---

6. We base our analyses on publicly available data from the following 14 polls: New Haven 2002; Greece 2004; Northern Ireland 2007; EU 2007; US GE Online 2004; NIC 1996; UK Crime 1994; Australian Referendum 1999; China Zeguo 2005; Argentina La Plata 2009; Brazil Porto Alegre 2010; Bulgaria 2008; Japan 2012; Poznan 2009.

7. http://cdd.stanford.edu/polls/argentina/

8. For instance, Argentinian La Plata 2009 seems like a good candidate for a poll where things did not go according to plan. Keeping in mind that statistical significance is a function of the size of the sample, and that there were 62 participants, the researchers find that 10 of the 55 attitude items have significant differences, a batting average of nearly 1 in 5 (http://cdd.stanford.edu/polls/argentina/).

Effective participation

> Throughout the process of making binding decisions, citizens ought to have an adequate opportunity, and an equal opportunity, for expressing their preferences as to the final outcome. They must have adequate and equal opportunities for placing questions on the agenda and for expressing reasons for endorsing one outcome rather than another (Dahl 1989: 109).

According to Dahl, a democratic process must give everyone an equal opportunity to have his say. But even where the opportunity is formally the same for everyone, in practice, major disparities can still occur. For reasons already discussed, imperfections in recruiting mean that some people have less of an opportunity to participate than others. But even those who participate may not be able to participate on an equal footing. The garrulous, those strongly attached to their views, those who think the issue is important, the self-righteously knowledgeable, among many other species, all prefer talking to listening, often at the expense of giving others the chance to air their views. Then there are those who, even when they have the opportunity to talk, talk very little. In short, to ensure equality of opportunity, one typically cannot rely on formal rules alone.

Unfortunately, proactive measures can fail. For instance, deliberative polls use trained moderators to facilitate the small-group discussions.[9] Their purpose is to 'maintain an atmosphere of civility and mutual respect, encourage the diffident, restrain the loquacious and ensure that all the major arguments for and against in the briefing document get aired' (Fishkin and Luskin 2005: 288). Even so, the fact remains that many participants hardly speak at all (Kim, Siu and Sood 2010).[10] Insofar as they do not speak because they are crowded out by other participants, deliberative polls fail, in practice, to facilitate effective participation.

This latter worry extends to the plenary-session component of a Deliberative Poll®. Unlike, say, the participants in a citizens' jury, participants in a Deliberative Poll® are not asked to reach a decision, let alone a consensus, on the policy issue under discussion. Rather, what they are asked to do is to come up with an agreed set of questions that are then put the expert panel in the plenary sessions. Yet insofar as some people hardly speak at all, the questions that are put to the panel are generated under conditions in which actual equality of opportunity falls short of the ideal.

The near silence of so many participants would be yet more troubling if members of socially disadvantaged groups were especially less likely to talk. At first glance, this fear appears well founded. Women and the less educated do indeed speak less than men and the more highly educated. But after adjusting for prior

---

9. The training they receive usually lasts no more than a few hours. *See also* Landwehr in Chapter Six of this volume.

10. The evidence is from two online Deliberative Polls® and may not generalise to face-to-face Deliberative Polls®.

levels of knowledge, and some other background characteristics, speaking-time is not predicted by socio-demographic characteristics (Siu 2009).[11] Even so, one cannot simply say that deliberative polls meet the criterion of equal participation. While on average participants from socially disadvantaged groups may be no less likely to speak, they may speak less in certain kinds of small group. Random assignment to small groups generally produces a fair amount of 'variation in variation'– some groups are more internally diverse than others. So, while certain minorities are well represented in some small groups, they are not well represented in others. Consequently, in some cases they may lack the 'critical mass' and hence the confidence to voice their own concerns (James 2008: 120–3). Again, we do not know to what extent this is so but we recommend that scholars investigate this issue further.

What we do know, however, is that the more knowledgeable participants do speak vastly more than the less knowledgeable participants. On the face of it, one might not see this as especially troubling. For although there is no necessary relation between a person's being informed and his offering an informed argument, it seems likely that the more informed participants will, on average, offer a greater number of relevant facts when presenting arguments than the less informed participants.

On the other hand, one cannot simply assume that the more knowledgeable will speak for the ignorant or for those who are too diffident to speak. But even if we could assume this, democrats could still not rest content. Democrats do not want one group to speak for another but instead want each group to speak for itself.[12] In short, while there may be nothing about the design of deliberative polls or other mini-publics that biases the discussion process in favour of some participants, in practice much more needs to be done to ensure greater – that is, genuine, as opposed to merely formal – equality of opportunity.

A similar concern arises with respect to adequacy of opportunity. Deliberative polls usually take place over a weekend. But since some time must be spent organising the participants into groups, showing them to their rooms, explaining how the sessions will work, introducing them to one another, hearing from the moderator and so forth, the actual time available to participants for formal discussions is far less than one might imagine. A small group of 20 participants allowed five hours to discuss multiple issues leaves only ten minutes for each

11. Evidence for participation rates in Siu (2009) comes from two online Deliberative Polls®. *Cf.* Setälä *et al.* 2010, who suggest that women may, in fact, speak less than men. Whereas Siu bases her argument on coded transcripts, Setälä *et al.* rely on self-reports, which are vulnerable to social desirability biases. Indeed, the authors themselves modestly interpret their findings as 'Women seem to play down their own activity compared to men' (Setälä *et al.* 2010: 710).

12. As John Stuart Mill argued, we 'need not suppose that when power resides in an exclusive class, that class will knowingly and deliberately sacrifice the other classes to themselves: it suffices that, in the absence of its natural defenders, the interest of the excluded is always in danger of being overlooked; and, when looked at, is seen with very different eyes from those of the persons whom it directly concerns' (Mill 1991 [1861]: 246).

participant on average.[13] We do not know if this is adequate but we would like to signal it as yet another issue that deserves closer attention. One way to study the problem would be to simply survey the participants about whether they thought the time available for discussion was adequate. There are, however, potential complications, including the fact that 'adequate' time is likely to vary by issue and by diversity of opinions (and information) on the issue.

Enlightened understanding

> Each citizen ought to have adequate and equal opportunities for discovering and validating (within the time permitted by the need for a decision) the choice on the matter to be decided that would best serve the citizen's interests. (Dahl 1989: 112).

As we explained above, the principle of political equality entails that each person has the right to say what her interests are. The right is predicated on the assumption that each person is the best judge of his own interest, which is, of course, what many critics of democracy doubt. Yet deliberative democrats are not only committed to treating each person as the best judge of his own interest, but are also committed to ensuring that each person has the opportunity to learn what he needs to know to arrive at an informed judgement (Dahl 1998: 39).

So what is it that a person needs to know to make an informed judgement? Unsurprisingly, the list is dauntingly long: policy-relevant facts on all sides of the issue; logic and evidence behind conjectures about the probability of success of various alternatives; potential implications of the policy for oneself and others; the policy preferences of others and the reasons for their preferences; opportunity costs of adopting one policy as opposed to another; and much, much more. Not only is the list long, but each item on it is potentially overwhelmingly large – for instance, the domain of facts relevant to a single piece of legislation can easily run into thousands of pieces of information, if not more.

It follows, then, that any deliberative forum can no more than *aspire* to provide all the information that participants need to know. Yet it is also likely that some mini-publics go further than others in satisfying this *desideratum*. Unfortunately, the task of comparing different mini-publics is hampered by lack of common measures; so, again, we restrict our analysis here to evidence from deliberative polls. In particular, we investigate which particular features of the Deliberative Poll® design appear to bolster learning and which appear to be problematic.

Deliberative Polls® provide especially rich opportunities for acquiring information about the different sides to a policy issue, including balanced briefing

---

13. Although Deliberative Polls® normally take place over a weekend, administrative and organisational matters take up a fair bit of time. For evaluation purposes, it would be useful to know how much time exactly.

materials, moderated discussions and access to experts during plenary sessions. As one might therefore expect, on average, people learn a fair amount of policy-relevant factual information (Luskin *et al.* 2009). However, closer inspection reveals a fair bit of systematic variation around the mean – for example, better educated participants who start out ill-informed learn more than similarly ill-informed but less well-educated participants (Luskin *et al.* 2009).[14]

Some of this variation is explained by the different design elements of the Deliberative Poll®. For instance, data suggest that roughly two-thirds of the acquisition of 'public' information, including that contained in the briefing materials, happens *before* the small-group deliberations (*see* Hansen 2004; Luskin *et al.* 2009). Hence, it is likely that mini-publics that do not provide briefing materials to participants come up short in this respect. Of course, briefing materials are not a panacea. A non-trivial proportion of the Deliberative Poll® participants report that they do not read the briefing materials completely.[15] There is, moreover, a pattern to who reads the briefing materials, with women and the better-educated reading more of them. This matters because the extent to which people read briefing materials affects how much they learn (Luskin *et al.* 2009).

Selective attention, processing and retention of information are common human traits. This means that, even where participants are provided with balanced briefing materials, most of the learning is limited to attitudinally congenial information (Hansen 2004). While this bias in information acquisition is mostly corrected by small-group deliberations (Hansen 2004), the pattern of adverse side-effects to good remedies continues. Varying composition of small groups creates variation in opportunities to learn. For instance, those assigned to groups whose members are more knowledgeable and those assigned to more attitudinally diverse groups learn more policy-relevant facts than those assigned to groups whose members are less knowledgeable or those assigned to groups whose members are less attitudinally heterogeneous (Luskin *et al.* 2009).[16] This problem affects not just the learning of 'public' information but also the learning of 'private' information that only emerges during the course of the small-group discussions; the learning of private information also varies across groups because different people have different private information.[17] In all, the opportunities for learning are unequal and, courtesy of randomisation (where that is practised), arbitrarily so.

---

14. This has potentially crucial implications. Given that knowledge gain is positively correlated with attitude change (Luskin *et al.* 2002), it is likely that the less educated change their opinions less than the more educated.

15. The true proportion of those who read the briefing materials fully is likely to be even lower, given the prevalence of social-desirability-induced inflation on these kinds of questions.

16. While the evidence comes from Deliberative Polls®, it is likely that it generalises to other mini-publics.

17. Given at least some information is only available to a particular person, it also means that pertinent private information available to be shared varies by the sample. We would like note that this point has deeper implications for statistical inference when members of the group 'treat' each other (i.e. person A is persuaded by information offered by person B in the group).

There are a variety of other, hitherto unexplored, concerns. Here we only mention two. First, participants who feel strongly about a particular side of an issue may act strategically to raise doubts about correct information or, if it better suits their purposes, withhold correct information to which they are privy. Hence, participants may fail to learn correct information or end up doubting its veracity. Secondly and, arguably, more worryingly, since at least some participants are liable to be misinformed and since information offered in small groups is not vetted, it is likely that incorrect information is offered in group discussions. Correcting misinformation offered by others in small groups depends on those holding correct information speaking up, which may or may not happen. Consequently, it is possible (indeed, likely) that small-group discussions impart both correct *and* incorrect information. To date, we do not know to what degree this occurs.

Some of the points that we have just raised readily translate into guidance for the design of a mini-public. In our view, all mini-publics should consider providing briefing materials in advance of deliberation. Ideally, such materials should be as accessible as possible – for example, in response to worries about citizen competence, briefing materials could contain illustrations to help elucidate complex points. Their designers may also want to explore instructor-led (online or in-person) sessions as a way of addressing the fact that some participants do not (for one reason or another) read the briefing materials on their own. In order to reduce variation across small groups one could employ stratified random assignment, with the relevant strata being 'knowledge' and 'policy preferences'. Where learning is hampered by unequal ability, 'affirmative action' may be necessary to produce equal learning. For example, the less cognitively-able could be provided with additional help in the form of supplementary video materials. Finally, in order to judge whether people really are learning (or gaining the information that they need to make an informed judgement), designers could survey the participants multiple times over the course of their discussions to see how their attitudes change across survey times (*see* Goodin and Niemeyer 2003). Here the thought is that the rate of change will decline as people proximate their 'fully informed preferences'. Of course, the proposal assumes that the information that is presented, both in the briefing materials and in the small-group discussions, is balanced. Failure on this count means that lack of change in attitudes may not indicate a normatively defensible stasis but, in fact, reflect an end result of one-sided persuasion.

Voting equality at the decisive stage

At the decisive stage of collective decisions, each citizen must be ensured an equal opportunity to express a choice that will be counted as equal in weight to the choice expressed by any other citizen. In determining outcomes at the decisive stage, these choices, and only these choices, must be taken into account (Dahl 1989: 109).

While deliberative polls and other mini-publics are not decisive in the way Dahl intends – that is, they do not usually result in universally binding policy decisions – we can nevertheless ask about the extent to which they guarantee participants 'an equal opportunity to express a choice'.

While those responsible for designing deliberative polls and other mini-publics have mainly been concerned about the conditions that ought to precede the making of a choice, there is a need to think further about the implications of how exactly choices are registered. Some deliberative forums – for example, town hall meetings – use public voting. Yet those who hold unpopular preferences may lack the courage to express them openly and hence either stay silent or adapt their preferences in ways that bring them more into tune with those of the majority (*see* Elster 1983).

Worries of this sort may be attenuated by means of the secret ballot, the approach adopted by the BC Citizens' Assembly (*see* Warren and Pearse 2008), or the confidential questionnaire, the approach used by deliberative polls. However, confidential questionnaires bring problems of their own. At least partly as a result of lower social pressure to register a choice, some people may leave a question unanswered on the questionnaire, despite having a view about that question. The numbers here may be small (*see*, for example, Luskin *et al.* 2006: 187; Hansen 2004) but they are likely to come disproportionately from the ranks of the less educated, racial minorities and other socially disadvantaged groups (*see* Berinsky 2004).

There are, therefore, worries about how choices are registered. There are also worries about what exactly gets counted. While participants in a Deliberative Poll® are surveyed both before and after the event, there are problems in interpreting changes. Due to lack of motivation, social desirability pressures and other such problems linked to the fact that initial surveys are typically done over the phone (*see* Holbrook, Green and Krosnick 2003), measurement error can be much greater in pre-deliberation surveys than post-deliberation surveys. The latter are typically 'self-complete' questionnaires and respondents are often highly motivated to respond accurately, having gone through an extensive process. For example, when survey questions are asked in 'agree or disagree' format, 'yea-saying' tendencies can disproportionately contaminate pre-deliberation responses, thereby rendering any pre-post movement suspect (*see* Weiksner 2008). Insofar as this occurs, the worry is that bogus 'votes' are being tallied.

In addition to questions about the processes of registering and counting preferences, imperfections in the participant sample must again be taken into account. As we noted above, even if self-selection is precluded, the sample may still differ from the population. It is common to correct such imperfections using post-stratification, reverse entropy weighting, regression, matching and so forth. However, as far as voting equality is concerned, such techniques may not be enough. Suppose that a mini-public assigns people to small groups randomly and that the small-group composition has some influence on the outcome we plan to tally. It naturally follows then that, for the same sample, different random assignments will produce different outcomes. The potential outcomes (decisions, preferences or what not) of each person are now a great many more than two, which means that the traditional way to estimate the effect of the 'treatment' – simple difference in means between the treatment and control group – may be inadequate. In response to such concerns, we suggest the following: either work to make small groups similar to each other,[18] making any talk of group composition moot, or estimate a model for how small-group composition matters for all variables of interest and then simulate all random assignments to small groups. This will give us a distribution of effects, with each potential treatment effect having its own standard error. Of course, there may be other approaches that one could take. But the point remains that we need to work harder to ensure that mini-publics do more to ensure equality at the decisive stage.

Control of the agenda

> The demos must have the exclusive opportunity to decide how matters are to be placed on the agenda of matters that are to be decided by means of the democratic process (Dahl 1989: 113).

The power to control the political agenda is the power to determine which political issues will be discussed, the order in which they will be discussed and the options that will be decided on (Bachrach and Baratz 1962). While in principle that power should be distributed equally amongst the members of a democratic society, popular control over the agenda is notoriously difficult to secure (*see*, for example, Riker 1982).

It will therefore come as little surprise that deliberative polls and other mini-publics have, to date at least, fared poorly on this criterion (Bua 2012). The Danish model of the consensus conference seems to allow the freest rein: participants get to participate in setting the agenda and also have a say in the selection of the experts to be heard (Hendriks 2005). Yet even here there is little control over the basic terms of reference or, more specifically, which area of technological development is to be discussed (Co-Intelligence Institute 2003). To take another example, participants in the BC Citizens' Assembly were charged with reviewing the provincial electoral system and, if necessary, recommending an alternative system which would then be put to a referendum. On the face of it, this was a serious democratic responsibility involving a great deal of political agency and control. Yet participants were severely hamstrung from the start. While they could recommend a new electoral system, they could not recommend any attendant changes to the composition of the provincial legislature (which was to remain at 79 seats). That ruled out electoral systems that needed a relatively large number of legislative seats to work well – including MPP, which, as a number of commentators

---

18. Of particular interest are differences in group composition that have an impact on the outcome. For instance, if the mean knowledge-level of a group has a uniform impact on knowledge gain, one may want to make groups as similar as possible with regards to mean knowledge-levels.

have argued, might have delivered the stronger sense of local representation that most participants seemingly desired (Lang 2008: 92; Smith 2009: 89).[19]

In fairness, part of the failure to devolve control of agenda to participants is simply a consequence of extant funding realities. For the most part, deliberative polls and other mini-publics are funded by organisations (governments, political parties, NGOs and so on) interested in answering a particular question. It is our sense that most if not all mini-public designers would happily hand some control of the agenda over to participants if the right sort of organisational support were to become available (*see*, for example, Dryzek 2009: 5). But even if mini-publics were to devolve control over the choice of issue to be discussed, other concerns would remain – including concerns about the framing of the issue in the briefing materials, the choice of alternatives on which participants may offer their opinions, and the order in which issues are considered.

Lack of control over the crafting of the briefing materials naturally gives rise to concerns about their neutrality, comprehensiveness and correctness, not least because the process by which briefing materials are constructed tends to be woefully opaque. We need to know a lot more about where the information they contain comes from, what resources were expended in drawing them up, how the order in which information is presented was determined, which organisations (or 'experts') were consulted and how they were consulted (for example, did any organisation have a veto?), and so on. The lack of data (a consequence of opaque procedures) means that it is hard to make progress on these issues, other than by relying on reports from participants, which may not be very diagnostic. Unsurprisingly, then, our recommendation is for greater transparency.

The construction of the questionnaire is another area of concern. Deliberative polls typically ask participants to mark their preferences on closed-ended scales, such as 'on a scale of 0 to 10, where 0 is opposing something as strongly as possible, 10 is supporting it as strongly as possible, and 5 is exactly in between, how strongly would you support or oppose policy X?' Yet, partly as a result of the structure of the questionnaire and partly as a matter of constraints on available time, closed-ended scales have the potential to poll people only on a subset of concerns about any one topic – concerns chosen by the creators of the questionnaire. As such, closed-ended scales provide inadequate opportunities for participants to note their own concerns about the issue, which one might view as an analogue of failure of control over the agenda. This is not to denigrate instruments of this sort; closed-ended measures are extremely valuable – they are efficient and cost-effective, and can capture a fair bit of important information.[20] But it does suggest that Deliberative Poll® designers ought to consider making greater use of open-format

---

19. A sceptic might say that, in restricting the agenda in this way, political elites in BC were seeking to ensure that whatever the Assembly finally recommended, that recommendation would not be contrary to their interests (*see* Dahl 1998: 40).

20. Efficiency comes from the fact that the information that they capture is structured and already reduced to numbers.

measures, soliciting people's opinions about the issues under discussion in more general terms, especially as we continue to make gains in analysis of textual data.

Finally, when multiple issues are discussed, one must worry whether a participant's judgement about one issue will be inappropriately affected by his judgement about another. The graver worry that emerges here concerns the possibility of manipulating outcomes by carefully choosing which issues get discussed. For instance, an organisation with a hidden anti-immigration agenda might seek to pair immigrant rights with terrorism, while a pro-immigration organisation might seek to pair immigrant rights with globalisation of capital. And then, of course, there are worries about the order in which issues are discussed: which issue is discussed first may be consequential. Indeed, there is evidence from a Deliberative Poll® to suggest that the order of discussion may have an effect on how much people learn about each issue and on how their attitudes change (*see* the tables in Farrar *et al.* 2010).

Clearly, the issues here are vast and multifaceted. Yet for whatever reason, mini-public designers have been slow to confront them. This is surprising, given the seriousness with which political scientists in general regard the power that attaches to being able to control the policy agenda.

Conclusion

Deliberative polls and other mini-publics have been widely trumpeted as a panacea for various democratic ills and, in particular, for the 'democratic deficit' in liberal democracies (Dryzek and Dunleavy 2009: chapter 9). Yet while deliberative polls and other mini-publics hold out much promise, their democratic credentials have been largely left untried. In this chapter we have sought to redress this lacuna. We find that the Deliberative Poll® scores poorly on some of Dahl's criteria and hence, to that extent at least, fails to create suitable conditions for *democratic* deliberation. In particular, there are serious concerns about effective participation (at least in online deliberative polls) and agenda control. Yet, as we pointed out in our introductory remarks, one would not necessarily expect every democratic institution to satisfy every democratic standard to the same degree. What ultimately matters is the democratic framework as a whole: is it sufficiently balanced? Is institutional reform a realistic possibility? And so forth.

Unfortunately, such questions far exceed the scope of this chapter. But it is worth pointing out that deliberative democrats interested in the prospects for, and design of, mini-publics are acutely aware of such problems. In particular, there is a growing sense that what is required is a more panoptic view of their place within the democratic system as a whole (for example, Smith 2009; Newton and Geissel 2011; Parkinson and Mansbridge 2012). We need to know much more about their possible contribution to the policy process and where that contribution might be best placed. The sheer breadth of these questions (and more besides) necessarily means that our effort here has been a modest one; we have tried to identify places where there is some slippage between claims and practice, between assumptions and empirical reality and between different assumptions. We have given our reasons and, where possible, proposed some solutions.

Surprisingly, we have found the going hard even on this modest venture. Both lack of data and incommensurability of measures (either due to lack of co-ordination or different underlying theoretical assumptions) have occluded our analytical lens. Naturally, then, our first recommendation is to urge designers and practitioners to collect more data and to make it more broadly available. To this end, they might seek to learn from the extensive efforts of political scientists to jointly collect data on different democratic systems (for example, the Comparative Constitutions Project, Comparative Study of Electoral Systems, and so on). For more foundational differences across mini-publics, it is important to be as clear as possible about criteria, principles, values and guiding assumptions – which, among other things, means that normative and empirical deliberative democrats need to work closely together. But if it is important to be explicit about how we understand each criterion, principle or value, we also need to be clearer about the relationships between them – and in particular about the difficult trade-offs that will sometimes need to be made (Thompson 2008). This matters not just for scholarly reasons but for ensuring accountability. Mini-publics can seem artificial; they can also seem designed to further the interests of those who promote them. To some they will seem too liberal, to others they will seem too 'otherworldly', which may explain why 'uptake' often proves so patchy (Goodin and Dryzek 2006). If such problems are to be addressed, then greater transparency will be needed.

Mini-publics have long been criticised by advocates of the status quo. They argue that deliberative alternatives are at best unnecessary and at worst distinctly poorer than current institutional arrangements. We are not part of that cabal which requires its members to elide over inconveniences such as the large chasm between foundational assumptions and reality (for example, the US Congress was conceived of as a deliberative body but most observers would agree that today it is anything but that). In fact, we are card-carrying members of that other cabal that sees distinct hope in deliberation as a way to solve some of the ills of contemporary democratic institutions. And none of the deficiencies we find in mini-publics have dimmed our optimism, although they have made us more keenly aware of the work that needs to be done to fulfil their promise.

References

Ansolabehere, S. and Schaffner, B. (2011) 'Re-examining the validity of different survey modes for measuring public opinion in the US: findings from a 2010 multi-mode comparison', working paper.

Bachrach, P. and Baratz, M. (1962) 'Two faces of power', *American Political Science Review*, 56 (4): 947–52.

Berinsky, A. J. (2004) *Silent Voices: Public opinion and political participation in America*, Princeton, NJ: Princeton University Press.

Bua, A. (2012) 'Agenda setting and democratic innovation: the case of the Sustainable Communities Act', *Politics* 32 (1): 10–20.

Co-Intelligence Institute (2003) *Consensus Conference: a Danish description.* Online. Available http://www.co-intelligence.org/P-ConsensusConference1.html (accessed 1 October 2013).

Dahl, R. (1989) *Democracy and Its Critics*, New Haven, CT: Yale University Press.

— (1998) *On Democracy*, New Haven, CT: Yale University Press.

Dryzek, J. (2009) 'The Australian Citizens' Parliament: a world first', *Journal of Public Deliberation* 5 (1). Available http://services.bepress.com/jpd/vol5/iss1/art9 (accessed 1 October 2013).

Dryzek, J. and Niemeyer, S. (2008) 'Discursive representation', *American Political Science Review* 102 (4): 481–93.

Dryzek, J. and Dunleavy, P. (2009) *Theories of the Democratic State*, Basingstoke: Palgrave Macmillan.

Elster, J. (1983) *Sour Grapes: Studies in the subversion of rationality*, Cambridge: Cambridge University Press.

Farrar, C., Fishkin, J. S., Green, D. P., List, C., Luskin, R. C. and Levy Paluck, E. (2010) 'Disaggregating deliberation's effects: an experiment within a Deliberative Poll', *British Journal of Political Science* 40 (2): 333–47.

Fishkin, J. S. (1995) *The Voice of the People: Public opinion and democracy*, New Haven, CT: Yale University Press.

Fishkin, J. S., He, B., Luskin, R. C., and Siu, A. (2010) 'Deliberative democracy in an unlikely place: deliberative polling in China', *British Journal of Political Science* 40 (2): 435–48.

Fishkin, J. S. and Luskin, R. C. (2005) 'Experimenting with a democratic ideal: deliberative polling and public opinion', *Acta Politica* 40 (3): 284–98.

Fishkin, J. S., Luskin, R. C., Panaretos, J., Siu, A., Xekalaki, E. 'Returning deliberative democracy to Athens: Deliberative polling for candidate selection', paper presented at the American Political Science Association Annual Conference, Boston, August 2008.

Fung, A. (2003) 'Recipes for public spheres: eight institutional design choices and their consequences', *Journal of Political Philosophy* 11 (3): 338–67.

Golden, M. M. (1998) 'Interest groups in the rule-making process: Who participates? Who gets heard?', *Journal of Public Administration Research and Theory*, 8 (2): 245–70.

Goodin, R. E. (2005) 'Sequencing deliberative moments', *Acta Politica* 40 (2): 182–96.

— (2007) 'Enfranchising all affected interests, and its alternatives', *Philosophy & Public Affairs*, 35 (1): 40–68.

Goodin, R. E. and Dryzek, J. S. (2006) 'Deliberative impacts: the macro-political uptake of mini-publics', *Politics & Society*, 34 (2): 219–44.

Goodin, R.E. and Niemeyer, S. (2003) 'When does deliberation begin? Internal reflection versus public discussion in deliberative democracy', *Political Studies* 51 (4): 627–49.

Groves, R. (2004) *Survey Errors and Survey Costs*, London: Wiley.

Hansen, M. H. (1989) *Deliberative Democracy and Opinion Formation*. PhD dissertation, University of Southern Denmark.

Hendriks, C. M. (2005) 'Consensus conferences and planning cells: lay citizen deliberations', in J. Gastil and P. Levine (eds) *The Deliberative Democracy Handbook: Strategies for effective civic engagement in the 21st century*, San Francisco: Jossey-Bass.

Holbrook, A. L., Green, M. C. and Krosnick, J. A. (2003) 'Telephone vs. face-to-face interviewing of national probability samples with long questionnaires: comparisons of respondent satisficing and social desirability response bias', *Public Opinion Quarterly* 67 (1): 79–125.

Iyengar, S., Luskin, R. C. and Fishkin, J. S. (2003) 'Facilitating informed public opinion: evidence from face-to-face and online deliberative polls', working paper, The Center for Deliberative Democracy, Stanford University. Online. Available http://pcl.stanford.edu/common/docs/research/iyengar/2003/facilitating.pdf (accessed 1 October 2013).

James, M. R. (2008) 'Descriptive representation in the British Columbia Citizens' Assembly', in M. Warren and H. Pearse (eds) *Designing Deliberative Democracy: The British Columbia Citizens' Assembly*, Cambridge: Cambridge University Press.

Jowell, R., Hedges, B, Lynn, P., Farrant, G. and Heath, A. (1993) 'The 1992 British election: the failure of the polls', *Public Opinion Quarterly* 57 (2): 238–63.

Keeter, S., Courtney Kennedy, A. C., Tompson, T. and Mokrzycki, M. (2007) 'What's missing from national landline RDD surveys? The impact of the growing cell-only population', *Public Opinion Quarterly* 71 (5): 772–92.

Kim, N., Siu, A. and Sood, G. 'Minority report: impact of opinion minorities on deliberation', paper presented at the Annual Meeting of the International Communication Association, Singapore, 2010.

Luskin, R. C., Fishkin, J. S. and Jowell, R. (2002) 'Considered opinions: deliberative polling in Britain', *British Journal of Political Science* 32 (3): 455–87.

Lang, A. (2008) 'Agenda-setting in deliberative forums: expert influence and citizen autonomy in the BC Citizens' Assembly', in M. Warren and H. Pearse (eds) *Designing Deliberative Democracy: The British Columbia Citizens' Assembly*, Cambridge: Cambridge University Press.

Luskin, R. C., Hahn, K. S., Fishkin, J. S. and Iyengar, S. (2006) 'The deliberative voter', working paper, The Center for Deliberative Democracy, Stanford University. Online. Available http://cdd.stanford.edu/research/papers/2006/deliberative-voter.pdf (accessed 1 October 2013).

Luskin, R. C., O'Flynn, I., Fishkin, J. S. and Russell, D. (2014) 'Deliberating across deep divides', *Political Studies* 62 (1): 116–135.

Luskin, R. C., Sood, G., Fishkin, J. S. and Kim, N. (2009) 'Deliberation and learning: Evidence from the deliberative polls', paper presented at the American Political Science Association Annual Conference, Chicago, 2009.

Lynn, P. and Jowell, R (1996) 'How might opinion polls be improved? The case for probability sampling', *Journal of the Royal Statistical Society* 159 (1): 21–8.

Mill, J. S. (1991 [1861]) 'Considerations on representative government' in J. Gray (ed.) *John Stuart Mill: On Liberty and other essays*, Oxford: Oxford University Press.

Miller, D. (2009) 'Democracy's domain', *Philosophy and Public Affairs* 37 (3): 201–28.

Moser, C. A. and Stuart, A. (1953) 'An experimental study of quota sampling', *Journal of the Royal Statistical Society* Series A, 116 (4): 349–406.

Newton, K. and Geissel, B. (eds) (2011) *Evaluating Democratic Innovations: Curing the democratic malaise?*, London: Routledge.

Parkinson, J. and Mansbridge, J. (2012) *Deliberative Systems: Deliberative democracy at the large scale*, Cambridge: Cambridge University Press.

Riker, W. H. (1982) *Liberalism Against Populism: A confrontation between the theory of democracy and the theory of social choice*, San Francisco, CA: W. H. Freeman & Co Ltd.

Setälä, M., Grönlund, K. and Herne, K. (2010) 'Citizen deliberation on nuclear power: a comparison of two decision-making methods', *Political Studies* 58 (4): 688–714.

Siu, A. (2009) *Look Who's Talking: Examining social influence, opinion change, and argument quality in deliberation*, PhD dissertation, Stanford University.

Smith, G. (2009) *Democratic Innovations: Designing institutions for citizen participation*, Cambridge: Cambridge University Press.

Thompson, D. (2008) 'Deliberative democratic theory and empirical political science', *Annual Review of Political Science* 11: 497–520.

Warren, M. and Pearse, H. (eds) (2008) *Designing Deliberative Democracy: The British Columbia Citizens' Assembly*, Cambridge: Cambridge University Press.

Weale, A. (1999) *Democracy*, Basingstoke: Palgrave Macmillan.

Weiksner, M. 'Measurement error as a threat to causal inference: acquiescence bias and deliberative polling', paper presented at the Society for Political Methodology Annual Summer Conference, Ann Arbor, MI, 2008.

Westwood, S. and Sood, G. 'Assessing quality of deliberation and its consequences: evidence from deliberative polling', paper presented at the Annual Meeting of the International Communication Association Meeting, Singapore, 2010.

Yeager, D., Krosnick, J. A., Chang, L., Javitz, H. S. Levendusky, M. S., Simpser, A. and Wang, R. (2011) 'Comparing the accuracy of RDD telephone surveys and internet surveys conducted with probability and non-probability samples', *Public Opinion Quarterly* 75 (5): 861–71.

Chapter Five

Normative Theory and Experimental Research in the Study of Deliberative Mini-Publics

Maija Setälä and Kaisa Herne

Introduction: On the relationship between the empirical and the normative

Generally speaking, normative theories of democracy are related to empirical political science in two ways. First, following Teorell (2006: 788), normative theory '[...] suggests what questions are important to ask and it provides the standards needed to evaluate the empirical findings'. An example of a question that is 'important to ask' is who votes and who abstains in elections. If it is found that particular groups of people are more likely to abstain than others, we may ask whether the representative system really fulfils the idea of political equality central to democratic theory. Second, normative theories of justice and democracy include causal statements that are empirically testable. For example, theories of participatory democracy suggest that participation in democratic politics increases participants' capacities to participate in politics and their sense of political efficacy (*see*, for example, Barber 1984). Pateman (1970: 45) argues that 'the experience of participation in some way leaves the individual better psychologically equipped to undertake further participation in the future'.

The experimental method is nowadays widely used in the social sciences and its use has also increased in political science. In their recent book on political science experiments, Morton and Williams (2010) report a clear increase in publications in the three top journals (*APSR, AJPS, JP*). A majority of these experiments concerns tests of descriptive theories or models. From the point of view of this chapter, it is noticeable that the experimental method has also been used to test certain claims made in normative theories. This chapter deals with the question of how deliberative mini-publics can be used as experiments, testing claims relevant to normative democratic theories of democracy and, in particular, theories of deliberative democracy.

Our first aim is to review how mini-publics have been used as democratic innovations and also, more recently, as experiments. After that, we take a closer look at how the conditions of experimental research have been met in the study of mini-publics and consider the interpretation of these results and their implications for democratic theory. Finally, we raise some critical questions and suggestions concerning the use of mini-publics as experiments. While this chapter focuses on experiments based on mini-publics, it is important to point out that discursive aspects of democracy have also been studied in other types of experiments (*see* for example, Karpowitz and Mendelberg 2011).

Deliberative mini-publics as democratic innovations and experiments

The term 'deliberative mini-public' was first used by Fung (2003). Following Goodin and Dryzek (2006), the term is used to refer to forums of citizen deliberation in which particular attention has been paid to the representativeness of participants (inclusion of different viewpoints). Deliberative mini-publics are democratic innovations (see, for example, Smith 2009) that are expected to expand and improve the quality of citizen participation in policy-making. Some formats of mini-publics, such as planning cells and citizens' juries, were developed as early as the 1970s to bridge the observed gap between citizens and policy-makers. However, there has been an increased interest in deliberative citizen participation since the 1990s, due to the 'deliberative turn' in democratic theory.

In deliberative mini-publics, the aim is to form a citizen panel on which different viewpoints on the issue are represented (Brown 2006). Participants are provided information on the topic and they interact with experts and stakeholders and, most importantly, engage in moderated small-group discussion. All these features are expected to encourage the weighing of different arguments, which is the central idea of democratic deliberation. There is an increasing body of research on deliberative mini-publics. Several case studies on deliberative mini-publics around the world have been undertaken. Sometimes, although not always, these include qualitative content analyses of discussions and analyses of impacts on policy-making (such as Dunkerley and Glasner 1998; Smith and Wales 2000).

The Deliberative Poll® was developed in the 1990s to provide a new method of measuring people's opinions: an alternative to traditional opinion polls, which do not encourage reflection or deliberation. The need to develop a method of measuring considered opinions was directly motivated by the theories of deliberative democracy (*see*, for example, Fishkin 2003). In the recruitment of participants, Deliberative Polls® apply the sampling methods used in opinion polls. From the sample representing the whole adult population, a group consisting of 100–300 participants is recruited through self-selection or, in some cases, a combination of self-selection and sampling. It is notable that, unlike deliberative mini-publics that aim to provide policy recommendations, Deliberative Polls® primarily aim to measure individual participants' opinions and knowledge before and after deliberation.

Otherwise, Deliberative Polls® share the basic features of other mini-publics, most notably, exposure to information and moderated group discussions. However, Deliberative Polls® involve some elements of experimental research, most importantly, the random allocation of participants to small groups and the pre-test/post-test measurement of individual opinions, attitudes and knowledge.

Deliberative Polls® were motivated by the idea of testing what appears a counterfactual claim, in other words, what people *would* think about political issues *if* they had more information and had deliberated on the issue (Fishkin and Luskin 2005: 294).

Quantitative analyses of Deliberative Polls® take advantage of the panel data gained from surveys conducted before and after deliberation. These studies frequently report significant opinion changes among participants, as well as increases of knowledge on the issues discussed. Moreover, it has been found that opinion changes do not depend only on information (Luskin, Fishkin and Jowell 2002). Luskin *et al.* (2002) have also shown that group polarisation has not taken place in Deliberative Polls®, which can be regarded as an indication of the absence of group pressures. Moreover, studies based on Deliberative Polls® often take advantage of a quasi-control group, that is, people who participate in surveys conducted before and after deliberation but who do not participate in deliberations. The use of a quasi-control group has lent support to the proposition that opinion changes were actually due to participation in deliberation and not to other ongoing developments in the society. The term quasi-control group is used here because participants in Deliberative Polls® are not randomly assigned to the experimental group and the control group, which gives rise to a self-selection bias (*see* below).

In the following, we review some results gained from experimental studies in which the mini-public format has been applied. The Deliberative Poll® on the euro in Denmark in 2003 generated a panel study in which opinions were measured at four points. The control sample was used to show that the changes are actually due to the experimental treatment, that is, to participation in deliberation. On these grounds, the authors call their study a 'quasi-experiment' (Andersen and Hansen 2003; Hansen and Andersen 2007). Like other Deliberative Polls®, the results from the Danish experiment include opinion changes and increase of knowledge. Andersen and Hansen also find that deliberation increases participants' understanding of the arguments used by those who have an opposing view on the issue. This study thus provides a more sophisticated analysis of the effects of deliberation and confirms the idea put forward by theorists of participatory and deliberative democracy that democratic deliberation increases understanding of conflicting viewpoints.

When testing various hypotheses, some studies of deliberative mini-publics apply content analyses of discussions in addition to the survey data collected before and after experimental treatment. Stromer-Galley and Muhlberger (2009) use data from an experiment in which moderated deliberations were conducted online. The authors make a content analysis of the expressions of agreement and disagreement in small-group deliberations and find that exposure to expressions of disagreement did not affect satisfaction with the deliberative event or motivation to future engagement. The results of their analysis contest the prevalent view that people find it uncomfortable to face political disagreements (for example, Mutz 2006); at least, this does not seem to be the case in organised deliberation.

There are studies on the effects of group composition on deliberation. Farrar, Green, Green, Nickerson and Shewfelt (2009) use three multi-site Deliberative

Polls[®] as an experiment, in which they study the effects of composition in randomly assigned groups. Their results show only sporadic evidence that group composition has effects on participants' post-deliberation attitudes. This result challenges the body of social psychological research, typically based on laboratory experiments, which finds significant group-composition effects on group deliberations and decision-making (for example, Schkade et al. 2000). The authors discuss the possible reasons for their findings. Among other things, specific features of Deliberative Polls[®], such as the use of moderators and the heterogeneity of participants, seem to encourage open-mindedness and decrease social pressures.

There are also more systematic experimental procedures designed to observe particular treatment effects among a group of deliberators. Setälä, Grönlund and Herne (2010) analyse the effects of two different decision-making methods – common statement and secret ballot – on the outcomes of deliberation. The participants, or the experimental subjects, were randomly assigned to two treatments, and to small groups within the treatments. The treatments differed according to the group decision-method; in other words, whether the decision was reached by writing a common statement or conducting a secret ballot. The experiment followed the procedures used in Deliberative Polls[®] in other respects, including measurement of opinions and knowledge before and after deliberation. The authors do not find significant effects from the decision-making method on participants' post-deliberation opinions on nuclear energy and other energy issues but they did find that participants' knowledge on energy issues increases more in the common statement treatment.

Farrar, Fishkin, Green, List, Luskin and Levy Paluck (2010) test the hypothesis that deliberation causes preference structuration, in other words, increased proximity to single-peakedness of participants' preference profiles. Half of the participants of the Deliberative Poll[®] deliberated first on the low-saliency question of revenue sharing and then on the high-salience issue of airport expansion; the other half deliberated on the same issues in a reverse order. This split design of the experiment allowed the authors to test the impact of the salience of the issue on preference structuration. The authors find that deliberation causes some preference structuration and this occurs especially on issues of low salience.[1]

---

1. A different method of analysing the outcomes of deliberation has been developed by Niemeyer (2011), who shows that deliberation increases meta-consensus and the intersubjective rationality of participants' opinions. Instead of traditional survey methods, Niemeyer uses the Q-methodology to measure participants' opinions, which allows the making of in-depth analyses of the changes of participants' attitudes.

Deliberation experiments as experiments in political philosophy?

Thought experiments and real experiments

As this brief and by no means comprehensive review of published studies illustrates, experimental methods have been applied in the study of deliberative mini-publics. In this section, the aim is to clarify the central ideas of experimental research and especially the use of experimental methods to study normative theories. A scientific experiment studies a certain phenomenon that is influenced by a number of factors. In an ideal case, we know what those factors are; and an ideal experiment holds N-1 factors constant and manipulates one factor. Controlled variation, which is the key to testing cause–effect relations, is possible only in the laboratory.[2] When other factors are held constant, we know that any variation in the outcomes of the experiment is due to variation in the manipulated factor. In reality, however, we do not know all factors and cannot ensure that we control all of them (*see* below). In addition to experimental manipulation, an experiment is also characterised by random assignment of subjects into experimental and control groups, which is expected to minimise systematic variation not due to experimental manipulation.

While normative theories cannot be tested as such, experimental study of political philosophy is possible to the extent that it tests the empirical claims embedded in normative arguments. As pointed out above, normative theories may include causal statements, such as the claim made by participatory democrats that political participation affects readiness to participate. Moreover, normative theories sometimes include thought experiments that elaborate what would happen under specified conditions. These conditions are often counterfactual, in the sense that they do not describe political reality as it is. Thought experiments call attention to specific circumstances and encourage the reader to imagine what would happen under these conditions; they start with a set of assumptions and proceed by making claims about what would happen if these assumptions held. Famously, Rawls (1971) presents a thought experiment about the choice of principles of justice in an Original Position specified by counterfactual assumptions such as the Veil of Ignorance.

Mitchell and Tetlock describe the relationship between thought experiments and laboratory experiments as follows (2006: 3): '[t]hought experiments help philosophers isolate and clarify the role of different principles and assumptions in their normative arguments, to see what is essential and what is not to a theory, much like laboratory experiments help to identify the role of different variables in cause-effect relationships'. When talking about experiments on theories of justice, Mitchell and Tetlock (2006) call the technique of testing thought experiments 'the hypothetical society' paradigm. The accounts of thought experiments in normative theories have varied from 'arguments' to 'elaborations of actual experiments'

---

2.   In social scientific experiments, the laboratory refers simply to a classroom, often equipped with computers but not necessarily.

(Souder 2003). In the latter case, it can be argued, it is only a question of time and resources that prevents such experiments from actually being conducted. Of course, the set of assumptions in some theories of political philosophy, such as Rawls' theory of justice, are so complex that they cannot be fully simulated in experimental conditions.

It can be argued that experimental testing of empirical claims made in normative theories is more scientific than just relying on speculation or thought experiments. If a testable, empirical claim is made, we should try to test it empirically rather than use imagination. An experiment is not necessarily the only possible way of testing such claims as these could, in principle, also be tested, for example, by using survey data. However, experiments often seem to be the best way. Thought experiments in political philosophy often rely on counterfactual conditions that do not exist in the real world and, therefore, may only be approximated in the laboratory.

Testing normative arguments experimentally involves the same problems that are encountered in other types of experiments. One argument against laboratory experiments is that they lack realism and do not therefore provide adequate tests of theories. In effect, there has been a call for more realistic field experiments, conducted in subjects' natural environments. While field experiments bring about certain advantages, they cannot often achieve the same degree of control as laboratory experiments (for a comparison, *see* Morton and Williams: 2010, 278–308). The issue of realism may not, however, be as acute when the claims of normative theories are studied. Thought experiments in normative theories do not necessarily mimic conditions of 'the real world' but may describe theoretically defined, counterfactual conditions.

Furthermore, Falk and Heckman (2009) list the common objections concerning the validity of social scientific experiments. These points concern both the internal and external validity of experiments. They include the use of university students as experimental subjects; trivial incentives; small numbers of participants; inexperienced participants; the Hawthorne effect; and self-selection of experimental subjects. The Hawthorne effect refers to the problem that being observed can influence the behaviour of the participants of an experiment. Some of these problems may not be relevant in experiments in normative theories; but, at the least, the problems of incentives, self-selection of participants and the Hawthorne effect are certainly relevant. These problems are discussed more in detail in the following section.

Mini-publics as experiments in democratic deliberation

Theories of deliberative democracy are based on the idea of an unconstrained process of mutual justification among equal individuals who represent different viewpoints on a political issue. In a deliberative process, deliberators judge each others' arguments only by their merits and are expected to revise their own epistemic beliefs and value judgements in the light of better arguments. In the course of deliberation, participants should reach more agreement on the qualities of policy alternatives as well as facts and values related to the decision. Habermas' idea of 'consensus-generating force of argumentation' has been further elaborated by Dryzek and List (2003), who identify preference structuration as an outcome of deliberation, and Dryzek and Niemeyer (2006), who introduce the idea of meta-consensus. The collective decisions reached through deliberative processes should be thus more legitimate (Habermas) or reasonable (Rawls) than the outcomes achieved by, for example, mere aggregation of preferences.

The theory of deliberative democracy seems to make counterfactual or, as it is sometimes argued, idealised assumptions about the nature of communication. However, Habermas (2005) denies the idealised character of his theory of communicative action; he thinks, rather, that the theory describes 'the rules of the game' of arguing. Without going deeper into the question of whether the idea of democratic deliberation is idealised or not, we can conclude that it seems to be counterfactual in most contexts of political talk. This is despite the fact that theorists of deliberative democracy have argued that the concept of deliberation should involve not just rational argumentation but also other forms of communication, such as certain types of rhetoric and story-telling (for example, Dryzek 2000: 50–6). Real-world political discussions seem to fall short of the standards of communication depicted in deliberative theory as they often include, among other things, bargaining, coercive and deceitful rhetoric and stories as well as appeals to emotions such as prejudice and hatred. Moreover, political discussions in informal or formal forums seem to be characterised by different social inequalities based on level of education, occupational status, gender and so on.

Proponents of deliberative mini-publics seem to maintain that mini-publics are designed in such ways that they can be regarded as experiments in democratic deliberation. The procedural features of mini-publics, such as the random selection of participants, information, interaction with experts and stakeholders and moderated small-group deliberations, can be assumed to facilitate deliberation among people representing different viewpoints (*see*, for example, Fishkin 2009). In this respect, mini-publics seem to follow the idea of experiments in a 'hypothetical society'. Consequently, mini-public experiments should not necessarily be regarded as tests of political talk in real-world contexts but rather as tests of what happens in conditions that are the closest to ideal in terms of democratic deliberation. However, if deliberation experiments are expected to shed light on the processes of political discussion and opinion-formation in the real world, for example, everyday political talk or parliamentary discussion, the question of realism may arise.

It is also notable that at least some results from deliberative mini-publics have been different from the results gained from political (or social) psychological research on discursive participation and political talk (*see* Delli Carpini *et al.* 2004 for a review). The experiments of political psychology differ from mini-public experiments in two important respects. First of all, most of these studies use students as experimental subjects and thus subjects are not representative of the adult population at large. Second, these studies do not necessarily aim to study deliberation understood as a process of weighing and judgeing arguments, just as discussion. The differences in the results of political psychological experiments and mini-public experiments seem to highlight the importance of the institutional context of political deliberation; and to support the view that the procedural features of mini-publics make a difference.

Although mini-publics have increasingly been used as experiments in democratic deliberation, it seems that, in most cases, mini-public experiments do not qualify as truly controlled experiments. So far, there have been only a couple of mini-public experiments meeting the standards of properly controlled experiments (for example, Farrar *et al.* 2010), whereas most of them seem to be less controlled quasi-experiments. However, more controlled experiments would be needed if we want to draw more reliable conclusions about various causal relationships related to democratic deliberation.

Of course, it may be asked to what extent experimental control can be applied in the study of democratic deliberation, which is a multi-faceted and free-form process of communication and reasoning (Kittel and Marcinkiewicz 2012: 38). However, certain efforts can be made to increase experimental control in mini-public experiments. First, participants should be randomly assigned to an experimental group and a control group. Second, in order to examine the impact of deliberation on dependent variables, such as opinion changes, political knowledge and efficacy, participants in the experimental and in the control group should be located in comparable circumstances and surveys completed under similar conditions. Third, in order to detect more specific causal effects, such as the impact of information, group composition or decision-making methods, separate experimental manipulations would be required. For example, Mutz (2006: 61) has encouraged studies which would disentangle these different aspects of the deliberative 'package' into smaller, more specifiable components.

Certain problems of experimental research are also involved in mini-public experiments. The question of incentives is relevant in deliberation experiments, not least because deliberation requires a lot of time and attention. People may be less motivated to participate in deliberation if it does not influence political decision-making. Indeed, the processes of deliberation may be quite different in purely experimental designs and in situations where deliberation is actually expected to influence or lead to collectively binding decisions. Mini-public experiments are also likely to be vulnerable to certain types of self-selection biases. It has been shown that participants in deliberation experiments tend to be more politically interested and knowledgeable; this seems to have been the case in both mini-publics primarily designed as scientific experiments and in those used primarily as democratic innovations (*see*, for example, Fishkin *et al.* 2005; *see also* Karpowitz and Mendelberg 2011: 268). It seems also plausible that the deliberative set-up attracts participants who are prepared to 'hear the other side'. The monetary compensation given to participants of mini-publics may help to alleviate the self-selection bias to some extent.

The Hawthorne effect seems to play a role in all kinds of experiments. For example, participants of mini-public experiments may refrain from showing very extreme opinions or they may adopt a position that they think pleases the organisers. In mini-public experiments, Hawthorne effects may be particularly hard to distinguish from the 'civilising' effects of public deliberation or other group dynamics involved in deliberative settings. However, it must be pointed out that these kinds of objections are not necessarily specific to the experimental method. For example, the self-selection bias and the Hawthorne effect are concerns for survey research as well.

Interpreting the results of mini-public experiments

In the second section of this chapter, we reviewed some experiments in deliberative mini-publics and their results. The question is now how these results should be interpreted and what their implications are for the theory of deliberative democracy. The Duhem-Quine thesis (Duhem 1906; Quine 1951; *see also* Guala 2005; Bardsley *et al.* 2010) deals with the problem that when certain hypotheses have been tested and certain results obtained, the experimentalist should decide whether the hypotheses can be rejected or accepted based on the results. The Duhem-Quine thesis states that this decision always involves some degree of interpretation, because we can never test a single hypothesis in isolation (Bardsley *et al.* 2010: 96). Instead, what we test is a set of hypotheses, the target hypothesis plus a set of auxiliary hypotheses. The problems of interpretation are related to the fact that we cannot be sure whether the results of an experiment have implications with respect to the target hypothesis or one or several of the auxiliary hypotheses. If the result is interpreted to depend on any of the auxiliary hypotheses, the question arises whether there are ways to change the experimental set-up so that these auxiliary effects vanish or, alternatively, to study the exact impact of these auxiliary effects.

Assuming that we use a deliberative mini-public as an experiment to test the claims of the theory of deliberative democracy, the target hypothesis is usually that democratic deliberation brings about certain types of outcomes or effects. In other words, we assume that the procedures of the mini-public actually foster the kind of reasoning and communication depicted in the theory of deliberative democracy. As a consequence, we rely on various auxiliary hypotheses pertaining to procedures applied in mini-publics, for example, that participants really represent different viewpoints on the issue discussed, the information given to participants is unbiased, moderators help to facilitate the exchange of arguments and there is sufficient time for participants to exchange and reflect on arguments. There are also other types of auxiliary hypotheses pertaining to the experimental setting, such as that the participants understand and follow the instructions of the experiment and that they interpret the survey questions correctly and answer them honestly.

It looks like our understanding of certain auxiliary hypotheses involved in mini-public experiments is still limited. Careful experimental designs in mini-public experiments could help to resolve some of the concerns related to the Duhem-Quine thesis. In the vein of Mutz's idea of separating different aspects of deliberation, effects of information, moderation, group composition or the duration of deliberation could be studied in separate controlled experiments manipulating one of these factors. One reason for the lack of such studies may be the fact that mini-publics are a costly way of conducting experiments compared, for example, to experiments using student subjects.

Furthermore, mini-publics typically also have another purpose, that is, democratic innovation. Some experimental designs, although desirable from the scientific point of view, may not be compatible with this purpose. The manipulation of certain aspects of the design of mini-publics, such as information or group composition, involves the risk of decreasing the quality of deliberations to the degree that a mini-public can no longer be regarded as a method of enhancing democratic engagement. It would therefore be recommendable that auxiliary hypotheses related to the procedures of mini-publics would be studied through controlled experiments that use students as experimental subjects.

In experimental research, the external validity of results can be increased by repeating the test of the hypothesis with some modifications. For example, mini-public experiments could be repeated with different subject pools, slightly different designs, different issues, and in different political contexts. If similar results are always gained, it is possible to conclude that the finding is robust despite variations in the experimental setting. It looks like that some of the findings of deliberative mini-publics have gained support in experiments with different designs, issues and contexts; for this reason these findings could be regarded as robust. For example, participants of mini-publics have unexceptionally learned about the facts related to the issue. However, it is not self-evident that this learning effect has necessarily been due to deliberation. The set-up of Deliberative Polls®, especially, does not usually allow us to infer whether participants' increased knowledge has been caused by the provided information rather than by deliberation. There is some evidence about the positive effects of the deliberation (Setälä *et al.* 2010), but experimental studies properly separating information from deliberation effects would be needed.

Moreover, there have been significant opinion shifts among participants of mini-publics. Results showing non-polarisation (Luskin *et al.* 2002), increased preference structuration (Farrar *et al.* 2010) seem to support the view that deliberation leads to the kinds of opinion shifts depicted in the theory of deliberative democracy. Naturally, opinion shifts do not necessarily follow from deliberation but they may be a result of other types of group dynamics. In order to distinguish the effects of deliberation from other group dynamics, it is recommendable that experiments would include more groups and that the relationship between deliberative processes and outcomes would be established at the group level (*see*, for example, Karpowitz and Mendelberg 2011: 267–9).

In experimental research, repeating the test increases confidence with the conclusion that a certain hypothesis can be rejected or supported. Indeed, it appears that some claims based on normative theories of democracy have been challenged by experimental research on democratic deliberation. There is some evidence showing that, contrary to the suggestion of participatory democrats, participation in public deliberation does not necessarily increase internal efficacy. Morrell (2005) finds out that deliberation did not have much effect on measures of internal political efficacy. In Morrell's experiment, there were two treatments: a 'parliamentary' form of deliberation that aimed at a collective decision and a 'generative' form of deliberation that did not end in a decision; a control group did not deliberate.

It is notable that Morrell's experimental subjects were students and, in this respect, his experiment does not qualify as a mini-public experiment. However, Morrell's experimental design was similar to the design of deliberative mini-publics because it involved the provision of information and moderated deliberations. In fact, evidence from mini-public experiments seems to be in line with Morrell's findings and suggests that participation in deliberation has very little impact on internal efficacy (for example, Stromer-Galley and Muhlberger 2009; Grönlund *et al.* 2010). It may therefore be argued that experimental evidence challenges the view that discursive participation necessarily increases internal political efficacy. On the other hand, these results contrast with the findings of social psychological research on political talk, indicating that facing disagreement decreases people's sense of efficacy (for example, Mutz 2006). All in all, these kinds of results have led to the refinement of some of the causal claims made in theories of democracy.

The fact that mini-public experiments test claims derived from normative theory raises further complications. It may be argued that normative claims pertaining to legitimacy and justice in deliberative democracy are not testable; but certain hypotheses related to them can be tested. Namely, normative theories may be understood as also giving descriptive representations of how people reflect on moral issues. For example, Swift (1999) discusses the relationship between people's thinking about justice and normative theories of justice. Descriptive studies, experiments or surveys could be used to investigate whether people actually think about ethical issues in the way normative theories suggest. Mitchell and Tetlock (2006) review studies of typical patterns of people's judgements on justice.

In a similar manner, it is possible to ask whether democratic deliberation corresponds to the way in which people perceive ideal collective decision-making processes. For example, it could be possible to analyse whether deliberative processes actually increase participants' perception of the fairness or legitimacy of a collective decision. This could be tested experimentally by comparing subjects' perceptions of the fairness and legitimacy of outcomes based on a deliberative process versus, for example, those based on mere voting. It seems that mini-public experiments have not been used to examine this topic, although there are some other experimental studies on the effects of discursive participation (for example, Sulkin and Simon 2001; Esaiasson *et al.* 2010; Persson *et al.* 2013).

How should we interpret those findings of deliberative experiments that seem to challenge some of the core assumptions of theories of deliberative democracy? As we are talking about a normative theory, these findings cannot be used to falsify the theory but rather to raise questions about its feasibility. For example, there are findings suggesting that different inequalities existing in the society arise in deliberative mini-publics despite the fact that particular efforts have been made to facilitate inclusive deliberation. For example, women and the less educated tend to participate less actively in deliberations (Mendelberg and Karpowitz 2007; Setälä *et al.* 2010).

One can find two possible reactions to the findings suggesting that deliberative mini-publics have failed to bring about such processes and outcomes depicted in deliberative democracy. The first reaction is to raise questions concerning the auxiliary hypotheses and ask whether procedures in mini-publics in general or in a particular mini-public in question have actually provided such ideal conditions for deliberation. In mini-public experiments, particular attention has been paid to procedures that should enhance deliberation. However, the designs of deliberative mini-publics may not create the most favourable conditions for deliberation, after all. As pointed out above, there is not sufficient theoretical or experimental research on how various procedural aspects of mini-publics, such as information, group composition or moderators, actually affect the quality of deliberation. Alternatively, the organisation of a particular mini-public may fail because of problems in the recruitment of participants or moderation, for example.

The second reaction is to challenge the theory of deliberative democracy itself. At the most extreme, this could mean the outright rejection of the standards of deliberative democracy. For example, the finding that different inequalities prevalent in the society arise also even in the 'most favourable' conditions of mini-publics can be seen as a confirmation of the unfeasibility of the ideas of deliberative democracy. These kinds of results may persuade especially those inclined to think that deliberative democracy does not provide a plausible theory of political justice or legitimacy (for example, Sanders 1997). A more typical reaction has been to redefine the concept of deliberation. For example, it has been suggested that the concept of deliberation should be broadened so that it would allow not just argumentation but also other forms of communication, such as rhetoric and story-telling, as far as they non-coercive and truthful.

The interpretation of the results of deliberative mini-publics would gain support from the analysis of processes of discussion and, especially, the evaluation of quality of democratic deliberation. The Discourse Quality Index by Steiner, Bächtiger, Spörndli and Steenbergen (2004) is one of the most prominent methods of analysing the quality of deliberation. It was originally developed for the analysis of parliamentary deliberations but it has been applied to the analysis of citizen deliberation as well (*see*, for example, Himmelroos 2011; *see also* Bächtiger and Gerber in Chapter Eight of this volume). Other authors assessing the quality of deliberation have paid more attention to the purpose of speech acts, based on the distinction between arguing and bargaining (Holzinger 2005; Holzinger and Landwehr 2010).

One may criticise all these measures of the quality of deliberation for the reason that they focus on speech acts and that they do not pay attention to cognitive processes taking place 'within' deliberators (for example, Goodin 2000). Indeed, these kinds of cognitive processes have largely remained unobservable or they have been examined indirectly through outcomes of deliberation. Outcomes of deliberation have been operationalised and measured, for example, in terms of the increase of knowledge, opinion changes, non-polarisation of opinions, increased understanding of others' viewpoints; or in more sophisticated terms, such as meta-consensus or preference-structuration. Indeed, scholars of deliberative democracy seem to have quite divergent views on outcomes of deliberation. Furthermore, these differences may reflect deeper theoretical disagreements on the nature of deliberation. Some authors follow Habermas and emphasise the 'consensus-generating force of argumentation' (for example, Niemeyer), whereas others take a more 'liberal' approach and emphasise changes in individual deliberators' values and beliefs (for example Andersen and Hansen 2007; Fishkin).

Conclusions: Prospects and limits of mini-publics as experiments

The use of mini-publics as experiments has provided new insights on processes of political communication and reasoning. Some of these results have challenged the results of social psychological research concerning group dynamics. In many respects, experimentation on deliberative mini-publics has helped to overcome the problem that normative theories and positive political science 'grow out of literatures that proceed, for the most part, on separate tracks, largely uninformed by one another' (Shapiro 2002: 235). Mini-public experiments allow researchers to study deliberation on real-world political conflicts and, sometimes, to give participants real incentives to participate due to political impacts of mini-publics. However, the role of mini-publics as democratic innovations seems to rule out such experimental designs, which would clearly violate central features of democratic deliberation such as inclusion and informed deliberation.

It can be argued that the experimental testing of causal statements in normative theories of democracy is more scientific than just relying on speculation or thought experiments. There seems to be two reactions to observed failure of deliberative mini-publics to meet the standards of theories of deliberative democracy. In the vein of Duhem-Quine thesis, it is possible to raise questions about the auxiliary hypotheses involved in the deliberative setting. These seem to highlight the issues related to the experimental set-up of the mini-public in question or mini-publics in general. This chapter suggests that the auxiliary hypotheses related to moderation, group composition, decision-making methods, time used for deliberation and so on call for more experimental research, either in controlled mini-public experiments or in deliberation experiments using students as subjects. The second possible response to the failure of mini-publics to bring about expected outcomes is to question the feasibility of the theory of deliberative democracy or, typically, to redefine the concept of democratic deliberation.

However, it seems clear that before making any conclusions, more and better experimentation would be needed to test various issues raised above. It should be kept in mind that experimental results only get external validity after several repetitions in different circumstances and with slight variations in the design. Although repeated testing appears recommendable, the practical problem is that the results of replicated experiments are difficult to get published. This problem is particularly pressing in the case of mini-public experiments, which are very expensive. The results gained from deliberative mini-publics are hard to interpret, not just because of the typical problems in experimental research but also because a consensus on how to operationalise and measure a deliberative process and its outcomes has not been reached. Moreover, there seem to be differences in views on the extent to which processes or outcomes should be emphasised when studying deliberation. Sometimes these disagreements reflect a lack of theoretical consensus on what, exactly, constitutes a deliberative process and its outcomes (*see* Chapter Thirteen of this volume).

References

Andersen, V. N. and Hansen, K. M. (2007) 'How deliberation makes better citizens: the Danish Deliberative Poll on the euro', *European Journal of Political Research* 46: 531–56.

Bardsley, N., Cubitt, R., Loomes, G., Moffat, P., Starmer, C., and Sugden, R. (2010) *Experimental Economics: Rethinking the rules*, Princeton and Oxford: Princeton University Press.

Barber, B. (1984) *Strong Democracy: Participatory democracy for a new age*, Berkeley, CA: University of California Press.

Brown, M. B. (2006) 'Survey article: citizen panels and the concept of representation', *Journal of Political Philosophy* 14: 203–25.

Delli Carpini, M. X., Cook, F. L. and Jacobs, L. R. (2004) 'Public deliberation, discursive participation, and citizen engagement: a review of the empirical literature', *Annual Review of Political Science* 7, 315–44.

Dryzek, J. S. (2000) *Deliberative Democracy and Beyond*, Oxford: Oxford University Press.

Dryzek, J. S. and List, C. (2003) 'Social choice theory and deliberative democracy: a reconciliation', *British Journal of Political Science* 33: 1–28.

Dryzek, J. S. and Niemeyer, S. (2006) 'Reconciling pluralism and consensus as political ideals', *American Journal of Political Science* 50: 634–49.

Duhem, P. (1906/1954) *The Aim and Structure of Physical Theory*, translated from French by P. P. Wiener, Princeton, NJ: Princeton University Press.

Dunkerley, D. and Glasner, P. (1998) 'Empowering the public? Citizens' juries and the new genetic technologies', *Critical Public Health* 8: 181–92.

Esaiasson, P., Gilljam, M. and Lindholm, T. (2010) 'The voice of the pupils: an experimental comparison of decisions made by elected pupil councils, pupils in referenda, and teaching staff', *Educational Assessment, Evaluation and Accountability* 22: 73–88.

Falk, A. and Heckman, J. (2009) 'Lab experiments are a major source of knowledge in the social sciences', *Science* 326: 535–38.

Farrar C., Fishkin, J. S., Green, D., List, C., Luskin, R. and Levy Paluck, E. (2010) 'Disaggregating deliberation's effects: an experiment within a Deliberative Poll', *British Journal of Political Science* 40: 333–47.

Farrar, C., Green, D. P., Green, J. E., Nickerson, D. W. and Shewfelt, S. (2009) 'Does discussion group composition affect policy preferences? Results from three randomized experiments', *Political Psychology* 30 (4): 615–47.

Fishkin, J. S. (2003) 'Consulting the public through deliberative polling', *Journal of Policy Analysis and Management* 22: 128–33.

—— (2009) *When the People Speak*, Oxford: Oxford University Press.

Fishkin, J. S. and Luskin, R. (2005) 'Experimenting with a democratic ideal: deliberative polling and public opinion', Acta Politica 40: 284–98.

Fung, A. (2003), 'Survey article: recipes for public spheres: eight institutional design choices and their consequences', *Journal of Political Philosophy*, II (3): 338–67.

Gastil, J., Deess, P. E. and Weiser, P. (2002) 'Civic awakening in the jury room: a test of the connection between jury deliberation and political participation', *The Journal of Politics* 64 (2): 585–95.

Goodin, R. E. (2000) 'Democratic deliberation within', *Philosophy & Public Affairs*, 29 (1): 81–109.

Goodin, R. E. and Dryzek, J. S. (2006) 'Deliberative impacts: the macro-political uptake of mini-publics, *Politics and Society* 34: 219–44.

Grönlund, K., Setälä, M. and Herne, K. (2010) 'Deliberation and civic virtue: lessons from a citizen deliberation experiment', *European Political Science Review* 1: 95–117.

Guala, F. (2005) 'The methodology of experimental economics', Cambridge and New York: Cambridge University Press.

Habermas, J. (2005) 'Concluding comments on empirical approaches to deliberative politics', *Acta Politica* 40: 384–92.

Hansen, K. M. and Andersen, V. N. (2003) 'Deliberative democracy and the Deliberative Poll on the euro', *Scandinavian Political Studies* 3: 261–86.

Himmelroos, S. (2011) 'Democratically speaking: can citizen deliberation be considered reasoned and inclusive?', paper presented at the workshop Frontiers of Deliberation at the ECPR Joint Sessions of Workshops, St Gallen, April 2011.

Holzinger, K. (2005) 'Context or conflict types: which determines the selection of communication modes? *Acta Politica* 40: 239–54.

Holzinger, K. and Landwehr, C. (2010) 'Institutional determinants of deliberative interaction', *European Political Science Review* 2: 373–400.

Karpowitz, C. F., Mendelberg, T. (2011) 'An experimental approach to citizen deliberation', in J. N. Drukman, D. P. Green, J. H. Kuklinski and A. Lupia (eds) *Cambridge Handbook of Experimental Political Science*, Cambridge: Cambridge University Press.

Kittel, B. and Marcinkiewicz, K. (2012) 'Voting behavior and political institutions: an overview of challenging questions in theory and experimental research', in B. Kittel, W. J. Luhan and R. B. Morton (eds) *Experimental Political Science: Principles and practices*, Basingstoke: Palgrave Macmillan.

Luskin, R. C., Fishkin, J. S. and Jowell, R. (2002) 'Considered opinions: deliberative polling in Britain', *British Journal of Political Science* 32: 455–87.

Mendelberg, T. and Karpowitz, C. (2007) 'How people deliberate about justice: groups, gender, and decision rules', in S. Rosenberg (ed.) *Deliberation, Participation and Democracy*, Palgrave: Basingstoke.

Mitchell, G. and Tetlock, P. E. (2006) 'Experimental political philosophy: Justice judgements in the hypothetical society paradigm', University of Virginia Law School Public Law and Legal Theory, Working Paper Series 52.

Morrell, M. E. (2005) 'Deliberation, democratic decision-making and internal political efficacy', *Political Behavior* 27: 49–69.

Morton, R. B. and Williams, K. C. (2010) *Experimental Political Science and the Study of Causality: From nature to the lab*, Cambridge, NY: Cambridge University Press.

Mutz, D. C. (2006) *Hearing the Other Side: Deliberative versus participatory democracy,* Cambridge: Cambridge University Press.

Niemeyer, S. (2011) 'The emancipatory effect of deliberation: empirical lessons from mini-publics', *Politics & Society* 39: 103–40.

Persson, M., Esaiasson, P. and Gilljam, M. (2013) 'The effects of direct voting and deliberation on legitimacy beliefs: an experimental study of small group decision-making', *European Political Science Review* 5 (3): 381–400.

Pateman, C. (1970) *Participation and Democratic Theory,* Cambridge: Cambridge University Press.

Quine, W. V. (1951) 'Two dogmas of empiricism', *Philosophical Review* 60(1): 20–43.

Rawls, J. (1999[1971]) *A Theory of Justice. Revised Edition,* Oxford: Oxford University Press.

Sanders, L. M. (1997) 'Against deliberation', *Political Theory* 25 (3): 347.

Schkade, D., Sunstein C. R. and Kahnemann, D. (2000) 'Deliberating about dollars: The severity shift', *Columbia Law Review* 11: 497–520.

Setälä, M., Grönlund, K. and Herne, K. (2010) 'Citizen deliberation on nuclear power: a comparison of two decision-making methods' *Political Studies* 688–714.

Shapiro, I. (2002) 'The state of democratic theory', in I. Katznelson and H. V. Milner (eds) *Political Science: State of the discipline,* New York and London: W.W. Norton and Company.

Smith, G. (2009) *Democratic Innovations: Designing institutions for citizen participation,* Cambridge: Cambridge University Press.

Smith, G. and Wales, C. (2000) 'Citizens' juries and deliberative democracy', *Political Studies* 48: 51–65.

Souder, L. (2003) 'What are we to think about thought experiments?', *Argumentation* 17: 203–17.

Steiner, J., Bächtiger, A., Spörndli, M. and Steenbergen, M. R. (2004) *Deliberative Politics in Action: Analysing parliamentary discourse,* Cambridge: Cambridge University Press.

Stromer-Galley, J. and Muhlberger, P. (2009) 'Agreement and disagreement in group deliberation: effects on deliberation, satisfaction, future engagement, and decision legitimacy', *Political Communication* 26: 173–92.

Sulkin, T. and Simon, A. F. (2001) 'Habermas in the lab: a study of deliberation in an experimental setting', *Political Psychology* 22 (4): 809–26.

Swift, A. (1999) 'Public opinion and political philosophy: the relation between social-scientific and philosophical analyses of distributive justice', *Ethical Theory & Moral Practice* 2: 337–63.

Teorell, J. (2006) 'Political participation and three theories of democracy: a research inventory and agenda', *European Journal of Political Research* 45 (5): 787–810

Chapter Six

Facilitating Deliberation:
The Role of Impartial Intermediaries
in Deliberative Mini-Publics

Claudia Landwehr

Introduction

In Habermas' counterfactual ideal speech situation, speakers are equals and co-ordinate their beliefs and action plans through a rational discourse. They make and challenge validity claims, resolve disputes and eventually arrive at a consensus that is both rational and dispels conflict, thus warranting a two-fold claim to superior legitimacy. In political practice, Habermas locates democratic deliberation in the public sphere, where communication is free-flowing, boundless and subject-free. While the contexts of justification in the public sphere can clearly be more or less democratic, Habermas and other proponents of a two-track-model of political decision-making that contrasts the public sphere and the political system are, for several reasons, less interested in the institutionalisation of deliberation in mini-publics (*see* Schmalz-Bruns 2009: 451–2). Bächtiger *et al.* have distinguished Habermasian deliberation as 'deliberation Type 1' from a more comprehensive understanding of deliberation – 'deliberation Type 2' – which not only considers less ideal instances of interaction as at least potentially deliberative but is also more concerned with the institutionalisation of deliberation (Bächtiger, Niemeyer, Neblo *et al.* 2010). Where deliberation is organised and institutionalised, however, some of the people involved in the process assume a role that is different from that of those who are to deliberate under conditions of equality: they function as organisers, agenda-setters, chairpersons, moderators, mediators or facilitators.

These intermediaries are ideally impartial and enable structured communication where it would otherwise be impossible, due to the intensity of conflict or simply to a lack of co-ordination. Understanding institutions as sets of rules (Ostrom 1986), those who organise and institutionalise communicative interaction must be seen as rule-setters; and those who keep it going within institutions must be seen as rule-keepers. Impartial intermediaries thus constitute a kind of personification of discourse rules, whatever these rules are in the given case.

Deliberation in mini-publics is always organised and structured by rules: the convenors typically choose the topic for a deliberative event, invite and select participants and set up a time schedule for deliberation. Typically, intervention does not end here: in most cases, deliberation is attended by a professional mediator, moderator or facilitator. Where this is not the case, participants may be advised to choose a chairperson from their midst or may even do so on their own initiative. While intermediaries in different types of mini-publics share the role of rule-keepers, the way they fulfil this role, and thus their impact on interaction and function in deliberation, vary widely – both in theory and in practice.

In this chapter, in the first section I will try to structure arguments for the use of impartial intermediaries in mini-publics and suggest a list of possible tasks and functions for them, before I review existing research on the role and impact of intermediaries in deliberative practice in the second section. In the third section, I will argue that the appropriate role of intermediaries – as chairpersons, moderators, mediators or facilitators – depends on the mode of interaction that is institutionalised and on the role of participants in communication. I conclude by pointing to open questions and possible routes for further research.

Intermediaries in mini-publics: Tasks and functions (theory)

Communication needs organisation – at least in groups of more than about five speakers, particularly where opinions conflict and where the aim is making some sort of decision. While fears of domination and censorship apparently deter many deliberative theorists from openly discussing organisational requirements such as agenda-setting and rule-enforcement, preventing disorder or even chaos in communication is a more practical concern: 'Free speech without regulation becomes just noise; democracy without procedure would be in danger of degenerating into a tyranny of the loudest shouter' (Blumler and Coleman 2001: 17–18).

Considering reasons for and against intermediation, it seems that there are strong normative reasons against it but also strong pragmatic reasons in favour. Taking Habermas' idea of the ideal speech situation as a reference point, it is clear that intermediation violates the condition that all speakers interact as equals: the intermediary possesses powers that are not based on the 'forceless force of the better argument' but associated with the special role assigned to him or her. Thompson and Hoggett point to a 'huge lacuna in the theory of deliberative theory', consisting in the 'absence of an account of leaders' (Thompson and Hoggett 2001: 360). Those who study the practice of deliberative democracy in mini-publics, however, are aware of the requirements of organised communication and groups' need for organisation and even leadership. Accordingly, they use intermediaries in the set-up of deliberative forums, although apparently often without reflecting on their role and impact. Deliberative democrats' lack of interest in leadership may thus result in a neglect of intermediation (which is nonetheless practised for pragmatic reasons) and thus a failure to connect practical experiences with theory.

In the surprisingly scarce literature on intermediation in deliberative forums, we find different functions and tasks assigned to impartial intermediaries (for example, Wright 2006: 553; Edwards 2002: 6). I suggest grouping these tasks as follows, ranging from minimal regulation to significant intervention in the discourse.

Task 1: Constitutionalise deliberation (institutionalisation and organisation)

Communication in mini-publics is, as noted before, always organised communication. As a minimum, someone needs to set up a website or book a venue and invite participants. Typically, this kind of initial organisation also includes the selection of a topic for communication. Consensus conferences or planning cells address very specific topics, such as genetic engineering or school reform. In participatory budgeting, too, the subject that is dealt with is clear – the allocation of a given budget. Citizen juries, focus groups or online forums can be more open where the subjects to be addressed are concerned but they still focus on controversial issues of contemporary relevance (such as issues in upcoming elections or problems in the community). In general, it seems that the more closely mini-publics are connected with macro-political institutions and decision-making processes, the more institutionalisation and organisation will be required.

The institutionalisation and organisation of deliberation also comprises the setting of conversational maxims or constitutive rules of reciprocal interaction.[1] Such maxims include the abjuration of physical and verbal violence and a commitment to minimal co-operation, in the sense that speakers refrain from speaking all at once and generally try to listen to one another. Participants in mini-publics are usually asked to accept a set of rules of procedure provided by the organisers. While details may be subject to change within the deliberative process, these rules are the initial constitution of a deliberative forum.

Task 2: Enforcing procedural rules

After the initial steps that organise and institutionalise communication, intermediation is typically taken over by a different group of people: chairpersons, mediators, moderators or facilitators. The motivation for this change in intermediaries is the legitimate fear that organisers could steer deliberation in a direction that suits their own preferences or research hypotheses. The choice of professional intermediaries who are not only impartial between the participants but also independent from the organisers is thus a requirement of good research practice.

The first and least controversial task for these intermediaries is to ensure that the rules of procedure, which are constitutive of the forum, are kept. In practice, this task ranges from preventing violence and enforcing compliance with discourse rules (for example, by banning insulting contributions) to keeping a list of speakers and admitting speakers to the floor. The enforcement of rules of procedure becomes more important the larger the group is. In small groups, speakers may manage to co-ordinate themselves if they have internalised the rules of procedure. However, the larger a group and the more controversial the issue at hand is, the

---

1. H.P. Grice pointed out a co-operation principle that regulates communication and is constitutive of it (Grice 1979).

more challenging and the more important keeping the rules of procedure becomes. If a group is left to itself, this task is often taken up by dominant participants. By assuming this responsibility these people do provide a service to the group; but they are not impartial and may tend to press their own views upon the other participants in illegitimate ways.

Task 3: Rationalising communication and keeping emotions at bay

The third task for intermediaries is far more controversial than the first two. Intermediaries can try to 'rationalise' communication by insisting on generalisable arguments and trying to keep emotions at bay. Interventions can range from the explicit rejection of contributions ('this is not an argument'; 'your emotions are not of interest here'; 'we don't want to hear about your personal experiences') over exhortations ('let's not get too emotional here'; 'let's return to the general question') to pacification or the rephrasing of personal stories into general arguments ('I see why you get upset here'; 'you probably mean to say that [...]').

Whether or not contributions other than reasonable and generalisable arguments should be permitted in deliberation is a hotly debated topic in current deliberative theory. Several authors have highlighted the legitimate significance of emotions in politics (for example, Hall 2005; Krause 2008) and argued that non-argumentative contributions such as greetings and, in particular, personal stories or 'testimonies' have important inclusive functions in deliberation and should therefore not only be permitted but encouraged (for example, Lara 1999; Young 2002). The present positive appraisal of emotions and personal narratives in democratic decision-making goes so far that the diagnosis that an emotional or narrative turn has followed the cognitive turn in democratic theory is surely correct.

Nonetheless, it is important to remember the benefits of rational argumentation; there are contexts in which it is the most appropriate and goals to which it is the most conducive form of communication. In particular, where mini-publics are to produce recommendations to become inputs to legislative processes at the political macro-level, comprehensible and generalisable arguments are essential for any real and justifiable impact on collectively binding decisions.

Task 4: Ensuring internal inclusion and pluralistic argumentation

A common problem with mini-publics is that, even if they are inclusive in the sense of being representative of the population at large, some participants are more assertive and eloquent than others, leading to a kind of domination that undermines the equality of speakers. Iris Marion Young was the first to remark on the importance of 'internal' as well as external inclusion (Young 2002). While it is easy to see how internal inclusion may be lacking, for example, when some speakers do not contribute at all or when they are not listened and responded to, it is difficult to say when precisely it has been properly achieved. Simply counting minutes of floor time or references to contributions by single speakers may be simplistic as a way to measure inclusion. Maybe internal inclusion is best conceived of as a regulatory ideal that intermediaries pursue, keeping in mind that it is notoriously difficult to achieve. Pursuing this ideal, it will help to be aware of the fact that dominant participants tend to be male, white and better educated, meaning that power relations within mini-publics tend to reproduce those in the society at large (Sanders 1997).

Intermediaries can try to counter undesirable power dynamics by encouraging ('A, what is your opinion on this?'; 'I think A can say something about this') and protecting ('I think A had not finished his point'; 'you're missing A's point here') shy participants and by thwarting too-dominant ones ('B, I think everyone's got your point'; 'B, please don't interrupt A'; 'I would like to hear what the others think'). However, inclusiveness can concern not only participants but also arguments. As Dryzek and Niemeyer (2008) argue, discursive representation is given where all relevant arguments and counter-arguments are heard and where different world-views and discourses are brought to bear on deliberation (Dryzek and Niemeyer 2008). Where the intermediary herself brings in missing arguments and views, however, she loses her impartiality. The intermediary can thus ensure argumentative inclusiveness legitimately only by encouraging and protecting the participants who make the respective arguments. Moreover, while deliberative theorists stress the importance of internal inclusion and organisers of deliberative events are usually positive about encouraging interventions by intermediaries, participants themselves may view such interventions as patronising.

Task 5: Summarising, aggregating and decision-making

The final task for intermediaries is the most problematic one. Particularly where communication is goal-oriented, for example, where a joint report or vote is to be produced, the intermediary is under some pressure not only to enforce rules of procedure but also to keep to a schedule and to structure the discourse accordingly. Structuring the discourse can mean to sum up results, to define the issue at hand, to close a topic and open a new one or to establish agreement. A more interventionist form of structuring and summarising consists of actively suggesting solutions or compromises or defining options to be put to a vote. Some models for deliberative mini-publics, such as the planning cell (*see* Hendriks 2005) do not force participants to take a decision but reserve the task of aggregation for organisers and intermediaries. The same path was taken in one of the most famous experiments in alternative citizen participation, the Oregon Health Plan (*see* Oberlander, Marmor and Jacobs 2001). In Oregon, the results of large-scale citizen hearings were aggregated by an expert group that merely registered the frequency with which certain topics were raised (for example, 'mental health', 'access to care', 'efficiency'). These 'results' of the citizen hearings then served as an input to an expert ranking of medical services according to priority, leaving the actual significance of deliberations for the decision entirely obscure.

Where aggregation and decision-making are not left to deliberators themselves but taken over by intermediaries, deliberation runs into the danger of becoming no more than an input to a technocratic decision-making process. Fears that deliberation mainly serves to win consent for predetermined decisions and ease the implementation of unpopular policies are clearly warranted here. Nonetheless, there are cases where the heat of a conflict renders agreement or acceptance of a majority vote unrealistic goals and where an arbitral award that takes the interests and arguments of all parties into account is better than no solution at all.

Intermediaries in mini-publics: Roles and impact (practice)

While the importance of intermediaries in mini-publics is frequently discussed, research on the effects of facilitation is surprisingly scarce. Deliberative events are typically intensively documented and studied. However, reports often mention facilitation only in the description of the set-up, not as a factor whose effects are systematically controlled for and analysed. As Wright notes: '[...] it is often claimed that "skilled" or "trained" moderators are used, but no details are given as to what this means in practice' (Wright 2006: 551). Given that intermediation is more or less universally used in mini-publics and widely appreciated for its benefits, how can it be that we know so little about what these benefits are?

I believe that one reason for this gap in research on deliberation is that it is – for eventually normative reasons of good research practice – in most cases hardly possible to organise a control group that deliberates without some sort of intermediation. As noted before, communication needs organisation, at least where group size exceeds a limit of five to ten participants. Where deliberation is 'cold', that is, where participants have no or little vested interest and emotions involved in the conflict at hand (*see* Fung 2003), communication without intermediation may simply be unorganised and unconducive to decision-making, with the resulting frustration possibly leading to a high number of drop-outs. In 'hot' deliberation, however, especially in divided societies or even between former combatants in a civil war, unmediated interaction may lead to physical violence – violence that in this case would in a highly problematic way have been caused by researchers themselves. In hot conflicts, setting up a control group without intermediation would thus amount to deliberative 'malpractice' and clearly constitute a violation of research ethics.

For cold deliberation, by contrast, the potential insight to be gained from comparing facilitated deliberation with non-facilitated deliberation appears worth risking a little frustration on the participants' side. However, given that researchers rarely have funds to realise more than a single mini-public and that they have strong interests in the success of their own event, it is understandable that they do not opt for unmediated communication.

A more systematic and therefore more serious reason for the neglect of the role of intermediaries may lie in deliberative theorists' aforementioned lack of interest in leadership: proponents of deliberative democracy, who organise mini-publics, accept intermediation for pragmatic rather than normative reasons and may seek to downplay its effects because these call into question the theory's premise that communication is best when it takes place among equals. A final reason, both normative and pragmatic, to refrain from organising mini-publics without intermediation is that participants conceive of themselves as engaging in democratic deliberation, not as guinea-pigs in an experiment. What if a control group without intermediaries asks the organisers for facilitation or elects a facilitator from its midst? Would the academic interest in the effects of intermediation justify its denial to a group of democratically engaged citizens?

Given these obstacles, existing studies on the effects of intermediation come from a context where risks and costs are lower: they are studies of virtual, rather than face-to-face communication in online discussion forums. Let us take a look at their main findings. Given that the number of studies is small, this look can be brief.

Trénel (2009) finds that 'advanced facilitation' that actively encourages reticent participants improves the internal inclusion of women and non-whites. Wright compares two types of moderation in online forums. *Content moderation* involves censoring the content of contributions and, if necessary, deleting entries with offensive messages. *Interactive moderation* is even more interventionist than content moderation: the moderator not only controls content and seeks to maintain civility but also brings in new users and even participates in debates himself. Wright finds that the interactive moderator 'can have a positive role in promoting both the levels of discussion and bringing in users from the outside'; but he also notes that, where moderation and censorship are not perceived as independent and unbiased, the legitimacy of the forum may be undermined (Wright 2006: 563). Edwards describes the moderator in online forums as an 'emerging democratic intermediary', arguing that 'moderators will establish themselves as elements of the information and communication infrastructure between the citizenry and public administration' (Edwards 2002: 18). His analysis of several forums, however, mainly serves to illustrate this claim rather than providing evidence to prove it. Moreover, all three studies (Trénel, Wright and Edwards) compare forums with more intermediation (advanced / hands-on / interactive moderation) with ones with less intermediation. None of them refers to a 'control forum' without any intermediation, which would be required for a comprehensive assessment of the effects of intermediation.

Chair, moderator, mediator, facilitator: Roles and functions for intermediaries in organised communication

Given the reluctance of deliberative theorists to address intermediation theoretically and the scarcity of empirical research on the effects of intermediation, a systematic appraisal of the possible roles and functions of intermediaries in organised communication appears to be a clear desideratum. Assuming that 'one size fits all' is hardly ever true, I want to argue that different types of forums and different types of conflicts require different types of intermediation. Cold deliberation in a rather 'expertocratic' forum can, where the requirements for intermediation are concerned, hardly be compared with hot deliberation in a divided society like, for example, Colombia (described in Steiner 2012). Deliberation on emotional issues like the rebuilding of the World Trade Center (described by Polletta 2006) is difficult to compare with deliberation on distributive or informational issues. I suggest four possible roles for intermediaries, each suited to a particular mode of interaction.[2]

The chair

Where interaction is highly formalised, for example, in parliamentary debates, the forum is typically 'chaired' by one member or a committee of members. Who is the 'chair', and what are his tasks and functions? Literally, a chair is a piece of furniture, not a living participant in interaction. The description of a person in charge of keeping rules of procedure, of leading discursive interaction, as a chair, comes from the position this person assumes at the table or in the plenum: he or she is seated in the front and in the middle, not on the side of either of the factions. The tasks of the chair were described above as task 2: enforcing rules of procedure. The chair keeps a list of speakers and admits speakers to the floor. He or she takes action against violations of discourse rules, depending on how these are specified. Typically, insulting remarks and physical violence are ruled out and interruptions are allowed only if the speaker on the floor permits them. In addition, speaking time will often have to be limited to ensure equal floor time for all groups and factions. However, the chair will refrain from evaluating contributions as adequate or inadequate and from encouraging members to express their opinion. Some 'chairs' may also summarise results. The chair in a parliamentary debate, though, aggregates opinions by calling a vote that also closes the exchange on a given subject.

In what kinds of conflicts and for what modes of interaction is the role of the chair the appropriate one for an intermediary to assume? I have noted above that intermediaries are commonly described as 'chairing' interaction where this is highly formalised, in a parliamentary debate, for example. The debate, as a mode of interaction, is characterised by antagonism between groups or factions. It is public, but in the way that speakers address an audience rather than one another. The audience that listens to the debate cannot contribute to it and, in this sense, the debate is not discursive (*cf.* Landwehr 2010). Accordingly, speakers seek to convince the audience, not one another, and admitting to a change in opinions or preferences may amount to admitting defeat or even losing face. Ideal-typically, opponents in a debate do not seek to reach an agreement or co-ordinate their action plans. Rather, they act out a conflict 'on stage' for an audience whose preferences are formed and transformed in listening. Nearly ideal-typical debates may be seen in the events organised by debating clubs, where positions are assigned by lot and the debate itself is a game, played according to specified rules, in which speakers seek to *score* by making arguments. To what extent parliamentary and

---

2. I have suggested a typology of modes of political interaction – debate, discussion, bargaining and deliberation – elsewhere (Landwehr 2009; Landwehr 2010). I do not explicitly draw on this typology here but it is no coincidence that each of the possible roles for intermediaries corresponds to one of those four modes of political interaction.

other debates in a given political system resemble this ideal-type will depend on the set-up of its polity and its political culture.

Why is the chair the appropriate role for an intermediary in the kind of antagonistic interaction we find in a debate? Where factions merely act out a conflict as a tennis match, where positions are fixed and where co-ordination is neither aimed at nor realistic, it is particularly important that the intermediary does not take sides. The chair's role is not only to be impartial but to be as neutral as a sports referee. In the context of a debate, any attempt to influence interaction that goes beyond taking action on rule violations will be frowned upon by the debating parties and would undermine the intermediary's authority.

The moderator

A second possible role for intermediaries is that of a moderator. The Latin origin of the word moderator is moderare, meaning 'to check/slow down/control'. The tasks for this type of intermediary were described above as task 3, the task of rationalising communication and keeping emotions at bay. The moderator, as I wish to define the role here, thus does significantly more than the chair: he or she evaluates contributions as relevant or irrelevant to the topic and may even admonish participants for digressions or emotional outbursts.

When is the role of the moderator the appropriate one for an intermediary to assume? A moderator is required where the goal of interaction is one of tracking truth and assessing justification, or at least of establishing rational, justified premises for decision-making, and where passion and rhetoric may impede the pursuit of this goal. I have termed this mode of interaction 'discussion' (Landwehr 2010). A discussion is a highly discursive mode of interaction, where claims and arguments are conscientiously assessed. All hearers can also become speakers, in contrast to the debate, where listeners are confined to a passive role. In their logic, discussions are public: what is said is being said for everyone to hear and to judge. The reasons named are supposed to be general and transferable to hearers. In other words, speakers, when giving reasons, claim that these are not only reasons for themselves but that they should constitute reasons for anyone else, too. However, participants in a discussion do not so much aim at a consensus as at tracking truth or assessing justification. Consensus on a given assumption or conclusion may well be an indicator of its truth or justification. In a discussion, however, consensus is not an end in itself. Accordingly, it would be inappropriate for an intermediary in a discussion to suggest a compromise – truth is nothing to be bargained about.[3]

The pursuit of truth through discussion also requires discursive inclusion (or representation) in Dryzek and Niemeyer's sense (Dryzek and Niemeyer 2008): if important information is missed out or if relevant perspectives are not considered, results – if achieved at all – are likely to be biased. Political institutionalisation of the discussion as a mode of interaction can be found in advisory forums and expert

---

3. For a somewhat contrary argument, *see* Goodin and Brennan 2001.

committees. In the selection of expert members for their (supposedly) superior knowledge and understanding, convenors typically seek to ensure external inclusion by drawing on scholars for different disciplines or schools of thought. Internal inclusion appears to be less of a problem here, assuming that experts have won their status in part through the confident articulation of their positions within their respective peer groups. However, given that they do not have material interests in results, participants in a discussion may feel inclined to drop out of the process when their arguments do not meet with resonance. While it may seem patronising in the intermediary to encourage more reticent expert members in a discussion, he or she could still ask for opinions or prevent a premature closure of the discussion in order to ensure discursive inclusion.

The central role for the intermediary in a discussion, however, derives from the fact that experts can, in practice, be highly emotional about their position and may resort to rhetorical means they would disapprove of if taken to task. Assuming that all members of the forum aim at a rational, measured exchange – which is the kind of interaction most conducive to truth and justification – moderating interventions from the intermediary are likely to be approved of in factual discussions.

The mediator

A far more interventionist role for the intermediary to assume than that of either the chair or the moderator is that of a mediator. The word is of Latin origin, too, originally meaning 'to intervene' or 'to divide in the middle'. The meaning 'one intervenes between disputing parties' is first attested in the fourteenth century.[4] Today, intermediaries described as mediators play a role in the out-of-court settlement of legal conflicts, for example over custody of children. In political contexts, mediation is used in conflicts between stakeholder groups with vested interests, where hierarchical direction is not likely to be effective and a decision by majority vote not feasible.

I define the mediator role for intermediaries in political interaction by the primary task connected with it, which is the one I outlined above as task 5: the mediator not only guards rules of procedure and moderates interaction where necessary, he or she also seeks to enable solutions by aggregating opinions, by exposing shared interests and areas of agreement and by summarising results. In situations where no other form of aggregation (through voting, majority rule or compromise) is possible, the mediator may even make an arbitral award on the basis of an evaluation of the participants' interests, positions and arguments. In any case, it is particularly important for the mediator to be accepted as impartial by all parties involved.

In what kinds of situations is the mediator role the appropriate one for an intermediary to play? As noted before, mediators seek to settle disputes between stakeholders with vested interests. Mediation would be pointless, however, if

---

4.   *Source*: Online Etymological Dictionary, www.etymonline.com, accessed 17 February 2014.

besides the parties' diverging interests there was not also a shared interest. The analogy with child-custody proceedings holds well here: however fierce the couple's battle may be, they still have one interest in common – that of their child or children. Mediation is thus a viable option only in positive-sum games. The situation where an intermediary acting as mediator might enable superior outcomes is a classical bargaining situation. Bargaining, as a mode of interaction, is not public in the way a debate or a discussion is. The reasons, or motives, that drive participants need not be general and transferable. They do not even need to be justifiable, because interests are taken as given.

In such a bargaining situation, mediation may enable superior outcomes by encouraging participants to lay out their interests and positions more clearly and to explain them to the other side. This is why inclusion plays a role in bargaining situations as well. First of all, external inclusion needs to ensure that all relevant stakeholders are represented, as any results achieved in mediation are unlikely to win public approval otherwise. Moreover, internal inclusion requires that all participants get the chance to bring their interests (rather than only their positions) to bear on decisions. This is precisely what Fisher, Ury and Patton (1992) have pointed out as a prerequisite for win-win solutions to be achieved in negotiations (Fisher, Ury and Patton 1992 [1984]). Compared to more traditional bargaining situations (without or with only minimal intermediation), transparency of reasons may enable new deals and compromises that would have remained out of reach in a situation of mutual suspicion. Dryzek notes that, once a mediator has achieved such reasoned engagement between initially hostile parties, he or she can 'increasingly fade into the background' and allow the parties to work out solutions by themselves (Dryzek 1987: 668). However, and quite in contrast to the discussion case, consent, or rather compromise, on a joint solution, is a goal in itself in situations of bargaining between vested interests. Tracking truth or establishing which party's claims are better justified, by contrast, is not a goal to be pursued here and respective approaches from participants would be dismissed rather than encouraged by a mediator.

The facilitator

Neither of the situations, or modes of interaction, referred to so far comes close to the ideal of deliberative interaction. Deliberation is both discursive and aimed at co-ordination; and it is both about truth and about reaching meaningful compromises (cf. Landwehr 2010). Deliberation is a demanding mode of interaction to realise and intermediation that contributes to its success is demanding as well. I would like to argue that the appropriate role for an intermediary in deliberation is that of a facilitator. The word comes from French faciliter – 'to render easy'. What is the facilitator to render easy? In short, the facilitator is to help the group reach its own goals. As these goals are twofold – truth or normative justification on the one hand, co-ordination through compromise or consensus on the other hand – so are the facilitator's tasks. I have defined the facilitator's tasks and thus his role as task 4 above: the tasks of ensuring internal inclusion and pluralism.

Each of these tasks for the facilitator is conducive to one of the deliberating group's goals. Internal inclusion, which is notoriously difficult to ensure in deliberative mini-publics, is central for the goal of co-ordination. Only those participants who have actively contributed to the group's product, for example, a joint statement or report, are likely to fully support it. The facilitator's role here is to ensure that the absence of open dissent is not mistaken for consensus and thus successful co-ordination. More passive participants, particularly if they hold minority opinions, may opt for the exit rather than the voice option and drop out of a deliberative forum altogether. Encouraging passive members and thwarting too-dominant ones is not to be understood as an intervention in the discourse itself but as a kind of advanced enforcement of discourse *rules*. While in the context of a debate, in which opponents view themselves as equally equipped with the necessary professional skills to make themselves heard, it is sufficient to guarantee orderly proceedings by, for example, keeping a list of speakers, watching speaking time and penalising offences, deliberation among lay citizens requires somewhat more. Discourse rules may need to be more fully specified, particularly where they are supposed to ensure mutual respect. In a citizen conference on stem-cell research in Berlin, for example, participants set up the rule 'troubles first': whenever one of the forums members felt misunderstood, disrespected or offended, this irritation was dealt with before the group continued topical deliberation (*see* Landwehr 2009: 200).

Ensuring pluralism of different arguments and points of view is important with regard to the goal of tracking truth and assessing justification. Clearly, the scope of arguments and perspectives is limited by the composition of the forum. What if the forum's opinions and views turn out to be alarmingly biased? Although convenors of deliberative events will strive to assemble groups representative of the population at large, a group that is representative with regard to socio-demographic criteria may well turn out to have (or be dominated by) biased opinions on specific issues – and the smaller group is, the higher the likelihood of biased opinions occurring. Can or should the intermediary prevent the kind of polarisation and group think that is likely to evolve in such cases (Sunstein 2003)? If facilitators bring in issue-related arguments themselves, they leave the safe and important ground of impartiality. Whether preventing group-think or maintaining impartiality is more essential in any given case will be a practical and pragmatic decision. When choosing to leave the ground of impartiality, the facilitator should, in any case. present arguments not as his or her own opinion but in a more indirect way. Rather than saying 'you're wrong, because p, q!' he or she might suggest: 'what would you reply if someone argued that because p, q?' The facilitator could thus try to ensure 'discursive representation' (Dryzek and Niemeyer 2008) without taking sides.

To obtain a clear picture of how the intermediary in deliberation can act as a facilitator, it may help to differentiate this role from those of chair, moderator and facilitator and to point out what the facilitator should *not* do. Like the chair, the facilitator guards rules of procedure. However, the facilitator should not enforce rules too strictly and should be sensitive to situations where it helps to deviate from them, for example, by permitting immediate replies instead of sticking to a list of speakers or by allowing interruptions from participants who feel misunderstood or offended. Like the moderator, the facilitator may sometimes have to keep emotions at bay and calm down participants when they are upset. However, the facilitator should not seek to rationalise deliberation by disqualifying or evaluating contributions. In particular, accounts of individual experiences have important functions in citizen deliberation and storytelling should not be discouraged by insistence on generalisable reasons. Like the mediator, the facilitator may point out areas of agreement and summarise arguments. However, he or she should refrain from aggregating results or making suggestions. Where facilitators do so, they give rise to the suspicion that the outcome of a deliberative event does not depend on the course of argumentation in the forum itself but is pre-determined by its organisers. While epistemic progress (tracking truth and assessing justification) and co-ordination are goals of deliberation, neither of them is, in this context, an end in itself. Any result of a deliberative citizen forum bears legitimacy and is of relevance only in so far as it was achieved by citizens themselves, free from undue influence by organisers and intermediaries.

All this said, we must keep in mind that there exist very different models for deliberative forums (*see* Fung 2003). In particular, forums differ with regard to their size (ranging from 10–20 in consensus conferences to hundreds in Deliberative Polls®) and with regard to their goals (some aiming at consensus, others pursuing mainly goals of information and exchange). Clearly, the role and tasks of the intermediary will differ depending on the precise set-up of the deliberative forum. In very large forums, the intermediary may only be able to ensure internal inclusion in a rather mechanistic way, by keeping a list of speakers and perhaps favouring ones who have not contributed yet. The role of the intermediary will, under such circumstances, rather resemble that of a chair. Moreover, large forums, particularly where deliberation is hot, may require moderating interventions to prevent turmoil that could risk the success of the entire event. Where a consensual vote constitutes an important goal for a deliberative forum, in contrast, the intermediary may take on the role of a mediator and seek to aggregate reasons and results in order to achieve the kind of 'deep compromise' that is often a more realistic outcome of deliberation than consensus (Richardson 2002: chapter 11).

Conclusions

Both deliberative theory and deliberative practice in mini-publics have shown surprisingly little interest in the role of impartial intermediaries. As for the theorists, this lack of interest may be due to strong beliefs in the equality of speakers and a general suspicion of leadership. The intermediary, after all, possesses rights the other speakers do not. Those who study deliberation empirically in mini-publics seem to accept intermediation mainly for pragmatic reasons; controlled studies of its effects are not to be found. The fact that interaction in mini-publics without intermediation can be so problematic that the success of the entire forum is risked and that organising mini-publics without intermediation may even amount to an academic 'malpractice' is reason enough to address the issue more systematically. As long as little is known about the effects of (different elements of) intermediation, it may help to assume that intermediaries try to fulfil the tasks assigned to them and, more often than not, will succeed in doing so.

I have pointed out five central tasks for intermediaries. Sometimes, these can be pursued simultaneously; sometimes goal conflicts will arise in their pursuit. When deciding which tasks to assign to an intermediary, organisers of deliberative events should be clear about the character and goals of the forum: different roles for intermediaries are suitable for and conducive to different modes of interaction. I have suggested four possible roles for intermediaries that may be understood as ideal-types: the roles of chair, moderator, mediator and facilitator. The responsibility of organisers of mini-publics does not only lie in making sure that intermediaries are 'skilled' and 'trained', they also need to make clear – to both participants and intermediaries – what tasks intermediation is supposed to fulfil and what role the intermediary is to play in the forum. If interaction is to be deliberative, that is, aimed at co-ordinating participants' preferences through a discursive assessment and weighting of reasons, the intermediary should act as a facilitator. The facilitator will promote internal inclusion and a pluralism of differing points of view but refrain from an overly strict application of discourse rules as well as from attempts to 'rationalise' interaction and from summarising results.

References

Bächtiger, A., Niemeyer, S., Neblo, M. A. *et al.* (2010) 'Disentangling diversity in deliberative democracy', *Journal of Political Philosophy* 18 (1): 32–63.

Blumler, J. G. and Coleman, S. (2001) *Realising Democracy Online: A civic commons in cyberspace*, London: IPPR.

Dryzek, J. (1987) 'Discursive designs: critical theory and political institutions', *American Journal of Political Science* 31 (3): 656–79.

Dryzek, J. and Niemeyer, S. (2008) 'Discursive representation', *American Political Science Review* 102 (4): 481–93.

Edwards, A. E. (2002) 'The moderator as an emerging democratic intermediary: the role of the moderator in internet discussions about public issues', *Information Polity* 7 (1): 3–20.

Fisher, R., Ury, W. and Patton B. (1992 [1984]) *Getting to Yes: Negotiating agreement without giving in*, New York: Houghton Mifflin.

Fung, A. (2003) 'Survey article: recipes for public spheres: eight institutional design choices and their consequences', *Journal of Political Philosophy* 11 (3): 338–67.

Goodin, R. E. and Brennan, G. (2001) 'Bargaining over beliefs', *Ethics* 111 (2): 256–77.

Grice, H. P. (1979) 'Logik und Konversation', G. Meggle (ed.) in *Handlung, Kommunikation, Bedeutung*, Frankfurt-am-Main: Suhrkamp.

Hall, C. A. (2005) *The Trouble with Passion: Political theory beyond the reign of reason*, New York, Routledge.

Hendriks, C. M. (2005) 'Consensus conferences and planning cells: Lay citizen deliberation', in J. Gastil and P. Levine (eds) *The Deliberative Democracy Handbook*, San Fransisco, CA: Jossey-Bass.

Krause, S. R. (2008) *Civil Passions: Moral sentiment and democratic deliberation*, Princeton, NJ: Princeton University Press.

Landwehr, C. (2009) *Political Conflict and Political Preferences: Communicative interaction between facts, norms and interests*, Colchester: ECPR Press.

— (2010) 'Discourse and co-ordination: modes of interaction and their roles in political decision-making', *Journal of Political Philosophy* 18 (1): 101–22.

Lara, M. P. (1999) *Moral Textures: Feminist narratives in the public sphere*, University Presses of California.

Oberlander, J., Marmor, T. and Jacobs, L. (2001) 'Rationing medical care: rhetoric and reality in the Oregon Health Plan', *Canadian Medical Association Journal* 164 (11).

Ostrom, E. (1986) 'An agenda for the study of institutions', *Public Choice* 48 (1): 3–25.

Polletta, F. (2006) *It Was Like a Fever: Storytelling in protest and politics*, Chicago, IL: University of Chicago Press.

Richardson, H. S. (2002) *Democratic Autonomy: Public reasoning about the ends of policy*, Oxford: Oxford University Press.

Sanders, L. M. (1997) 'Against deliberation', *Political Theory* 25 (3): 347–76.

Schmalz-Bruns, R. (2009) 'Habermas' theory of democracy and critical policy studies: an (undistorted) elective affinity?', *Critical Policy Studies* 3 (3–4): 447–52.

Steiner, J. (2012) *The Foundations of Deliberative Democracy: Empirical research and normative implications*, Cambridge: Cambridge University Press.

Sunstein, C. R. (2003) 'The law of group polarization', in J. S. Fishkin and P. Laslett (eds) *Debating Deliberative Democracy*, Malden, MA: Blackwell.

Thompson, S. and Hoggett, P. (2001) 'The emotional dynamics of deliberative democracy', *Policy & Politics* 29 (3): 351–64.

Trénel, M. (2009) 'Facilitation and inclusive deliberation', in T. Davies and S. P. Gangadharan (eds) *Online Deliberation: Design, research, and practice*, Stanford, CA: CSLI Publications.

Wright, S. (2006) 'Government-run online discussion fora: moderation, censorship and the shadow of control', *British Journal of Politics and International Relations,* 8 (4): 550–68.

Young, I. M. (2002) *Inclusion and Democracy*, Oxford: Oxford University Press.

Chapter Seven

Online Deliberation: Theory and Practice in Virtual Mini-Publics

Kim Strandberg and Kimmo Grönlund

Introduction and background

The internet contains many favourable features for organising democratic discussions between lay citizens (Baek *et al.* 2011; Davies 2009: 2; Davies and Chandler 2011). As Coleman and Goetze remark (2001: 17) the internet 'makes manageable large scale, many-to-many discussion and deliberation'. Through removing many of the physical constraints – such as time, access, geographical distances and so forth – the online environment indeed appears to be a suitable venue for citizen discussions (see, for example, Grönlund *et al.* 2009; Kavanaugh *et al.* 2005; Manosevitch 2010; Luskin *et al.* 2004; Price 2009; Price and Capella 2002). Pertaining to deliberative discussions specifically, the internet could arguably be even more effective in combining face-to-face reasoning and mass politics than offline deliberation events, due to these logistic features. Also, as some scholars have remarked (for example, Stromer-Galley 2002; Witschge 2004), the anonymous and more non-verbal nature of the online sphere might free people from certain psychological barriers that would otherwise have made them less eager to engage in deliberation. Likewise, scholars have been quite optimistic regarding the possibility that the online setting will reduce the often adverse influence of status and social position on citizens' discussions (Dahlberg 2001; Gastil 2000: 359).

Some scholars have, however, raised concerns regarding the impact of the internet on public deliberation (*see*, for example, Price 2009: 37). The internet tends to attract like-minded people to interact with each other, possibly leading to a polarisation of opinions in online discussions (Sunstein 2001; 2006; Wilhelm, 1999: 172–83). Moreover, online discussions are often found not to meet the qualitative standards of deliberation (Coleman and Moss 2012: 6; Jankowski and Van Os 2004: 190; Papacharissi 2002: 16; Strandberg 2005; 2008).

It should be noted, though, that most of the research hitherto has assessed the extent to which online discussion boards, which are not *per se* designed to be deliberative and have not emerged with such a goal in mind, meet such standards of deliberative conversations. This observation is rather crucial in our opinion and raises the question of how online deliberation works in more rigidly designed discussion forums. It has been suggested by some scholars (such as Hamlett and Cobb 2006; Kies 2010; Manosevitch 2010; Wright and Street 2007) that online discussion venues built on principles derived from deliberative theory would be significantly more likely to bring about deliberative conversations than impromptu discussion boards. As Barber states (1998: 586) 'Technology then can help democracy but only if programmed to do so and only in terms of the paradigms and political theories that inform the program.'

Therefore, the purpose of this chapter is to provide an overview of 'the state of the art' within the emerging and growing field of research in which deliberative mini-publics – or similar guiding principles – have been applied in online discussion venues. As noted by Wright (2011: 14): 'studies of online deliberation experiments have afforded a number of insights that could be explored further'. To this purpose, we specifically focus on reviewing the important aspects surrounding online mini-publics in light of various experiments in online deliberation in order to provide a theoretical 'road-map' of sort concerning on-line mini-publics.

The aim of the study

The approach of the chapter is mainly descriptive. We do not seek to explain why online deliberations have been subject to certain design choices nor why they led to certain outcomes. Rather, our overarching purpose is to thoroughly and systematically describe these matters, in light of observations from studies of online deliberation. Specifically, we have three areas of focus that are aligned with the general themes of this volume:

1. The preconditions for online mini-publics;
2. The designs of online mini-publics;
3. The outcomes of online mini-publics.

In order to identify relevant cases for our study, we first conducted a search on the literature of online deliberation experiments. Judgeing from some earlier studies, such an approach seems clearly feasible and suitable for our purpose (for example, Bächtiger 2011; Davies and Gangadharan 2009; Delli Carpini *et al.* 2004; Manosevitch 2010; Towne and Herbsleb 2012). On a more general level, meta-analyses' benefits also lie in their ability to accumulate existing findings and thus better enable theory construction and testing (Peters 1998: 160–1).

After an initial glance at studies reporting on various experiments in online deliberations (for example, Albrecht 2006; Delborne *et al.* 2011; Grönlund *et al.* 2009; Luskin *et al.* 2006; Min 2007; Muhlberger 2005; Muhlberger and Weber 2006; Price 2009; Price and Capella 2002; Smith *et al.* 2009; Strandberg and Grönlund 2012; Rhee and Kim 2009) it became clear to us that the best manner in which to specifically conduct our literature review was to be somewhat more inductive than deductive. Thus, when reviewing the studies of online deliberation, we did so with an open mind and drew on these studies to illustrate the key components of our three focus areas throughout our empirical part. Hence, although slightly different in goals, our analytical approach is generally in line with that of Towne's and Herbsleb's review of online deliberative systems:

We strive to take a step beyond case studies by surveying the literature and its many single-point evaluations, examining them for common themes, and deriving a set of design considerations that can be used for the next iteration of online deliberation tools (Towne and Herbsleb 2012: 112).

Naturally, we do not have an ambition to include *all* studies of online deliberation. After all, the field is astonishingly broad and varied despite its relative novelty (*see* Davies and Gangadharan 2009). Our goal was, instead, to focus mainly on a census of studies reporting on *experiments* in online deliberation, in order to obtain a sufficient sample to describe the central aspects surrounding these experiments. Naturally, there are still several quasi-experiments – and in all honesty probably some experiments we have missed – in online deliberation that could have qualified for our analysis, which have been studied elsewhere (*see* Manosevitch 2010).

We also exclude all studies which discuss and test deliberative criteria on generic online forums (*see* Kies 2010: chapter four; Karlsson 2010 for examples of such studies). Naturally, purely theoretical studies are also excluded. However, we are aware that both of these areas are important in building our understanding of key aspects of online deliberation. From this point of departure we gathered the studies for our review using a 'snowball' method, in which search engines and online library resources as well as reference listings were utilised. In total, this process yielded ten experiments that are included in our literature review (Table 7.1).

Table 7.1: The experiments in online deliberation included in the review

Experiment	Country	Year	Study
Electronic Dialogue Project	USA	2000	Price and Capella 2002
Daum Deliberative Project	Korea	2004	Rhee and Kim 2009
National Citizens' Technology Forum	USA	2008	Delborne *et al.* 2011
Min's experiment	USA	2006	Min 2007
Virtual Agora Project	USA	2002–2005	Muhlberger 2005; Muhlberger and Weber 2006
Virtual Polity Project	Finland	2008	Grönlund *et al.* 2009; Strandberg and Grönlund 2012
Online Deliberative Polls®	USA	2003	Luskin *et al.* 2006; Iyengar *et al.* 2003
Deliberation and Internet Engagement	UK	2007–2009	Smith *et al.* 2009
Demos Debate in Hamburg	Germany	2002	Albrecht 2006
NCCR Experiment	Switzerland	2010	Bächtiger 2011

The subsequent empirical part of our chapter is organised in three sections, one for each of the areas of focus. Throughout the sections we draw on our cases in order to highlight, describe and accumulate empirical observations into themes concerning theoretically central aspects of online deliberations.

Analysis

Preconditions of online deliberation

When peering into the preconditions and how they have had a bearing on actual experiments with online mini-publics, the primary concern that emerges upon reviewing the literature generally pertains to the discussion on so-called 'digital divides' (Norris 2001; Price 2009: 42–3). Although divides in terms of internet access are being overcome in most developed countries, it is hardly convenient to take part in an online deliberation from a public internet access point such as a library or school. So even though internet access is much more widespread in developed countries nowadays, the type and ease of this access is nonetheless an important factor (Delborne et al. 2011: 367–8). Also, discrepancies in computer skills may have a significant bearing on conducting online deliberation experiments. In order to take part in an online deliberation, participants could be required to use webcams, headset and chat simultaneously, as in the Finnish Virtual Polity experiment for instance. In that experiment, severe problems arose precisely due to a lack in such skills on the part of the participants (Grönlund et al. 2009; Strandberg and Grönlund 2012). Hence, there is a risk that 'computer-savvy' citizens dominate the discussion (cf. Smith et al. 2009: 4). These issues of divides in access, and particularly skills, pertain, on a higher level of abstraction, to the aspect of discursive inclusion, which is often cited as one of the pillars upon which public deliberation rests and which is frequently mentioned in the literature (see, for example, Barber 1984; Dahlberg 2001; Gastil and Black 2008).

Differences in the level of motivation of citizens to take part are also a sub-issue brought to our attention in our literature review. Essentially, on-line engagement tends to reflect patterns in general political engagement (Norris 2001) so that citizens with a higher than average political interest would be the likeliest to be drawn to online deliberative events. As Smith et al. (2009: 7) remark: '[…] most citizens are typically unaware of (and generally uninterested in) these new opportunities to participate'. When considering this issue from a more general perspective on deliberative theory, the concern focuses on the representativeness of online deliberation (Luskin et al. 2004; Iyengar et al. 2003), which, in turn, affects its ability to function as a 'mini-public' or 'microcosm' reflecting the general public (Dahl 1989; Fishkin 1995). If the mini-public is skewed towards those with access, resources and motivation, the public to which the mini-public's results can be generalised would be equally skewed.

Shifting focus towards how these above-mentioned aspects have had a bearing on experiments with online deliberation, then, we observe that scholars have clearly been aware of this in their recruitment stages and taken appropriate measures. Hence, to battle inequalities in terms of internet access, the common solution has been to provide participants with the necessary technical equipment if they do not have access otherwise. In the Finnish Virtual Polity experiment (Grönlund *et al.* 2009; Strandberg and Grönlund 2012), for instance, participants were given free webcams and headsets. Likewise, Luskin *et al.* (2004) provided personal computers to those participants lacking them in recruiting to the online part of their Deliberative Poll® on foreign policy. Similar solutions have also been applied elsewhere, such as in the Virtual Agora project (*see*, for example, Muhlberger 2005; Muhlberger and Weber 2006). However, other scholars have tackled the access issue by drawing their sample of participants from existing online panels, maintain a representative sample of citizens amounting to several thousand people (for example, Delborne *et al.* 2011; Price and Capella 2002; Smith *et al.* 2009). Min (2007) used a strategy of having a student sample take part on-campus via university computers, to make sure all participants had access to the internet.

Evidently, access divides have been dealt with rather elegantly by scholars conducting experiments with online deliberation. But what about potential differences in computer skills: how can these be addressed? Obviously, using a sample of young citizens such as students (*cf.* Min 2007), has the positive side-effect that it erodes most differences in computer skills between participants. Another strategy, which has been applied in an experiment using text, speech and video, is to provide the participants with detailed instructions on how to use the necessary equipment needed to take part and also to train the moderators on how to provide the participants with technical assistance (for example, Grönlund *et al.* 2009; Strandberg and Grönlund 2012; *cf.* Muhlberger 2005; Muhlberger and Weber 2006). It should also be noted that many of the experiments in online deliberation have used mainly text-based communication methods (for example, Albrecht 2006; Bächtiger 2011; Delborne *et al.* 2011; Min 2007; Price and Capella 2002; Rhee and Kim 2009; Smith *et al.* 2009), which is, arguably, a form of modality (*see* Davies and Chandler 2011) that requires only basic computer skills compared to multimodal approaches. Hence, this type of input might serve to make differences in computer skills less relevant in the experiment. However, as Iyengar *et al.* (2003) note, text-based input might instead disadvantage less literate participants.

Concerning the strategies used for dealing with the challenges posed by a potential lack of motivation on the part of the general public to take part in online deliberations, a theme which emerges in the literature is the use of incentives at the recruitment stage. Hence, in order to attract a wider cross-section of citizens than only those with a high level of political engagement and interest, scholars have sometimes promised technical equipment or cash incentives for taking part in their deliberative experiment (for example, Grönlund *et al.* 2009; Luskin *et al.* 2004; Iyengar *et al.* 2003; Muhlberger 2005; Muhlberger and Weber 2006; Smith *et al.* 2009; Strandberg and Grönlund 2012). A closely related strategy was applied by Min (2007: 1375) who promised students extra credits for their courses if they took part in the online deliberation. In the case of the Demos Debate in

Hamburg (Albrecht 2006: 69), potential influence on city-planning policy was used as 'bait'. Regardless of what form incentives take, then, they appear to be widely accepted and applied within the field. It might be noteworthy, therefore, to consider that incentives can have methodological downsides in experiments. For instance, they could improve the participants' general 'mood' (Muhlberger 2005: 6), which could lead to mood-congruent answers to the experiment's surveys and thus damage the experiment's validity (*see* Göritz 2004 for a discussion). This discussion is, arguably, relevant to but beyond the scope of this chapter so we will merely highlight it here.

It is evident that the main theme in the preconditions needed to conduct a satisfactory online deliberation is inequality of access to the required equipment, computer and internet skills and motivation for taking part. Throughout the analysis, it was also evident that various techniques pertaining to the recruitment of participants are important to scholars as well as the form of communication (modality). Table 7.2 provides a summarising overview of these observations regarding the preconditions of online deliberations and how the analysed experiments have addressed them:

Table 7.2: Preconditions of online deliberations: summary of observations

	Preconditions		
	Access divides	Skill divides	Motivational divides
Electronic Dialogue Project	used online panel	less skill intense modality (text)	none
Daum Deliberative Project	none/self-volunteering	less skill intense modality (text)	none
National Citizens' Technology Forum	used online panel	less skill intense modality (text)	none
Min's Experiment	student sample/computer lab	student sample/computer lab	incentive (university credits)
Virtual Agora Project	provided equipment	instructions and assistance	incentive (equipment/cash)
Virtual Polity Project	provided equipment when needed	instructions and assistance	incentive (equipment/cash)
Online Deliberative Polls®	provided equipment	speech only argued to decrease divides	incentive (equipment/cash)
Deliberation and Internet Engagement	used online panel	less skill intense modality (text)	incentive (prize draw)
Demos Debate in Hamburg	none/self volunteering	less skill intense modality (text)	potential influence on policy
NCCR Experiment	none/self volunteering	less skill intense modality (text)	none

On an overarching level, beyond the themes discussed so far, it is noteworthy that both non-random sampling and random sampling have been used in recruiting to online deliberation experiments. In studies of online panel recruitment (for example, Baker *et al.* 2010; Van Selm and Jankowski 2006; Vehovar *et al.* 2008) it has been suggested that non-probability recruitment methods are generally more vulnerable to volunteering than probability-based methods and hence less likely to achieve representativeness of the general population. This is probably true for online deliberations and mini-publics as well, although a more systematic study of that specific aspect would be needed to gauge it properly (*cf.* Davies and Chandler 2011: 12). Nevertheless, the various techniques highlighted here appear to have been used rather widely, regardless of the overall sampling method. A slight discrepancy can be noted in that studies seeking representativeness more explicitly (for example, Grönlund *et al.* 2009; Luskin *et al.* 2006; Muhlberger 2005; Strandberg and Grönlund 2012) seem to apply a wider array of these techniques than studies using convenience samples (for example, Min 2007). Hence, the higher degree of representativeness one seeks to achieve, the more important it becomes to address the preconditions for online deliberations in the actual experiment.

Design of online deliberations

In the introduction we mentioned that the relatively anonymous online sphere might free people from psychological barriers when engaging in deliberation (for example, Stromer-Galley 2002; Witschge 2004) and that it could also serve to reduce the adverse influence of status and social position on deliberation (Dahlberg 2001; Gastil 2000: 359). We also noted, nonetheless, that there have been many concerns surrounding online deliberative processes, with scholars pointing particularly at potential 'polarisation tendencies' (Sunstein 2001; 2006) and discussions not meeting qualitative standards for deliberative conversations (Jankowski and Van Os 2004: 190; Papacharissi 2002: 16; Strandberg 2005; 2008). Taking a step from these assessments of deliberative designs online and looking at the ways in which design has been addressed and carried out in the experiments with online deliberations, then, what are the emerging themes?

Obviously, since we have only selected experiments for analysis here, all scholars have made explicit choices concerning experimental designs. Upon examination we find that variations of pre-test/post-test experimental design logic (*see* Campbell and Stanley 1963) – albeit often applied as a quasi-experimental design in practice – have generally been used within the field. Some have compared face-to-face deliberation to an online counterpart either directly or indirectly (for example, National Citizen's Technology Forum; Virtual Polity; Online Deliberative Polls®; Virtual Agora) while others have focused entirely on an online component (for example, Demos; NCCR; Electronic Dialogue; Deliberation and Internet Engagement; Daum Deliberation).

Moving beyond overall experimental designs, the main theme brought forth regarding design in our analysis is excellently summarised by Min (2007: 1374):

'[…] what is important to deliberation […] is to create an environment and process that are conducive to effective deliberation'. It is towards this end that most scholars within the field have striven. There are, however, discrepancies in the ways in which scholars have drawn on the norms of deliberation when designing the specific settings of their deliberative experiment. Firstly, there are differences in the modality, that is, the form of communication (Davies and Chandler 2011), used in the experiments. Only in the Finnish Virtual Polity Experiment has a full multi-modal approach incorporating text, audio and video in the deliberation sessions been used. Many studies only use text-based input in the deliberations (for example, Demos; National Citizens' Technology Forum; Deliberation and Internet Engagement; Min's project; NCCR; Electronic Dialogue) and some have mainly relied on audio as the main form (for example, Online Deliberative Polls® and the Virtual Agora Project). The form of communication might seem a technical detail of little relevance to the actual deliberations. However, these aspects concern the degree of anonymity in online deliberation, which has a direct connection to a potential erosion of social cues and other psychological barriers; this, in turn, has been argued to be a strong potential benefit of the online setting. Such benefits should logically be more evident the more an online deliberation experiment setting deviates from the face-to-face setting. Anonymity has, of course, also been blamed as the main factor behind the 'lack of civility and respect in online deliberations' (Coleman and Moss 2012: 8). In future studies, hence, a more systematic comparison of the impact of modality on the actual deliberation processes appears to be of interest.

Another aspect of the designs of online deliberation concerns the temporal considerations of the experiment, that is, the overall duration of the experiment and whether its discussions are synchronous or asynchronous (Coleman and Moss 2012: 8). As Muhlberger (2005) remarks, studies of Deliberative Polls® (for example, Iyengar et al. 2003; Luskin et al. 2006) indicate that one-day deliberation events are thought of highly by participants. These are, of course, offline events, requiring that participants are physically co-present in order to take part. The online setting makes it far easier to have multi-session experiments, both for the participants and for the scholars designing the experiment. As Luskin et al. (2006: 24) remark: 'An online sample could continue deliberating for eight weeks or eight months'. Asynchronous discussions have also been perceived as being able to provide more time for reflection and reasoning and could thus be more deliberative than synchronous discussions. In the studies analysed here, it appears that scholars have used one-off sessions and multi-session as well as synchronous and asynchronous discussions rather equally. Price's and Capella's year-long Electronic Dialogue experiment is arguably the longest of the experiments. During the year, synchronous discussions were incorporated in several waves in the experiment. Likewise, the online Deliberative Polls® hosted synchronous discussion sessions spread over a period of five weeks. Furthermore, Muhlberger's Virtual Agora Project had a two-phase approach, so that the long-term effects of deliberation could be assessed. In that particular project, the online discussions were synchronous. The Finnish Virtual Polity Experiment was mainly a one-off event with synchronous discussions, although it also contained a follow-up survey in order to gauge the long-term effects of the deliberation. The German Demos Project was open to the public for several weeks and hosted asynchronous discussion; this was also the case in the Korean Daum experiment. Other experiments, however, have been one-off deliberation events with both asynchronous (for example, Deliberation and Internet Engagement) and synchronous discussions (for example, NCCR, National Citizens' Technology Forum and Min's experiment).

A general observation, albeit a tentative one, which can be made regarding the duration of online deliberation experiments is that scholars appear to have opted for one-off deliberation (or similar) when they have been primarily concerned with the internal validity of the experiment – they seek to isolate the effects of the actual deliberation in more rigid experimental settings (for example: NCCR; National Citizens' Technology Forum; Virtual Polity; Min's experiment). Conversely, scholars whose experiments have been more tied to 'real life', and hence arguably have stronger external validity, have hosted deliberations of longer duration (for example: Demos; Online Deliberative Polls®; and the Electronic Dialogue Project). Hence, an overarching trade-off between experimental norms and the deliberative ideals of the 'mini-public' having external relevance beyond the actual experiment is often required.

Another observation pertaining to the design of online deliberations is the use of facilitators in the deliberation sessions. This has been one of the main aspects of process-design highlighted in the theoretical literature (*see* Coleman and Goetze 2001; Coleman and Moss 2012: 8). Judgeing from our analysis, the use of facilitators is indeed also widespread within the field of practice in online deliberation. In fact, facilitators or moderators were used in all experiments analysed here. Moreover, we note that the facilitators often have a dual role in the discussions: to provide assistance to participants (for example, the Virtual Polity and the Daum Deliberative Project); and also to ensure that the discussions follow guidelines derived from deliberative theory (for example, Daum; Electronic Dialogue; Virtual Polity; Online Deliberative Polls®). Hence, scholars appear to have taken measures to ensure that the deliberative quality of the actual deliberations is close to theoretical ideals.

Corresponding to the theoretical ideal of 'informed and rational reasoning', many scholars also provided participants with background information about the topic of deliberation (for example: NCCR; Online Deliberative Polls®; Virtual Polity; Daum; Min) and some have even provided the opportunity to watch experts debate the topic of deliberation (for example, Virtual Polity), or given participants the opportunity to submit questions to an expert panel (National Citizens' Technology Forum and the Online Deliberative Polls®). Evidently, thus, scholars seeking to study online deliberation explicitly – not merely to assess the deliberativeness of random online 'talk' – apply most of the same designs used in offline equivalents such as Deliberative Polls® (Fishkin 1995) and consensus conferences (*see* Delborne *et al.* 2011).

In wrapping up the section on design of online deliberations, we firstly stress that the themes brought forth here are by no means the only aspects relevant to

Table 7.3: Designs of online deliberations: summary of observations

	Designs			
	Experimental design	Modality	Temporality	Facilitation
Electronic Dialogue Project	online only	single mode (text)	long-term synchronous	yes
Daum Deliberative Project	online only	single mode (text)	semi-long asynchronous	yes
National Citizens' Technology Forum	comparison online vs. F2F	single mode (text)	one-off synchronous	yes
Min's Experiment	comparison online vs. F2F	single mode (speech)	one-off synchronous	yes
Virtual Agora Project	comparison online vs. F2F	single mode (speech)	semi-long synchronous	yes
Virtual Polity Project	comparison online vs. F2F	full modality	one-off synchronous	yes
Online Deliberative Polls®	comparison online vs. F2F	single mode (speech)	semi-long synchronous	yes
Deliberation and Internet Engagement	online only	single mode (text)	one-off asynchronous	yes
Demos Debate in Hamburg	online only	single mode (text)	semi-long asynchronous	yes
NCCR Experiment	online only	single mode (text)	one-off synchronous	yes

online deliberative designs found in the experiments. Throughout the review, noteworthy design-related aspects included detailed features such as whether or not the participants' identities are known to each other, whether only information without discussion is used in parallel to the group discussions and whether or not the writing of common statements is applied at the end of the sessions. So even though there is coherence on a general level pertaining to the design of online deliberations, differences can be found in the details. Clearly, however, the overarching common theme in the design of the experiments analysed here is that deliberative norms – and especially the concept of an 'ideal speech situation' (for example, Habermas 1989) – appear to have served as guidelines for the designs of online deliberations. Table 7.3 shows the summary of our detailed observations of how scholars have designed their deliberative online processes.

Outcomes of online deliberations

In the two preceding parts, our analysis has examined both the preconditions and designs of these experiments in online deliberation. Throughout those sections, it was quite clear that scholars have been aware of the potential problems facing online deliberations and incorporated solutions to them in their recruitment strategies and when designing the process of their experiments. In other words, the experiments have truly been designed to host deliberative discussions and should, logically, be highly likely to bring about democratic conversations with positive effects (for example, Hamlett and Cobb 2006; Kies 2010; Manosevitch 2010; Wright and Street 2007). In this final section of our analysis we peer into the outcomes of the experiments.

Concerning outcomes, we start by making a distinction between external and internal outcomes. With the term 'external' we here refer to outcomes beyond the actual experimental context, such as the deliberation event having an influence on actual policy or a connection to civil society (*cf.* Hendriks 2006). Internal outcomes refer to the outcomes or effects – that is, opinion changes, knowledge gains, increased internal efficacy, increased generalised and interpersonal trust and so on – found amongst individual participants due to taking part in an online deliberation.

Firstly, it should be stated that there are very few traces of real policy-impacts found as a result of the experiments analysed in this chapter. This is partly caused by our main focus on scholarly experiments, which tend to be more theoretically and methodologically driven than practice-driven (*see* Albrecht 2006: 70 for similar reasoning). Thus, most of the experiments here deal with what Hendriks (2006) calls micro-deliberation, in which the focus is on procedures and creating ideal conditions for them and not on achieving connections to civil society in general. In the online deliberations assessed here, only the deliberation in the German Demos Project in Hamburg was explicitly tied to actual city planning, in as much as influence on city planning was promised to the best suggestion brought up in the deliberations. In Smith *et al.*'s Deliberation and Internet Engagement project, in which deliberations concerned social policy, the Secretary of State for Communities and Local Government 'committed herself to consider the issues raised by the participants'. Hence, whether the deliberations would have any real influence on policy was largely unknown. Besides these two studies, one might tentatively argue that the use of experts in some of the experiments (for example, Online Deliberative Polls® and the Virtual Polity) could give the participants the impression that their deliberation would be noted in 'the outside world'. In the Finnish Virtual Polity Experiment, for instance, some of the experts used were, in fact, well known politicians (*see* Grönlund *et al.* 2009). Overall, hitherto, evidence of external outcomes of online deliberation experiments is scarce. This, however, is by no means unique to online deliberation. So far, mini-publics and other deliberative forums have mainly been conducted as *ad hoc* phenomena and, with a few exceptions (*see* Pateman 2012; Goodin and Dryzek 2006), have seldom been used as an institutional part of democratic decision-making.

Looking at internal outcomes of the online deliberations, then, we firstly pay attention to an aspect which is arguably partially related to design and partially to internal outcome: the actual quality of discussion in online deliberations. Quite surprisingly, in light of how predominant the content analyses of the deliberative quality have been in studies of online discussions in other contexts (for example,

Papacharissi 2002; Wilhelm 1999; Witschge 2004), actual discussion quality has been given almost no systematic attention in the studies analysed here. We stress, however, that this could in part be a selection bias in our analysis and should not be regarded as a general assessment of the entire research field. Nonetheless, whether the discussions in the experiments covered here actually were deliberative – that is, sincere, rational, qualitative and so on – is judged based on user experiences (National Citizens' Technology Forum), either briefly noted in the form of annotation-based evidence (for example, Virtual Agora) or not analysed at all (for example, Virtual Polity and the Deliberation and Internet Engagement Project). Only in Albrecht's Demos experiment were more in-depth assessments made concerning the actual discussion. Hence, scholars mainly appear to rely on the deliberative design of the experiment to assure that actual deliberation takes place.

The main research focus pertaining to internal outcomes of the online deliberations that we have found in our analysis of the studies is on two aspects: opinion/attitude changes and knowledge gains/learning. These are, of course, effects which are often central to deliberative theory, especially opinion changes (Barber 1984; Gutmann and Thompson 1996) and have been reported in offline experiments as well (Luskin *et al.* 2002; Mendelberg and Karpovitch 2007). Concerning the former of these, most of the online deliberations analysed in this chapter report opinion changes as one of their main findings. Participants in the online Deliberative Polls®, for instance, reportedly changed their attitudes on US foreign policy in a somewhat more globalist direction concerning six of nine measured items. Also, group mechanisms such as opinion variance and group polarisation (Sunstein 2006) are given thorough attention. Concerning this, the findings of the online Deliberative Polls® show that online deliberation reduced variance in opinions, albeit that a slight tendency to polarisation was also noted. Participants in the Finnish Virtual Polity Experiment on energy policy also changed their opinions and became more environmentally friendly after deliberating. Smith *et al.* (2009: 21) similarly report findings of 'consistent changes in opinion for those who participate' in their Deliberation and Internet Engagement Experiment. Muhlberger (2005: 8) reports that even though mean opinions were mostly unaltered, the participants' opinions did become more coherent within the deliberation groups in the Virtual Agora Deliberation Experiment. Hence, deliberation reduced the variance in opinions. Price and Capella demonstrate significant changes in participants' opinions, changes which they prove were due to the arguments made during group discussions in the Electronic Dialogue Project. These findings were also stable over time. In the Swiss NCCR Experiment, opinion changes also took place and were 'consolidated' in the deliberation groups. Min, however, found no significant changes in group means concerning opinions.

Offline deliberations often report knowledge gains as significant findings, besides opinion changes (for example, Fishkin *et al.* 2000; Luskin *et al.* 2002). Indeed, the second main aspect concerning internal outcomes in online deliberations was an increase in knowledge. Price and Capella (Electronic Dialogue Project), for instance, demonstrate how taking part in group discussions increased participants' knowledge on certain issues. Luskin *et al.* (Online Deliberative Polls®) show that participants experienced small but statistically significant knowledge increases due to deliberation. Grönlund *et al.* (Virtual Polity Experiment) report that significant knowledge gains took place due to taking part in their online deliberation. However, they are uncertain whether most of the effects are due to reading information material prior to the discussion or whether the effects are due to an incorporation of this information in the discussions (Strandberg and Grönlund 2012: 9–10). Similarly, Muhlberger and Weber (Virtual Agora) argue strongly for the case of learning in the deliberation process, which, they also maintain, is closely tied to opinion shifts. However, they found no evidence to indicate that learning was due to discussion and not merely to reading and contemplating the information material. Min, on the other hand, found that there was a significant difference in knowledge between participants and a control group, indicating that deliberation brought about knowledge gains. Evidently, the studies we have analysed show that increased knowledge is a significant outcome of deliberation. However, in light of the experiments in which information and discussion are separated more thoroughly (for example, Virtual Agora and the Virtual Polity), it is still quite unclear how this learning is produced, although Bächtiger suggests that findings in the Swiss NCCR Experiment indicate that discussion seemed to increase the chances of participants keeping their knowledge gains in the long term.

Besides the two main internal outcomes of online deliberations, an array of other effects also emerge when reviewing the literature. These have sometimes been called 'side effects' (Grönlund *et al.* 2010) and entail aspects such as efficacy, interpersonal trust, other-regarding attitudes and increased likelihood of activity and engagement. Before summarising our analysis section, we thus briefly shed some light on these supplemental internal outcomes. Concerning these, Min found evidence that taking part in an online deliberation increased both participants' efficacy and their willingness to participate in politics significantly. Price and Capella report that participants in the Electronic Dialogue Project had become significantly more willing to engage in politics and other civic activities. They also show that discussion attendance was positively linked to increased generalised trust. Strandberg and Grönlund, however, only found a few weak side effects of deliberating online in the Virtual Polity Experiment. Surprisingly, they even found that participants had become slightly less eager to participate in politics after deliberating. Rhee and Kim also write that no significant findings were found concerning civility, trust and tolerance in their Daum Deliberative Experiment.

In summarising the section on outcomes, we firstly note that our census of experiments mostly echoes the sentiment of Coleman and Moss (2012: 11), who have highlighted a lack of focus on policy outcomes within the research field concerning online deliberation. By and large, the outcome-related aspects brought out in our analysis were almost entirely concerned with such internal outcomes and any external outcomes in the form of connections to real life policy were 'loose' at best. Arguably (*see* Hendriks 2006), the field would have more to gain from integrating the micro-perspectives employed in these experiments with the macro-

Table 7.4: Outcomes of online deliberations: summary of observations

	Outcomes			
	External outcomes	Opinion shifts	Knowledge gains	Side effects
Electronic Dialogue Project	none	yes	yes	yes
Daum Deliberative Project	none	n.a.	n.a.	no
National Citizens' Technology Forum	none	n.a.	n.a.	n.a
Min's experiment	none	no	yes	yes
Virtual Agora Project	none	more coherent	yes	n.a
Virtual Polity Project	none	yes	yes	no
Online Deliberative Polls®	none	yes	yes	n.a
Deliberation and Internet Engagement	potential policy influence	yes	n.a.	n.a
Demos Debate in Hamburg	potential policy influence	n.a.	n.a.	n.a
NCCR Experiment	none	yes	yes	n.a.

deliberations already found in civil society and in policy-making. Concerning the internal outcomes of the experiments, we find that scholars have mostly focused on the effects that offline studies have focused on as well. Of course, some of the experiments analysed here strive to compare online deliberations to offline counterparts (for example, Online Deliberative Polls®; Virtual Polity; Min) so it is only natural to apply roughly the same measures as in the offline deliberation experiments. Generally, our literature review showed that opinion changes and knowledge gains appear to be the main outcomes of deliberating online, which is in line with both theory (for example, Barber 1984; Gutmann and Thompson 1996) and findings from offline deliberations (for example, Fishkin *et al.* 2000; Grönlund *et al.* 2010; Luskin *et al.* 2002). The observations concerning the outcomes of online deliberations are summarised in Table 7.4.

Conclusions

The aim of this chapter was to accumulate empirical observations from experiments in online deliberation, in order to identify common themes. We also argued that such a descriptive overview of a rather novel and disparate field hitherto labelled by some as being full of the 'impressionistic sharing of experience, intuitive arguments, and the like' (Davies and Gangadharan 2009: 6) would help theory-construction and testing. So what are the main findings of our chapter that could serve as a basis for further testing and potentially even aid the construction of theory?

Arguably, the most relevant knowledge for future studies to be drawn from our study is that it has highlighted areas that have still not been sufficiently studied in the practices of online deliberations. To be more specific: we found that the preconditions have mostly been addressed thoroughly by scholars in the literature and likewise design. Within these two main areas, we also observed a general coherence in practices. It is perhaps only the scarce use of full modality in deliberative designs online that limits our findings. Certainly, more studies employing full modality would further our knowledge. Concerning outcomes, however, our findings provide further support for Coleman and Moss's (2102: 11) view that 'online deliberation researchers need to become more attendant to outcomes – not simply in terms of whether participants trusted the process, learned anything new, or would do it all again, but in terms of political efficacy and of policy outputs'. Hendriks (2006: 499) argues strongly for an 'integrated system of public deliberation', in which internal procedures and outcomes, or micro-deliberations as she calls them, are tied to wider civil society or to the macro-deliberative context in which they occur. Thus, a too-narrow focus on deliberations as experiments with which to test theoretical assumptions may end up generating elitist constructions with little relevance beyond the experiment itself (*see* Hendriks 2006).

In our overview, the combination of the aforementioned lack of external outcomes, the limited amount of attention paid to side effects, such as political efficacy, and insufficient knowledge of whether the discussions actually meet deliberative standards all indicate that there are still uncharted areas concerning the outcomes of online deliberation experiments. One could, of course, also argue that valuable knowledge concerning online deliberations might be found if scholars were to reverse their approach and experiment with less-than-ideal preconditions and deliberative designs, putting deliberative theory to a more critical test online instead of showing us 'the social and technical conditions under which it [online deliberation] is most likely to be successful' (*cf.* Coleman and Moss 2012: 6).

Regarding the potential construction of theory, then, overviews such as ours and those conducted by other scholars (for example, Davies and Gangadharan 2009; Delli Carpini *et al.* 2004; Manosevitch 2010; Towne and Herbsleb 2012) are probably to be regarded as first steps beyond an 'impressionistic sharing of experience' (Davies and Gangadharan 2009: 6). Although none of them can overview the entire research field nor all aspects relevant to it – ours being no exception – systematic literature reviews nonetheless provide researchers with more knowledge of the commonalities and discrepancies found among the experiences that are being shared in single-point studies. This accumulated evidence could, in the next step towards theory construction, serve as a basis for studies with explanatory ambitions. One could apply systematic analytical techniques such as Qualitative Comparative Analysis (*see* Ragin 1994 for description) in seeking to explain, for instance, under which preconditions and with what designs online deliberation produces certain outcomes. The term 'online deliberation' has also been used very broadly and studied in varying contexts (Towne and Herbsleb 2012: 99; *cf.* Davies and Gangadharan 2009), which serves to make recurring overviews all the more important in order to describe every 'nook and cranny' of the phenomenon. Hence, there are several paths for future studies – both single-point and accumulating ones – to explore within the field of online deliberation.

An intensive dialogue between scientists and policy-makers is also needed before we can design a democratic system in which (online) deliberation is an integrated part of the decision-making process. In order to engage citizens in time-consuming deliberation in which different policy options are reflected upon, governments must show that the outcomes of public deliberation really have an impact, not only in the deliberation event but also on actual policies (Coleman 2012: 390).

References

Albrecht, S. (2006) 'Whose voice is heard in online deliberation? A study of participation and representation in political debates on the internet', *Information, Communication & Society* 9 (1): 62–82.

Baek, Y. M., Wojcieszak, M. and Delli Carpini, M. X. (2011) 'Online versus face-to-face deliberation: Who? Why? What? With what effects?', *New Media & Society* 1–21.

Baker, R., Blumberg, S. J., Brick, M., Couper, M. P., Courtright, M., Dennis, J. M., Dillman, D., Frankel, M. R., Garland, P., Groves, R. M., Kennedy, C., Krosnick, J., Lavrakas, P. J., Lee, S., Link, M., Piekarski, L., Rao, K., Thomas, R. K. and Zahs, D. (2010) 'Research Synthesis. AAPOR Report on Online Panels', *Public Opinion Quarterly* 74: 711–81.

Bächtiger, A. (2011) *Deliberation in Swiss Direct Democracy: A field experiment on the expulsion initiative*, report, Switzerland: National Centre of Competence in Research.

Barber, B. R. (1984) *Strong Democracy: Participatory politics for a new age*, Los Angeles, CA: University of California Press.

— (1998) 'Three scenarios for the future of technology and strong democracy', *Political Science Quarterly* 113 (4): 573–89.

Campbell, D. T. and Stanley, J. C. (1963) *Experimental and Quasi-Experimental Designs for Research*, Chicago, IL: Rand McNally.

Coleman, S. (2012) 'Making the e-citizen', in S. Coleman and P. M. Shane (eds) *Connecting Democracy: Online consultation and the flow of political communication*, Cambridge, MA: MIT Press.

Coleman, S. and Goetze, J. (2001) *Bowling Together: Online public engagement in policy deliberation*, report, London: Hansard Society.

Coleman, S. and Moss, G. (2012) 'Under construction: the field of online deliberation research', *Journal of Information Technology & Politics,* 9: 1–15.

Dahl, R. A. (1989) *Democracy and Its Critics*, New Haven, CT: Yale University Press.

Dahlberg, L. (2001) 'The internet and democratic discourse: exploring the prospects of online deliberative forums extending the public sphere', *Information, Communication & Society* 4 (4): 615–33.

Davies, T. (2009) 'The blossoming field of online deliberation', in T. Davies and S. P. Gangadharan (eds), *Online Deliberation: Design, research, and practice*, San Fransisco, CA: CSLI Publications.

Davies, T. and Chandler, R. (2011) 'Online deliberation design: choices, criteria, and evidence', in T. Nabatchi, M. Weiksner, J. Gastil and M. Leighninger (eds), *Democracy in Motion: Evaluating the practice and impact of deliberative civic engagement*, Oxford: Oxford University Press.

Davies, T. and Gangadharan, S. P. (2009) *Online Deliberation: Design, research, and practice*, San Fransisco, CA: CSLI Publications.

Delborne, J. A., Anderson, A. A., Kleinman, D. L., Colin, M. and Powell, M. (2011) 'Virtual deliberation? Prospects and challenges for integrating the internet in consensus conferences', *Public Understanding of Science* 20 (3): 367–84.

Delli Carpini, M. X., Cook, F. L., and Jacobs, L. R. (2004) 'Public deliberation, discursive participation, and citizen engagement: a review of the empirical literature', *Annual Review of Political Science* 2004 (7): 315–44.

Fishkin, J. S. (1995) *The Voice of the People: Public opinion and democracy*, New Haven, CT: Yale University Press.

Fishkin, J. S., Luskin, R. C. and Jowell, R. (2000) 'Deliberative polling and public consultation', *Parliamentary Affairs* 53: 657–66.

Gastil, J. (2000) 'Is face-to-face citizen deliberation a luxury or necessity?', *Political Communication* 17 (4): 357–61.

Gastil, J. and Black, L. (2008) 'Public deliberation as the organizing principle of political communication research', *Journal of Public Deliberation* 4 (1): 1–47.

Goodin, R. E. and Dryzek, J. S. (2006) 'Deliberative impacts: the macro-political uptake of mini-publics', *Politics & Society* 34 (2): 219–44.

Göritz, A. S. (2004), 'Recruitment for online access panels', *International Journal of Market Research* 46: 411–25.

Grönlund, K., Strandberg, K. and Himmelroos, S. (2009) 'The challenge of deliberative democracy online: a comparison of face-to-face and virtual experiments in citizen deliberation', *Information Polity* 14: 187–201.

Grönlund, K., Setälä, M. and Herne, K. (2010) 'Deliberation and civic virtue: lessons from a citizen deliberation experiment', *European Political Science Review* 2: 95–117.

Gutmann, A. and Thompson, D. (1996) *Democracy and Disagreement*, Cambridge, MA: Belknap Press of Harvard University Press.

Habermas, J. (1989) *The Structural Transformation of the Public Sphere: An inquiry into a category of the bourgeois society*, Cambridge, MA: Cambridge University Press.

Hamlett, P. W. and Cobb, M. D. (2006) 'Potential solutions to public deliberation problems: structured deliberations and polarization cascades', *The Policy Studies Journal* 34: 629–48.

Hendriks, C. M. (2006) 'Integrated deliberation: reconciling civil society's dual role in deliberative democracy', *Political Studies* 34, 486–508.

Iyengar, S., Luskin, R. C. and Fishkin, J. S. (2003) 'Facilitating informed public opinion: evidence from face-to-face and online Deliberative Polls', working paper, The Center for Deliberative Democracy, Stanford University. Online. Available http://pcl.stanford.edu/common/docs/research/iyengar/2003/facilitating.pdf (accessed 1 October 2013).

Jankowski, N. and Van Os, R. (2004) 'Internet-based political discourse: a case study of electronic democracy in Hoogeveen', in P. Shane (ed.) *Democracy Online: The prospects for political renewal through the internet*, New York, NY: Routledge.

Karlsson, M. (2010) 'What does it take to make online deliberation happen? A comparative analysis of 28 online discussion forums', in F. De Cincio, A. Machintosh and C. Peraboni (eds) *Online Deliberation*, proceedings, Fourth International Conference, Leeds, UK.

Kavanaugh, A. L., Isenhour, P. L., Cooper, M., Carroll, J. M., Rosson, M. B. and Schmitz, J. (2005) 'Information technology in support of public deliberation', in P. Van Den Besselaar, G. De Michelis, J. Preece and C. Simone (eds), *Communities and Technologies 2005,* Netherlands: Springer.

Kies, R. (2010) *Promises and Limits of Web-deliberation*, New York, NY: Palgrave Macmillan

Luskin, R. C., Fishkin, J. S. and Jowell, R. (2002) 'Considered opinions: Deliberative Polling in Britain', *British Journal of Political Science,* 32: 455–87.

Luskin, R. C., Fishkin, J. S. and Iyengar, S. (2004) 'Considered opinions on U.S. foreign policy: Face-to-face versus online deliberative polling', working paper, The Center for Deliberative Democracy, Stanford University. Online. Available http://cdd.stanford.edu/research/papers/2006/foreign-policy.pdf (accessed 1 October 2013).

Luskin, R. C., Fishkin, J. S. and Iyengar, S. (2006) 'Considered opinions on U.S. foreign policy: evidence from online and face-to-face deliberative polling', report, California: The Center for Deliberative Democracy.

Manosevitch, E. (2010) 'Mapping the practice of online deliberation', in F. De Cincio, A. Machintosh and C. Peraboni (eds) *Online Deliberation*, proceedings, Fourth International Conference, Leeds, UK.

Mendelberg, T. and Karpowitz, C. (2007) 'How people deliberate about justice: groups, gender, and decision rules', in S. W. Rosenberg (ed.) *Can the People Govern?*, Basingstoke: Palgrave.

Min, S.-J. (2007) 'Online vs. face-to-face deliberation: effects on civic engagement', *Journal of Computer Mediated Communication* 12: 1369–87.

Muhlberger, P. (2005) 'The Virtual Agora project: a research design for studying democratic deliberation', *Journal of Public Deliberation,* 1 (1).

Muhlberger, P. and Weber, L. M. (2006) 'Lessons from the Virtual Agora project: the effects of agency, identity, information, and deliberation on political knowledge', *Journal of Public Deliberation* 2(1).

Norris, P. (2001) *Digital Divide? Civic engagement, information poverty and the internet worldwide*, New York, NY: Cambridge University Press.

Papacharissi, Z. (2002) 'The virtual sphere: the internet as a public sphere', *New Media & Society* 4 (1): 9–27.

Pateman, C. (2012) 'Participatory democracy revisited', *Perspectives on Politics,* 10 (1): 7–19.

Peters, G. (1998) *Comparative Politics: Theory and methods*, New York: New York University Press.

Price, V. (2009) 'Citizens deliberating online: theory and some evidence', in T. Davies and S. P. Gangadharan (eds) *Online Deliberation: Design, research, and practice*, San Fransisco, CA: CSLI Publications.

Price, V. and Capella, J. N. (2002) 'Online deliberation and its influence: the electronic dialogue project in campaign 2000', *IT & Society* 1 (1): 303–29.

Ragin, C. (1994) 'Introduction to qualitative comparative analysis', in T. Janoski and A. Hicks (eds), *The Comparative Political Economy of the Welfare State,* New York, NY: Cambridge University Press.

Rhee, W. J. and Kim, E. -M. (2009) 'Deliberation on the net: lessons from a field experiment', in T. Davies and S. P. Gangadharan (eds) *Online Deliberation: Design, research, and practice,* San Fransisco, CA: CSLI Publications.

Smith, G., John, P., Sturgis, P. and Nomura, H. 'Deliberation and internet engagement: initial findings from a randomized controlled trial evaluating the impact of facilitated internet forums', paper presented at the ECPR General Conference, Potsdam, Germany, 2009.

Smith, G. and Wales, C. (2000) 'Citizens' juries and deliberative democracy', *Political Studies* 48: 51–65.

Strandberg, K. (2005) ' "Town hall" meetings for the masses or "social clubs" for the motivated? A study of citizens' discussions on the internet', *World Political Science Review* 1 (1): 1–19.

——— (2008) 'Public deliberation goes on-line? An analysis of citizens' political discussions on the internet prior to the Finnish parliamentary elections in 2007', *Javnost – The Public* 15 (1): 71–90.

Strandberg, K. and Grönlund, K. (2012) 'Online deliberation and its outcome: evidence from the virtual polity experiment', *Journal of Information Technology & Politics* 9 (12): 167–84.

Stromer-Galley, J. (2002) 'New voices in the public sphere: a comparative analysis of interpersonal and online political talk', *Javnost – The Public,* 9(2): 23–42.

Sunstein, C. (2001) *Republic.com,* Princeton, NJ: Princeton University Press

——— (2006) *Infotopia: How many minds produce knowledge,* Oxford: Oxford University Press.

Towne, W. B. and Herbsleb, J. D. (2012) 'Design considerations for online deliberation systems', *Journal of Information Technology & Politics* 9: 97–115.

Van Selm, M. and Jankowski, N. W. (2006) 'Conducting online surveys', *Quality & Quantity* 40 (3): 435–56.

Vehovar, V., Manfreda, K. L. and Koren, G. (2008) 'Internet surveys', in W. Donsbach and M. Traugott (eds) *The Sage Handbook of Public Opinion Research,* London: Sage.

Wilhelm, A.G. (1999) 'Virtual sound boards: how deliberative is on-line political discussion?', *Information, Communication and Society* 1 (3): 313–38.

Witschge, T. (2004) 'Online deliberation: Possibilities of the internet for deliberative democracy', in P. Shane (ed.) *Democracy Online: The prospects for political renewal through the internet,* New York, NY: Routledge.

Wright, S. (2011) 'Politics as usual? Revolution, normalisation and a new agenda for online deliberation', *New Media & Society* 14 (2): 244–61.

Wright, S. and Street, J. (2007) 'Democracy, deliberation and design: the case of online discussion forums', *New Media & Society* 9 (5): 849–69.

Chapter Eight

'Gentlemanly Conversation' or Vigorous Contestation?: An Exploratory Analysis of Communication Modes in a Transnational Deliberative Poll® (Europolis)[1]

André Bächtiger and Marlène Gerber

Deliberation is quickly changing. Recent years have seen considerable conceptual shifts in defining deliberation. The classic approach, with its stress on rational discourse, is being superseded by an expanded programme of deliberation putting a stress on wider forms of communication, including story-telling and (emotional) rhetoric (*see* Bächtiger *et al.* 2010; Mansbridge *et al.* 2010). In recent years, several scholars (Manin 2005; Urfalino 2005; Bächtiger 2011) have advocated that deliberationists should also focus more on contestation in deliberative processes. Surely, all deliberationists stress the importance of what Habermas (1989) has called 'rational-critical debate', which, by definition, entails controversial argument and argumentative contestation. Yet many scholars are still wary of equating deliberation with fully fledged contestation, as we typically find it in adversarial debate formats. John Dryzek (2009: 3), for instance, notes: 'Deliberation is different from adversarial debate. The initial aim is not to win, but to understand.' Indeed, standard accounts of deliberation draw from a 'conversation' model of speech (Schudson 1997; Remer 1999) and frequently emphasise communication that entails civility, respect and constructiveness, in combination with a dispassionate attitude, open-mindedness and a focus on reasons that everyone can accept (*see* Bächtiger *et al.* 2010; Mansbridge *et al.* 2010).

But this gearing towards 'gentlemanly' and consensual discussion has somewhat obscured contestation's virtues for realising essential goals of deliberation. In recent years, 'epistemic fruitfulness' (or, the acquisition of better knowledge) has become a focal point in deliberative theory and is frequently advocated as a key goal of the deliberative process (*see* Mansbridge 2010). Vigorous contestation may be instrumental to this goal (Manin 2005; Bächtiger 2011) and contestatory

---

1.   We thank Seraina Pedrini, Jürg Steiner, Simon Niemeyer, Robert Goodin, and Regula Hänggli for excellent comments on earlier drafts of this chapter. We also thank the Swiss National Science Foundation (Grant: 100017_140265) and the Hanse Wissenschaftskolleg (Delmenhorst) for financial support.

modes of communication may also achieve it much more effectively than consensual ones. In particular, contestatory modes of communication may help to more fully explore all sides of an issue, uncovering unshared information and reducing confirmatory bias by focusing on the downsides of specific proposals and arguments (*see* Schweiger *et al.* 1986; Schulz-Hardt 2002; Stromer-Galley and Muhlberger 2009). There is also intriguing psychological research demonstrating the epistemological superiority of contestation. In a laboratory study, Schweiger *et al.* (1986) found that contestatory formats in the form of 'dialectical inquiry' and 'devil's advocacy' were conducive to a higher level of critical evaluation of assumptions and better-quality recommendations than consensual formats, even though the latter were not geared towards finding easy consensus. To be sure, contestatory modes of communication may have their own problems and pitfalls, especially when it comes to other deliberative aims, such as social acceptability and legitimacy: consensual modes of communication may be more apt to achieve these goals. Indeed, Schweiger *et al.* (1986) also found that subjects in the consensus groups expressed greater acceptance of their groups' decisions as well as a desire to continue to work with their groups, compared to participants in dialectical inquiry or devil's advocacy groups. But there is full agreement in the literature that good deliberation should reveal all available information on an issue at hand and be conducive to an unbiased evaluation of the merits and downsides of proposals and arguments. Following psychological research, this means that good deliberation requires a healthy dose of vigorous contestation in the deliberative process.

But what does actually happen in citizen deliberations? Do citizen deliberations contain vigorous contestation and 'clashes of conflicting arguments' (Manin 2005) or are they instances of 'gentlemanly' and consensual discussion? To date, we know surprisingly little about the deliberative process in citizen deliberation. The most prominent format of citizen deliberation, the *Deliberative Poll*®, aims at the systematic elaboration and evaluation of '*competing considerations*' on an issue at hand (Fishkin and Luskin 2005: 285). Random selection of participants combined with random allocation to small-group discussions support this goal by creating 'cognitive diversity' (*see* Landemore 2013) and confronting participants with diverse opinions. As such, Deliberative Polling® has in-built mechanisms for contestatory engagement and should not merely feature 'gentlemanly' and consensual discussion. Yet, Bernard Manin (2005: 9) has hypothesised that 'diversity of views' does not necessarily imply 'conflicting views'. Even in the face of opinion diversity, to Manin, group discussions may entail a number of psychological hindrances to the full deployment of contestation, ranging from conflict avoidance to satisficing logics. So, one wonders how much vigorous contestation there really is in Deliberative Polls®.

In this chapter, we make a first attempt to systematically explore the levels of contestatory and consensual modes of communication respectively in citizen deliberation. We do this in the context of *Europolis*, a pan-European Deliberative Poll®, which was carried out in Brussels in late May 2009. Almost 400 EU citizens from all 27 EU member-states were assembled over three days to discuss the topics of third-country migration and climate change. Focusing on four carefully selected small discussion groups, we explore to what extent ordinary European citizens were engaging in contestation, co-operation or other forms of communication. In this regard, we mainly focus on the amount of disagreement (representing contestatory modes of communication), agreement (representing consensual modes of communication) and neutral speeches (representing other forms of communication, such as sharing experience or the elaboration of a position). On this basis, we are in a position to judge whether the Europolis small-group discussions primarily employed polite and consensual discussion or whether they featured vigorous contestation.

In the following, we will not explore further which communication mode, contestation or consensus, is ultimately superior. Nonetheless, our chapter is based on two premises: first, good deliberation requires a healthy dose of controversial argument. If underlying disagreements do not come to the fore, then this must be considered a deliberative failure. Second, in order to systematically evaluate what effects are produced by different communication modes, we first need to put in some empirical spadework and check what actually happens in citizen deliberation. Our exploratory analysis makes a first attempt to shed light on this urgent topic. Of course, the specific and somewhat artificial setting of a Deliberative Poll® with no consequential decision-making at the end may not tell us much about contestatory and consensual behaviour under conditions of real political salience and real political costs. But given the prominence of DP-style designs for organising citizen deliberation worldwide, our results may still be highly instructive for practitioners of citizen deliberation events.

Conversation, contestation, consensus: some conceptual nuts and bolts

Modern-day deliberation is frequently categorised as an instance of the 'conversation' model of speech (Schudson 1997; Remer 1999; Manin 2005). Habermas was the first to theorise 'conversation' in the context of eighteenth-century salons and coffee houses (Manin 2005: 19) and many deliberative democrats have followed this line, by conceptualising deliberation in 'conversational' terms. In a nutshell, 'conversation' can be defined as 'face-to-face communication' combined with a stress on 'the egalitarian and cooperative features of ideal conversation' (Schudson 1997: 299). 'Conversation' is also frequently equated with the term 'interactive discussion' (Manin 2005). The distinctiveness of 'conversation' or 'interactive discussion', however, mainly arises from its juxtaposition to adversarial debate formats. In this regard, Remer's (1999) distinction between the 'conversation' and 'oratory' model of speech is instructive. Remer depicts this as follows: 'Where the orator aims in oratory to beat his opponent, the speaker's purpose in conversation is to seek out the truth, collectively, with the other interlocutors.' (1999: 49) Moreover, oratory is distinguished stylistically from the conversational model: in oratory, a single active speaker delivers to a passive audience, whereas conversation is dialogical and involves several interlocutors, 'reflecting, ideally, the give-and-take of their discussion.' (*Ibid.*: 44) Finally, oratory also starts from the premise that the 'average person's nature necessitates extra-rational appeals' (*Ibid.*: 42), achieved by the deployment of (emotional) rhetoric, while the conversational model is geared towards rational argument. In past decades, deliberative democrats have given the conversational model an additional consensual spin, by emphasising respect as well as a focus on reasons that other participants can accept. This consensual spin in deliberative theory is based on the premise that 'gentlemanly' and consensual forms of discussion provide an alternative to the standard adversarial and aggressive way of discussing public affairs in contemporary politics, which many deliberative democrats view as harmful for a well functioning democracy (*see* Tannen 1998). Of course, the 'conversational-consensual' model of deliberation is itself not devoid of contestation, since the very structure of a deliberative process – the succession of arguments and counter-arguments – has contestatory elements by design. But the problem here is not one of presence or absence of contestation but one of basic orientation and quantity: our hunch is that the 'conversational-consensual' model of deliberation privileges communication forms other than controversial argumentation, namely the pooling of information, the sharing of experiences, the elaborations of positions which are not sharply polarised or formally adversarial, as well as the identification of converging arguments and common ground. In other words, the 'conversational-consensual' model of deliberation may under-produce conflicting arguments.

However, when it comes to developing productive categories for empirically distinguishing among the various communication modes, the existing literature is confusing at best. In this regard, Remer's (1999) distinction between conversation and oratory remains underspecified, especially when it comes to citizen deliberation. In particular, it obscures that citizen deliberation may also entail vigorous contestation as well, although it lacks the further implications of oratory, especially oratory's exclusive orientation towards conflict and mobilisation, which would clearly be at odds with a deliberative approach. Next, Manin (2005) has translated Remer's distinction between the conversation and oratory into a distinction between 'discussion' and 'debate'. In the context of citizen deliberation, however, Manin's elegant distinction is problematic, for two reasons: first, most deliberative practitioners organise citizen deliberation in a discussion and not in a debate format. Thus, when we speak about contestation in citizen deliberation, we necessarily speak about *debate-style elements within a discussion format*. Second, as mentioned above, there is also a strong current in deliberative theory towards consensus and agreement, requiring that we also capture consensual and collaborative elements within the discussion format. To deal with these various challenges, we propose to distinguish between two variants of the discussion format, a contestatory and a consensual variant, which we treat as poles of a 'discussion continuum'. Empirically, we explore towards which pole concrete citizen deliberations drift.

First, a consensual variant of discussion is geared towards common understanding and identifying common ground. Its main feature is the search and identification of converging arguments and reasons that other discourse participants can accept. In operational terms, differentiated argumentation, respect, mediating proposals and different forms of agreement are primary features. From an evaluation perspective, we would speak of a consensual variant of discussion if the amounts of agreement and respect were high. We may also find a substantial amount of other forms of communication, such as the pooling of information, the sharing of experiences or the elaboration of positions. These other forms of communication may be instrumental for finding common understanding and consensus. Finally, disagreement and contestation are certainly not absent in consensual versions of discussion (and they may even make up a substantial part of the communication process), but they are mainly done in a constructive and differentiated way with a view to solving the conflict.

Second, a contestatory variant of discussion is geared towards the clarification of differences. It has debate-style features, even though it does not conform to a classic debate format. The main difference from a classic debate format (or oratory) is that the speaker's goal in contestation is still related to 'truth-finding', not only to win the debate by means of rhetorical persuasion and by discrediting other debaters (*see* Walzer 1999: 171). The main feature of a contestatory discussion process is the clash of conflicting arguments (Manin 2005). Hereby, we can identify three (interrelated) *modi operandi*: 'disputing', which refers to a process of argumentative challenges (and counter-challenges); 'questioning', which refers to a process of critical interrogation and (cross-)examination; and 'insisting', which refers to a sustained process of questioning and disputing (*see* Bächtiger 2011). Speakers may also use a bold style of communication (such as provocation and open disrespect), in order to create awareness among participants and to stimulate passionate discussions. Moreover, a contestatory variant of discussion may not be fully interactive, in the sense that it involves all participants in discussion, but may restrict interactive elements to a few disputants. From an evaluation perspective, we would speak of a contestatory variant of discussion when there was a high level of disagreement (in the form of disputing, questioning and insisting); agreement may occur but this will be a rare event. Other forms of communication, such as the sharing of experiences or the elaboration of positions, may occur as well; but they will remain marginal. If disputants use such elaborations and experiences then they use them in order to challenge other disputants.

Communication modes in Deliberative Polls®

The tantalising question is now which communication mode, contestation or consensus prevails in citizen deliberation. In this chapter, we shall focus on the most prominent variant of deliberative mini-publics, Deliberative Polls® (*see* Fishkin and Luskin 2005; Fishkin 2009). In Deliberative Polling®, the goal is to 'weigh' competing considerations in informed, balanced, civil and conscientious discussion (Fishkin 2009: 33 ff.). As such, Deliberative Polling® is neither explicitly geared towards contestation nor towards consensus. With regard to the latter, Fishkin and his associates are even strongly opposed to the idea that citizen deliberation should reach agreement and consensus. In their view, an initial gear towards consensual outcomes vitiates the deliberative atmosphere and leads participants to act in a strategic rather than an authentic way. To be sure, Fishkin and his associates are not against the spontaneous, participant-driven emergence of agreement and consensus; they are just opposed to a 'conceptually' prescribed orientation towards these goals. By contrast, there is an opening to contestation. Indeed, the systematic and 'balanced' evaluation of 'competing considerations' lies at the heart of Deliberative Polling®. Even though Deliberative Polls® – and especially the small-group discussions – are not construed as a debate format, Fishkin and his associates seem to be fully aware that a healthy dose of contestation is necessary in order to achieve a thorough evaluation of an issue at hand. In Deliberative Polls®, a number of institutional devices support this goal.

First, participants are presented with balanced information material, listing pro and con arguments of an issue at hand. This should confront participants with the reality that there are competing arguments and an 'other side' that they need to consider. Second, with regard to the small-group discussions, the goal is to attain a systematic and thorough evaluation of the issue under consideration, whereby 'competing considerations' – presented to participants in the information material in the form of pro and cons– are put to discursive scrutiny. In addition, random selection of participants combined with random allocation to small-group discussions ensures that participants are diverse, facilitating the emergence of divergent opinions and interests. Third, facilitators are also supposed to keep the discussions on-topic and focused on the arguments. Fourth, in the 'plenary sessions', competing experts and policy-makers answer participants' questions. Fishkin and Luskin (2005: 288) depict this process as follows: 'The panelists in the plenary sessions respond to the questions formed in the small groups. These are not simple questions of fact, to which there are undebatably right and wrong answers. Rather, they concern the policy alternatives' consequences and costs, the trade-offs they may entail, and the like.'

Yet, there are several reasons why the full deployment of contestation might be constrained in Deliberative Polls®. Actually, this might apply to all three institutional pillars of Deliberative Polls®: the information material, the small-group discussions and the plenary sessions. In this chapter, however, we concentrate on problems in the small-group discussions. A batch of subtle psychological and other factors may hinder the full deployment of contestation. First, since stakes in Deliberative Polls® are low (that is, no decision-making is consequential on the deliberation and no consensus is required at the end), participants generally do not enter group discussion with a competitive mindset, trying to convince others that their ideas are superior and win the debate. In Europolis, our study object, more than 80 per cent of the participants stated that it was important or very important to get to know people from different backgrounds. This emphasis on 'getting to know others' may spark a logic of mutual understanding: participants may want to know and understand what others think, share experiences, learn from others, bridge differences and identify common ground rather than entering into controversial and heated discussion with others and insisting on their positions. Regarding Europolis, Olsen and Trenz (2014: 128) also note that the two topics under discussion, third-country immigration and climate change, were discussed as topics that 'required collective choices and invited the single participants to speak as a "we" in defence of collective goods and not of personal interests'. From a psychological point of view, finding out what 'we can do' may have the consequence that the amount of controversial arguments becomes restricted even further. Second, when discussions are not organised according to a debate format, vigorously disputing other positions and insisting on one's own position may be frequently seen as stubbornness as well as violating the norms of good discussion. This may also curb the contestatory character of discussion. Third, the interactive structure of group discussion and the emphasis on allowing every participant a turn may hinder proper debating as well. Empowered participants may want to speak up and contribute to the discussion. The consequence may be that an ongoing confrontation is interrupted, the focus of the debate shifted and an evolving controversy defused. In sum, despite the clear conceptual openness of deliberative opinion polls towards contestatory forms of engagement, it is not clear how much this will pan out in practice. But to date, almost no one has taken the trouble to systematically investigate what is actually going on in Deliberative Polls® (one of the few exceptions is Siu 2009). Our chapter sets out to change this.

Empirical analysis

We analyse the different communication modes on the basis of Europolis, a pan-European Deliberative Poll® which took place in Brussels in May 2009. The topics of discussion were migration and climate change. The Europolis project started with interviewing a random sample of about 4,300 European citizens in April 2009. About 3,000 of them, randomly selected, were asked at the end of the interview whether they would be interested in attending the deliberative event. The other 1,300, randomly assigned, never received such an invitation to the event and constituted a control group. Out of the 3,000 randomly selected to be part of the test group, a random sub-sample of 348 actually participated at the Deliberative Poll®. This group was proportionally stratified according to the number of seats per member-state in the EU Parliament (*see* Isernia *et al.* 2013). During the three-day event in Brussels, the 348 participants were randomly assigned to 25 small discussion groups. The groups were created by 'randomly varying the languages spoken' (Isernia *et al.* 2013). The discussions were simultaneously translated in all languages spoken in the respective small groups. The small-group discussions were led by trained facilitators. The task of facilitators in Europolis included the promotion of civility and boosting participants' 'Europeanness'.

Selection of discussion groups

As mentioned before, a total of 25 small-group discussions took place in Europolis. Since transcribing and analysing deliberative processes empirically is highly demanding and time-consuming, we refrain from analysing all 25 small groups. In this chapter, we selected a purposive sample of four groups for an in-depth evaluation of different communication modes and forms. Moreover, we limited ourselves to the general discussion on migration and the more specific discussion on policy options that address third-country migration. Our selection criteria have mainly a demonstration purpose, rather than fulfilling representativeness. First, all groups selected should have serious underlying disagreement on the immigration topic in advance of the small-group discussions. Second, we wanted to have some groups where we knew in advance that they comprised 'devil's advocates', either in the form of participant devil's advocates or in the form of a facilitator who questioned participants. This concerns group B (involving a participant devil's advocate) and group A (involving a facilitator questioner). Admittedly, the facilitator in group A may not fully conform to the concept of a devil's advocate, since he only interrupted participants and insisted on clarifications. Even if the critical side of questioning was not fully deployed, the facilitator in group A nonetheless tried to provoke a more focused and dedicated debate on the topic of migration. Third, we wanted to have groups with underlying disagreement, where we knew that no devil's advocates were present, either in the form of participant devil's advocates or in the form of facilitator questioners. This concerns groups C and D. The four selected groups included 14 to 15 participants and were composed as follows: group A consisted of participants from France and Hungary; group B consisted of participants from Germany, Poland and one participant from Austria; group C consisted of participants from Germany and Spain as well as one participant from Austria; and group D consisted of participants from France and Germany and one participant from Austria and one from Luxembourg. In the pre-deliberative questionnaire, all four groups displayed considerable diversity of views regarding crucial attitudinal questions on migration.

Operationalisation

To measure different communication modes empirically, we draw from established research in communication sciences. Stromer-Galley and Muhlberger (2009) have developed a useful scheme for capturing disagreement and agreement via content analysis. In this scheme, disagreement refers to argumentative challenges and highlights contestatory forms of engagement, whereas agreement highlights co-operative and consensual forms of engagement. In order to identify and capture agreement and disagreement in discussion, Stromer-Galley and Muhlberger (2009) use so-called 'thought types' as the unit of analysis. We proceed in a slightly different way: our unit of analysis is a speech. In so doing, we omit the onerous task of (reliably) identifying 'thought types' in the first instance. In addition, focusing on whole speeches also eases the subsequent aggregation of the data.

Following Stromer-Galley and Muhlberger (2009), 'disagreement' is defined as a statement signalling disagreement with what a prior speaker said. Cues of disagreement include statements such as 'I don't agree', and 'that's not correct'. Moreover, disagreement also concerns statements which contain counter-arguments to a specific position (a participant says 'p' and the following participant says 'not p'). We also created an additional category dubbed 'partial disagreement'. This contains statements where speakers say 'I partially agree', or 'that is correct, but'. 'Agreement', in turn, is defined as a statement that expresses alignment with what a prior speaker said. Cues of agreement include statements such as 'I agree', 'that's right', and 'true.' However, with regard to statements signalling agreement, we confront a serious problem. There may be instances where speakers align with one side in a debate and in so doing explicitly say that they 'agree' with this side. Such statements are clearly not expressions of proper 'agreement'; actually, they are coded as 'disagreement' because they signal disagreement with another position. Finally, speeches that contain neither agreement nor disagreement are coded as 'neutral'. We conducted a test of intercoder reliability with an independent coder assessing a total of 30 speeches. The test revealed that the reliability of our coding was satisfactory.[2]

Moreover, we also investigate the amount of informational versus critical questioning. Informational questions are questions posed by participants who ask for more or better information. These are instances of conversational and consensual modes of communication. Critical questions, in turn, are challenging questions in which participants query and probe the validity of another participant's arguments or claims. These represent instances of contestatory modes of communication.

Next, we present a batch of indicators that allow us to take an in-depth look at the communication style. We distinguish between a 'bold' and a 'polite' style of communication. A 'bold' style of communication would be indicative of a contestatory process of discussion; a 'polite' style of communication would be indicative of a consensual process of discussion. A first indicator of 'bold' style is the amount of provocative statements. By provocative statements, we mean statements in which people make exaggerated claims that aim at provoking reactions from other participants. A second indicator of 'bold' style is the amount of disrespect. Disrespect refers to speeches where participants explicitly denigrate the contributions and arguments of other participants. Next, we focus on 'polite' styles of communication. A first indicator of 'polite' style is the amount of 'differentiated' argumentation. In concrete, this means that participants address the issue from different sides, 'weigh' pros and cons, or make self-critical statements. Frequently, differentiated argument occurs in the context of partial disagreement, even though the relationship is not constitutive (that is, partial disagreement does not always entail differentiated argument nor is differentiated argument limited to the former). A second indicator of 'polite' style is the amount of explicit respect. Explicit respect refers to speeches in which participants value or acknowledge what other participants have said, even if they do not fully agree with the latter's viewpoints or arguments.

---

2. Four tests of intercoder reliability were performed for the various communication modes (with the corresponding levels of agreement in parentheses): Ratio of Coding Agreement RCA (73.3%); Cohen's kappa κ (0.638); Spearman's r (0.822); standardised Cronbach's alpha α (0.889).

Finally, we also investigate whether there are sequences of direct confrontational exchanges in the small-group discussions. As mentioned before, direct confrontational exchanges are the hallmark of the debate format and a large amount of direct confrontation would be indicative of discussion drifting towards debate. By direct confrontational exchanges, we mean that two (or several) speakers engage in sustained controversial argumentation. It goes like this: speaker A makes a challenge, which is taken up by speaker B who makes a counter-challenge, followed by a response of speaker A or another speaker defending speaker A's position. In idealised notions of debating, such challenges and counter-challenges would entail 'insisting' and go over several rounds. Thus, we count how many 'rounds' confrontational exchanges exhibit. A particular point of interest is also how direct confrontational exchanges end. We investigate whether participants are really going into the 'heart of the issue' and insisting on their claims or quickly 'take back' their claims and agree with the other disputant (or questioner).

Results

Let us first look at the amount of agreement, disagreement and neutral speeches. In three discussion groups (B, C and D) the percentage of clear-cut disagreements ranges between 20 and 24 per cent (*see* Table 8.1). In group A, despite the presence of a facilitator questioner, the relevant percentage is only 9.3 per cent. The number of partial disagreements (including speeches containing both agreement and disagreement) is smaller, hovering around 11 to 17 per cent for all four groups. While partial disagreements do signal conflict, they do this in a more polite, open and differentiated way than clear-cut disagreements. The number of explicit agreements, in turn, is quite substantial: in groups A and C, explicit agreement characterises around 16 and 20 per cent of the speeches. In groups B and D, the share is lower, hovering at 11 and 12 per cent respectively. The large majority of speeches, however, are 'neutral', with respective shares from 47 to 55 per cent. 'Neutral' speeches entail informational statements, the sharing of experiences and the elaboration of positions that are neither polarised nor formally adversarial. It is also quite striking to see how participants produce multiple streams of arguments and 'storylines' around the immigration topic, which are complementary and additive rather than controversial and confrontational. Finally, the amount of critical and informational questioning is generally low. These figures indicate that the four Europolis discussion groups neither drifted towards a contestatory nor towards a consensual variant of discussion. But to further qualify this finding, let us first take a more in-depth look at the style of communication.

The style of communication in our four Europolis groups is generally very 'gentlemanly'. As Table 8.2 displays, the number of provocations, that is, the making of exaggerated claims, is none or very few, with the partial exception of group B for which this amounts to almost 8 per cent. Disrespect, too, is at a very low level, hovering between 5 and 8 per cent. Here, parliamentary debates might serve as a useful contrast: the amount of disrespect in parliamentary debates

Table 8.1: Agreement, disagreement, and neutral speech in four Europolis discussion groups

	Disagreement (%)	Partial disagreement (%)	Neutral (%)	Agreement (%)	Critical questioning n (%)	Informational questioning n (%)
Group A (Number of speeches =54)	9.3	16.7	53.7	20.4	2 (3.7%)	3 (5.6%)
Group B (Number of speeches =129)	23.3	14.9	51.2	10.9	9 (7.0%)	7 (5.4%)
Group C (Number of speeches =43)	20.9	16.3	46.5	16.3	2 (4.7%)	4 (9.3%)
Group D (Number of speeches =65)	21.5	10.8	55.4	12.3	5 (7.7%)	4 (6.2%)

Table 8.2: Communication styles in four Europolis discussion groups

	Provocation (%)	Disrespect (%)	Differentiated argument (%)	Explicit respect (%)
Group A (Number of speeches =54)	0.0	5.6	9.3	5.6
Group B (Number of speeches =129)	7.8	8.5	14.7	5.4
Group C (Number of speeches =43)	2.3	4.7	20.9	7.0
Group D (Number of speeches =65)	1.5	7.7	15.4	7.7

generally exceeds 20 per cent (*see* Bächtiger 2005). At the same time, the number of speeches with differentiated argumentation is quite substantial – in group C it even exceeds 20 per cent – and is clearly higher than shares of provocations and disrespect. Interestingly, the amount of explicit respect is not very high, ranging only between 5 and 8 per cent. Again, parliamentary debates may give context to these figures: in non-public committee debates with the goal of finding a common solution, the amount of explicit respect is much higher, at around 30 per cent (*see* Bächtiger 2005). But the fact that the percentages for provocation and disrespect are below 10 per cent in all groups is quite telling and surely indicative of the polite character of the discussion.

The small-group discussions do not entail many direct confrontational exchanges either. As mentioned before, direct confrontational exchanges are the hallmark of the debate format and imply that there is a direct 'clash of conflicting arguments', either in the form of a direct challenge and subsequent response from the addressee, or in the form of a critical question and a direct response from the addressee. In groups C and D, there are only two and three participant-induced direct confrontational exchanges respectively. Moreover, these are not sustained but die out almost immediately: the average number of rounds in the direct confrontational exchanges in group D is 2.3 (the minimum is two rounds). In group A, there are ten facilitator-induced questionings. The facilitator in group A repeatedly asked critical questions that forced participants to further substantiate (and defend) their statements. However, facilitator-induced questionings were not at all conducive to a subsequent unfolding of a controversy: participants responded to the facilitator in a neutral way by providing additional justifications, with no participant engaging in controversial argumentation.

In group B, we find two longer instances of direct confrontational exchanges out of a total of seven. Both confrontational exchanges were initiated by a participant 'devil's advocate' (person A, a male participant from (Western) Germany). Let us

Table 8.3: Direct confrontational exchanges in four Europolis discussion groups

	Resolution (take back)	Participant-induced	Rounds (average)	Direct confrontational exchanges
	N	N	N	N
Group A (Number of speeches =54)	0	1	2.4	10
Group B (Number of speeches =129)	3	7	4.0	7
Group C (Number of speeches =43)	0	2	4.5	2
Group D (Number of speeches =65)	2	3	2.3	3

give a taste of one of these confrontational exchanges. In the following example, person A confronts person D, a female participant from (Western) Germany.

A (1): 'I'd like to ask the lady next to me what she would do when she would receive unsolicited visit. When she returns and there is somebody, right inside her apartment. What would she do?'

B (male, Western Germany) (2): 'Illegally in her apartment?'

A (3): 'Right.'

C (male, Austria) (4): 'In this case I'd like to ask how you can compare an apartment, meaning intimate living space, with a country that has far more space.'

A (5): 'Isn't it the same? Do you see any difference? This guy (in the apartment) I will kick out or arrest or whatever and to the other one (irregular immigrant in a country) I say "you can stay". And that is, that – you cannot do that, can you? Aren't that double moral standards?'

[…]

D (9): 'Well, I owe you an answer to your question. I see a very clear difference between my privacy sphere, between my apartment, and […] First of all, I move in my private sphere – in my own rooms, I have my family, they are my closest. And then I am part of a community […] and then I am a German national and furthermore, Germany is a country within the EU. Thus, we need to differentiate and I really cannot just say: "This is my home, I close the borders and devil-may-care" – this is not as simple as that. Let's turn the whole thing around: In Germany, we are the ones driving cars, possessing warm homes, power plants, making greenhouse gas emissions. We just release that into our beautiful environment. Thus, we actually need to build the wall high enough, such that our waste and everything stays with us. We cannot say on the one hand that we want to live a good life but when it comes to the people, we close the door and say: "Here's the boundary. Thanks and bye."'

Interestingly, the discussion changed considerably after this confrontational exchange. Before the confrontational exchange, there was quite a bit off-topic discussion among participants. After the confrontational exchange, participants focused on one particular aspect of immigration (which was aligned with the confrontational exchange): how an immigrant with a regular status can slide into an irregular status. In order to discover the relevant facts, participants even consulted the briefing material. Following this systematic exploration of the topic, some participants came up with proposals on how to improve the legal situation of irregular immigrants. Thus, the direct confrontational exchange had highly 'productive' implications.

However, even in group B, three direct confrontational exchanges ended with an immediate 'take back' of previous claims. This means that challengers were not insisting and instead tried to chart consensual ground. This may be illustrated by the following example in group B, an exchange between two (Western) German participants (person A male, person B female):

A: '[...] In my opinion, the EU should care more that its external borders are closed, in order to monitor that no illegal immigrants may infiltrate the countries and, yes, maybe even take away jobs from the native inhabitants [...]'

B: 'According to me, it shouldn't be the EU's task to close the borders because – we need to look at that a bit more globally – we are one world and the world does consist of a multiplicity of countries and then we need to care that all the people that we exploited for so many years are feeling well in some way [...]'

A: 'That's not what I meant by "closing borders". I think that a selective migration may indeed be reasonable but: we have to concentrate [...] on letting people in that dispose of adequate working experience, not that they take away the jobs from the lowest income class. [...] And concerning people from poor countries, of whom you say that they have been exploited in the times of colonialism; we should give them the opportunity to build up something in their own country and not as refugees [...] They should develop themselves at home in order that they do not need to migrate and to drown.'

This is a familiar scenario in our Europolis discussion groups. Even though there was clearly underlying disagreement, participants acted in a very constructive way by taking up the concerns and trying to propose a solution that both disputants could possibly agree with.

Evolving controversies are also hindered by the fact that other participants frequently act as 'mediators', shifting the controversy in other directions and thus defusing it at the same time. One such example can be found in group D. Here, participant A (female, (Eastern) Germany) argues for increasing development aid in developing countries in order to prevent immigration to Europe. In the following, person B (female, France) contradicts by saying that preventing migration is the wrong solution. In so doing, she highlights the importance of a better cultural understanding and refers to the Erasmus student exchange programme. Then, person C (male, France) jumps in the discussion, taking B's side by emphasising the importance of multiculturalism and tolerance and arguing against development aid. In reaction to that, person D (female, Luxembourg) intervenes with the following statement:

'I think there is already a fundamental difference by referring to certain projects. For some people that are already in a privileged situation and can afford tertiary education and the luxury of profiting from the Erasmus programme and living abroad – if you compare this contemporary situation with the people that suffer and feel bad – well, I wouldn't say that those people should absolutely stay home, but they should in their country already have good future perspectives, wealth. And this has to be said and repeated with regard to development aid in their countries, in that they do not sense the urge to emigrate.'

Without taking sides, D uncovers that the participants A and B were probably talking of two different immigration situations. In the second part of his speech, D searches for consensual ground. On the one hand, D implicitly refers to something that B mentioned, in saying that she does not see the solution in zero migration. On the other hand, D also implicitly refers to A, by arguing that development aid is of crucial importance in improving a country's situation. Thus, by taking a differentiated perspective, D succeeds in defusing an emerging conflict. In other words, the highly interactive setup in Deliberative Polls® seems to stall potentially ongoing controversies.

In some cases, it is also the facilitator who interrupts and stops a potentially evolving controversy. In group A, the facilitator kept asking detailed questions on different aspects of immigration, sometimes in a challenging manner. Although this might be a technique to bring latent disagreements to the fore, it did not work well in this particular case. Rather, by performing a questioner role, the facilitator somewhat freed participants from asking (critical) questions of their own. Moreover, the frequent interruptions by the facilitator also hindered coherent discussion and was conducive to what Ryfe (2006: 88) has called 'scattershot' discussion.

In sum, these findings provide a strong indication that our four small-group discussions in Europolis are mainly instances of 'gentlemanly conversation'. Contestation is not absent but it is neither the most important communication mode nor is it deployed in a bold manner. Only group B (involving a participant devil's advocate) has partial debate-style features, whereas group A (despite the presence of facilitator questioner) is so low on contestation that one might wonder about its 'critically reflective' character. As Manin (2005) has speculated, despite the fact that there is diversity and underlying disagreement in the groups, this is not automatically conducive to vigorous contestation. By the same token, our four Europolis groups also had no discernible drift towards consensual discussion: agreement was present, but consensual modes of communication were not particularly marked. As such, the discussions in the four groups were polite and 'gentlemanly' but not really consensual.

To be sure, we cannot make bold generalisations out of an analysis of four purposively selected discussion groups in one Deliberative Poll® on one specific issue. Future research will require more comparative data to give context to our findings and to support our interpretations. For instance, we need to compare our results with fully fledged debate formats (such as debating clubs) in order to determine what idealised notions of contestation actually look like, that is, what are the exact shares of contestatory and consensual modes of communication as well as of other forms of communication in such formats.

Conclusion

Bernard Manin's (2005) intuition was right. Opinion diversity in citizen deliberation does not automatically spark vigorous contestation and a 'clash of conflicting arguments'. Despite strong opinion diversity and their transnational character, the four Europolis small-group discussions that we analysed are a far cry from an adversarial inquiry as we find it in devil's advocacy or in cross-examination, for example. Rather, the small-group discussions are largely instances of 'gentlemanly conversation', with a bit of contestation surely but definitely with no drift in the direction of vigorous contestation.

Clearly, one might object that participants in Europolis have been provided with 'competing considerations' in the information material and also had the possibility to critically question experts from different sides. That might add to the contestation part and compensate for the lack of vigorous debating in the small-group discussions. But the core of a deliberative event is the actual deliberation phase. The very idea of deliberation, so Parkinson (2012) argues, is that preferences are constructed in the deliberative process. So, if contestation is as low as in our group A, one starts questioning the truly contestatory character of citizen deliberation.

But would more contestation in the small-group discussions really be superior to the 'gentlemanly' conversation mode that we found in our four groups? In other words, if the amount of disagreement and direct confrontation had been higher, would that have changed the outcome, both in epistemic and substantial terms? In the context of this chapter, we must leave this question open. However, as our example in group B underlines, after conflicting viewpoints had clashed in a direct controversial exchange, the discussion became much more focused, in-depth and creative. This finding may also be in line with psychological research arguing that pre-discussion preferences are hard to crack. The problem is that there is a human tendency to quickly dismiss preference-inconsistent information (*see*, for example, Greitemeyer and Schulz-Hardt 2003). As such, only direct confrontations – rather than merely 'hearing' counter-arguments or reading lists of pro and con arguments – might lead people to take proper notice of the disagreement; and, by forcing them to give answers, people might also begin to seriously reflect about the merits and downsides of counter-arguments.

Nonetheless, Fishkin and his associates might remain sceptical of pushing Deliberative Polls® in direction of a debate format. First, they might rebut that people actually change their minds in Deliberative Polls® and frequently do so in more public-spirited directions. This is also true for Europolis. First results show that participants in Europolis became more European and more tolerant towards immigrants (Cabrera and Cavatorto 2009). Moreover, individual satisfaction with the small-group discussions in Europolis was high. Furthermore, the participants experienced the event as extremely balanced and the quality of the group discussions as high (Isernia *et al.* 2013). Indeed, the mere presentation of diverse viewpoints as well as the release and pooling of private information may fulfil epistemic purposes. Argument in itself can be a learning experience, expanding perspectives and provoking insights. One might add that contestatory modes of communication may have their own pitfalls. There is a long debate in educational philosophy about the downsides of adversarialism. Educational philosophers (for example, Ikuenobe 2001) have emphasised that pure adversarialism might be counter-productive, making people entrench their position and become more dismissive of challenges. Clearly, the example in group D speaks a different language, namely that contestation can yield productive consequences. But much more research is needed to corroborate this positive outcome. Finally, a debate format may also increase the inequality of disadvantaged groups. Psychologists have shown that there is gender bias when roles such as the devil's advocate are assigned. Women's reputations can be harmed when they challenge men (Sinclair and Kunda 2000). Similar results were found when Kunda *et al.* (2002) examined reactions of whites to statements by blacks.

On the other hand, there is relatively broad agreement in the literature that vigorous contestation is essential for thoroughly exploring the downsides of proposals and unravelling inconsistencies and flaws in participants' arguments (*see* Schweiger *et al.* 1986; Schulz-Hardt 2002; Stromer-Galley and Muhlberger 2009; Bächtiger 2011). Thus, discarding debate-style formats as inappropriate for citizen deliberation would fully miss the point. As Schudson (1997: 299) has elegantly put it, good democratic discussion must be 'profoundly *uncomfortable*'. But if the goal is to enhance contestatory forms of engagement in citizen deliberation then this needs to be properly organised. In corporate business, for instance, special confrontation sessions are built into a decision-making process. As Herbert and Estes (1977) note, the institutionalisation of conflict and dissent 'may help de-personalize the conflict generated by criticism.' (*Ibid.*: 665). Another ingenious way of filtering controversial arguments into discussion is the 'Deliberatorium', an online deliberative forum developed by Mark Klein (2012). Klein and his team developed an algorithm that automatically evaluates argumentative quality. If argumentative quality turns out to be insufficient, the algorithm alerts the participants and provides them with additional and controversial insights on the topic. Finally, we might also enhance the amount of contestation via the facilitator's role (an under-studied topic, *see* Landwehr, this volume). Of course, the facilitator questioner in group A may not have performed her task well enough; but we may think of active facilitation designs where the facilitator is turned into a devil's advocate, especially when there is no participant devil's advocate in the discussion group.

In sum, this chapter has done some empirical spadework in analysing different communication modes in citizen deliberation. Future research will also have to deal with the consequences of different communication modes. For instance, it is an open question whether deliberation in DPs, based on the systematic discussion of 'competing considerations, has the same awareness and transformation effects as vigorous contestation. Having clarified such issues empirically, we may also be in a better position to rethink the merits and downsides of existing institutional designs for effective and productive citizen deliberation.

References

Bächtiger, A. (2005) *The Real World of Deliberation: A comparative study of its favorable conditions in legislatures*, Bern: Haupt.

—— (2011) 'Contestatory deliberation', paper presented at the Epistemic Democracy Conference, Yale University, October 2011.

Bächtiger, A., Niemeyer, S., Neblo, M. A., Steenbergen, M. R. and Steiner, J. (2010) 'Disentangling diversity in deliberative democracy', *Journal of Political Philosophy* 18(1): 32–63.

Cabrera, S., and Cavatorto, S. (2009) 'A Europe-wide Deliberative Polling experiment', *Professional Review of the Italian Political Science Association* 3.

Dryzek, J. S. (2009) 'The Australian citizens' parliament: a world first, *Journal of Public Deliberation* 5 (1): 1–7.

Fishkin, J. S. (2009) *When the People Speak: Deliberative democracy and public consultation,* Oxford: Oxford University Press.

Fishkin, J. S. and Luskin, R. C. (2005) 'Experimenting with a democratic ideal: Deliberative Polling and public opinion', *Acta Politica* 40 (3): 284–98.

Greitemeyer, T. and Schulz-Hardt, S. (2003) 'Preference-consistent evaluation of information in the hidden profile paradigm: beyond group-level explanations for the dominance of shared information in group decisions', *Journal of Personality and Social Psychology* 84 (2): 322–39.

Habermas, J. (1989) *The Structural Transformation of the Public Sphere: An inquiry into a category of the bourgeois society*, Cambridge, MA: Cambridge University Press.

Herbert, T. and Estes, R. (1977) 'Improving executive decisions by formalizing dissent: the corporate devil's advocate', *Academy of Management Review* 2 (4): 662–667.

Ikuenobe, P. (2001) 'Questioning as an epistemic process of critical thinking', *Educational Philosophy and Theory* 33 (3–4): 325–41.

Isernia, P., Fishkin, J. S., Steiner, J. and Di Mauro, D. (2013) 'Toward a European public sphere: the Europolis project', in R. Kies and P. Nanz (eds) *Is Europe Listening to Us? Successes and failures of EU citizen consultation*, Surrey: Ashgate Publishing.

Klein, M. (2012) 'Enabling large-scale deliberation using attention-mediation metrics', *Computer Supported Cooperative Work* 21 (4–5): 449–73.

Kunda, Z., Davies, P. G., Adams, B. D. and Spencer, S. J. (2002) 'The dynamic time course of stereotype activation: activation, dissipation, and resurrection, *Journal of Personality and Social Psychology* 82 (3): 283–99.

Landemore, H. (2013) 'Deliberation, cognitive diversity, and democratic inclusiveness: an epistemic argument for the random selection of representatives', *Synthese* 190 (7): 1209–1231.

Manin, B. (2005) 'Democratic deliberation: Why we should promote debate rather than discussion', Program in Ethics and Public Affairs seminar, Princeton University.

Mansbridge, J. (2010) 'The deliberative system disaggregated', paper presented at the Annual Meeting of the American Political Science Association, Washington DC, September 2010.

Mansbridge, J., Bohman, J., Chambers, S., Estlund, D., Føllesdal, A., Fung, A., Lafont, C., Manin, B. and Martí, J. L. (2010) 'The place of self-interest and the role of power in deliberative democracy', *Journal of Political Philosophy* 18 (1): 64–100.

Olsen, E. and Trenz, H.-J. (2014) 'From citizens' deliberation to popular will formation? Generating democratic legitimacy through transnational Deliberative Polling', *Political Studies* 62 (1S): 117–133.

Parkinson, J. (2012) *Democracy and Public Space: The physical sites of democratic performance*, Oxford: Oxford University Press.

Remer, G. (1999) 'Political oratory and conversation: Cicero versus deliberative democracy', *Political Theory* 27 (1): 39–64.

Ryfe, D. M. (2006) 'Narrative and deliberation in small group forums', *Journal of Applied Communication Research* 34(1): 72–93.

Schudson, M. (1997) 'Why conversation is not the soul of democracy', *Critical Studies in Mass Communication* 14 (4): 297–309.

Schulz-Hardt, S. (2002) 'Entscheidungsprozesse in Gruppen: Warum der Wissensvorteil von Gruppen oft ungenutzt bleibt und die Meinungsvielfalt diese Nutzung fördern kann', in E. H. Witte (ed.) *Sozialpsychologie wirtschaftlicher Prozesse*, Lengerich: Pabst.

Schweiger, D. M., Sandberg, W. R. and Ragan, J. W. (1986) 'Group approaches for improving strategic decision making: a comparative analysis of dialectical inquiry, devil's advocacy, and consensus', *Academy of Management Journal* 29 (1): 51–7.

Sinclair, L. and Kunda, Z. (2000) 'Motivated stereotyping of women: she's fine if she praised me but incompetent if she criticized me', *Personality and Social Psychology Bulletin* 26 (11): 1329 –42.

Siu, A. (2009) *Look Who's Talking: Examining social influence, opinion change, and argument quality in deliberation*, PhD dissertation, Stanford University.

Stromer-Galley, J. and Muhlberger, P. (2009) 'Agreement and disagreement in group deliberation: effects on deliberation satisfaction, future engagement, and decision legitimacy', *Political Communication* 26 (2): 173–92.

Tannen, D. (1998) *The Argument Culture: Stopping America's war of words*, Ballantine.

Urfalino, P. (2005) 'La délibération n'est pas une conversation', *Négociations* 4 (2): 99–114.

Walzer, M. (1999) 'Deliberation, and what else?' in S. Macedo (ed.) *Deliberative Politics: Essays on 'Democracy and Disagreement'*, Oxford: Oxford University Press.

Chapter Nine

Deliberative Democracy in Divided Belgium: An Alternative for a Democracy on the Edge?

Didier Caluwaerts and Dimokritos Kavadias

It is claimed both theoretically and empirically that a deeply divided public opinion undermines democratic stability. When groups are diametrically opposed, there are very few cross-pressures pushing citizens towards common ground. This is even more so in linguistically divided societies, where the language barrier raises the threshold for mutual understanding even higher. After all, language differences create multiple internally homogeneous public spheres in which citizens, media and politicians can develop an 'us versus them' ethno-nationalist discourse (Sinardet 2009).

Under such adverse circumstances, democracies face their greatest challenge, that of averting political disintegration: when inter-group contact is based on feelings of mutual hostility or distrust, the ground for democratic decision-making is not very fertile. One commonly made suggestion, therefore, is that political discussion should be left to elites, whereas the public should remain deferent (Lijphart 1968). After all, grass-roots activism will only jeopardise the already fragile balance between the social segments and deepen political cleavages (Bogaards 1998). Scholars of ethno-linguistic conflict seem to share this assumption when they suggest that a deeply divided public sphere indicates the unlikeliness of a viable deliberative democracy. As such, citizens of linguistically divided societies are, in all likelihood, unable to display the 'spirit of deliberation' that elites are supposed to show (Steiner 2009).

We would, however, like to push deliberative scholarship beyond its current limits, by asking whether contact between citizens of competing groups would, in fact, exacerbate political conflict. Put differently: can conflict accommodation between citizens of opposed groups live up to the deliberative ideal type? This, in turn, raises the question of under what conditions this would be so. What would happen if we put ordinary citizens together to deliberate under the institutional pressure of highly demanding decision-making rules?

Based on data from a deliberative experiment in deeply divided Belgium, we argue that both decision-making rules and group composition are important determinants of the quality of deliberation. Moreover, our findings suggest that deliberation across divides does not have to deepen political conflict. Facing the 'out-group' in person might even prove to be an incentive to adopting respectful and rational attitudes during the encounter.

In the remainder of this chapter, we first review the literature on inter-group deliberation and on decision-making rules in deliberation. Next, we explain why Belgium constitutes a particularly interesting case for studying citizen deliberation. In the fourth and fifth sections, we explain our experimental design and how we measured deliberation. In the final section, we report the rather unexpected findings from our experiments.

Theoretical perspectives on inter-group deliberation

Even though few scholars will deny that heterogeneity is essential to deliberation, they seem reluctant to contest Mill's statement that 'among a people without fellow-feeling, especially if they read and speak different languages, the united public opinion necessary to the working of representative government, cannot exist' (Mill 1991 [orig. 1859]: 428). Nevertheless, most of them do agree that inter-group interaction at the citizen level could be a key ingredient for peaceful conflict resolution (Dryzek 2005). Deliberation on issues of common concern could set in motion a trend towards conflict reduction: because equal consideration would be given to all perspectives and because the open-mindedness towards the arguments of others that deliberation requires is conducive to higher levels of mutual understanding. As such, a deliberative model of democracy could disrupt the never-ending spiral of conflict exacerbation and could transform strong antagonism into something more constructive for democratic sustainability (O'Flynn 2006).

Despite the optimism that deliberation could contribute to conflict resolution, most recent scholarship does not offer an assessment of the viability of democracy in the face of profound disagreement. However beneficial the application of deliberative principles might be for reducing conflict across deep divides, there is always the implicit – yet unsubstantiated – assumption that deliberation across deep divides is impossible. For instance, Michael Morrell concedes that democratic empathy might lead to 'toleration, mutual respect, reciprocity, and openness toward others' (Morrell 2010: 114) but, at the same time, reckons that empathy might be a rare sight in divided societies. Because very little is known about those on the other side, it is hard to empathise with them. Moreover, social identities in divided societies are partially constructed by the need to be different from, or even superior to, the other side in some way. Under such adverse circumstances, deliberation will at least require an unimaginable degree of deliberative restraint (McGraw 2010).

Along the same lines, Mutz (2006: 89) argues that 'the threat of a violent outcome is particularly great when those who have been living in segregated settings are first exposed to those of differing views'. This supports the idea that segmentation along dividing lines inhibits perspective-taking, which is necessary for deliberation. Contact with citizens from various backgrounds thus induces a defensive attitude likely to undermine deliberation.

The idea that participants in an inter-group context might stand firm on their initial stance, even if their opinions are obviously flawed, is also supported in social psychology. Whether we accept or reject arguments, according to social validation theory, depends on the source of the arguments rather than their intrinsic epistemic value (Lopes *et al.* 2007); and arguments from the out-group will always be invested with much less credibility. Or in the words of Mendelberg (2002: 161): 'When deliberation deals with an issue that has long generated deep conflict, it is unlikely that many novel arguments will be aired. And if novel and valid arguments are aired, they are not likely to persuade many people'. Strong feelings of social belonging thus undermine the fundamental openness to others' opinions that deliberation requires.

Despite the theoretical straightforwardness, there is some empirical ambiguity on whether inter-group deliberation actually leads to conflict exacerbation. After all, a recent Delibera in Northern Ireland sheds a rather more positive light on the potential of deliberation across divides. Despite the deep differences in opinions that Catholics and Protestants initially held on the issue under discussion, their preferences did tend to shift and inter-group relations improved after talking to each other (Luskin *et al.* 2012).

There are two possible explanations for these results. First of all, there are the characteristics of the setting. A Deliberative Poll® is a 'cold' deliberative setting, because only processes of social learning and political will-formation take place. In such a cold atmosphere, that is, one stripped of emotional involvement, resistance to persuasion might be lower because the stakes are lower (Dryzek 2005). Inter-group conflict might thus become particularly salient in 'hot' deliberative settings, where, formally binding decisions have to be made. Under these circumstances, in which the stakes of the decision increase dramatically, the willingness to remain respectful and open to other's opinions can be expected to be more limited. These conditions rather seem conducive to 'groupthink' and polarisation (Baron 2005; Sunstein 2000).

As a second explanation, the Northern Ireland results point in the direction of Allport's so-called 'contact hypothesis'. Allport (1954) acknowledges that stereotypes and prejudices form the basis of inter-group conflict but he also stated that contact between competing groups could mitigate inter-group conflict. To be successful, however, inter-group contact has to occur under the correct conditions. First, the groups had to have an equal status during contact. Privileging one of the groups through the contact would only result in conflict exacerbation. Furthermore, the groups had to depend on each other in order to attain common goals. Pursuing a common goal immediately reframes the discussion from an inter-group conflict into a search for a mutually beneficial solution. And finally, the contact should be long enough for personal ties and mutual recognition to arise. Brief interactions do little more than heighten tensions (Dovidio *et al.* 2003).

We conclude, therefore, by saying that division could impose a serious strain on deliberation. Competing interests, conflicting identities and psycho-cognitive processes significantly reduce the possibility of genuine deliberation at the grass-roots level in divided societies. Empirically, however, the evidence so far is rather limited and remains inconclusive.

Deliberation and decision-making rules

If social division turns out to have a negative impact upon deliberation in our experiments, this would also raise the question of how we could counter this effect. Research on the role of institutions in producing high-quality deliberation offers promising perspectives for reversing the downward spiral of inter-group deliberation. It is, after all, argued that submitting groups to certain institutional incentives might counter the dynamics of conflict exacerbation. If citizens participating in deliberative groups are asked not only to talk but also to reach a joint decision, there are constraints on the opinions they can utter.

The literature on the influence of decision rules on deliberation is based on the rupture between majority and unanimity rules. A simple majority, the argument goes, will inevitably lead to lower quality deliberation because the demands for inclusion, respect and justification are lower. After all, when only a limited number of people need to be convinced, very few concessions will have to be made. Joint decision-making under majority rule thus exhibits all the characteristics of a solution-driven (or verdict-driven) deliberation (Hastie *et al.* 1983). Majority rule stimulates deliberants to selectively provide evidence they think might convince just enough people to reach a solution, and it thus has important exclusionary characteristics. Majorities can simply ignore minority factions and will therefore put less effort into formulating persuasive arguments and more into discrediting the minority opinion. This is not to say, however, that deliberating groups under majority rule simply stop arguing as soon as a sufficient number of advocates is found. On the contrary, as Hastie *et al.* (1983: 235) contend: 'decision rules don't simply cut off deliberation at the point at which the required quorum is reached'. Majority members are thus found to keep deliberating even after a decision could be reached (Nemeth 1977).

A unanimity rule, on the other hand, gives rise to an information-driven (or evidence-driven) approach because it requires everyone's consent; and thus it needs a thoroughly deliberative process in which arguments pro and con a position are exchanged. It fosters reciprocity and respect and could function as the great unifier (Mansbridge 1983). Unanimity is therefore generally considered a good rule for producing high-quality deliberation, enhancing justificatory and respectful discourse. Unanimity is also believed to promote the substantive inclusion of all participants (Sanders 1997: 367) and it is accompanied by an attitude of friendliness and accommodation.

The role of unanimity in generating high-quality deliberation is, however, contested. For instance, Dryzek (1990) argues that the effect of unanimity is highly contingent on group characteristics: when the participants in deliberation do not share a common understanding, as in a divided group setting, the chances of reaching consensus are weak and the disagreements between the participants will be emphasised, leading to lower-quality deliberation (Mendelberg 2002). Moreover, Austen-Smith and Feddersen (2006) find that a unanimity rule is less likely to bring about a sincere and deliberative information exchange than simple majority rule. Deliberants under a unanimity rule have the power to deadlock the decision process, which inevitably leads to a downward deliberative spiral (Saward 1998: 70). Under majority rule, however, their power is much more limited and a decision is, strictly speaking, possible without their consent (Meirowitz 2007). As such, they are left with nothing more than the power of argumentation, possibly leading to more deliberative interactions.

As we will see later on, we have also included a two-thirds majority rule in our experiments because of its symbolic function in Belgian politics. It is one of the constitutional gridlocks and it is often depicted in the Belgian media and by politicians as the symbol of deadlock and minority tyranny. Theoretically, however, the effect of a two-thirds majority remains ambiguous. On the one hand, two-thirds majorities – or other types of supermajorities – were found to be more inclusive than majority rule because the threshold for the decision was raised; but the respect accorded to others and their arguments and justification of positions might still be less compared to unanimity rule. Davis and his colleagues (1975: 11) have demonstrated, however, that 'a simple majority decision scheme was very nearly as accurate for juries assigned a two-thirds majority rule'. This would mean that no matter what type of majority rule is demanded, the result will always be equivalent (Gerardi and Yariv 2007).

The general hypothesis is therefore that a unanimity rule fosters argumentative, respectful and open discussions, whereas less-than-unanimous rules lead to power-based encounters in which exclusion and disrespect set the tone. More generally, we hypothesise that the larger the quorum that is required, the higher the quality of the deliberation. As more participants need convincing, we expect that deliberation will yield more arguments and hence a higher quality of deliberation.

Why Belgium?

In order to test these hypotheses, we rely on data from a deliberative mini-public organised in 2010 in deeply divided Belgium. Since its foundation in 1830, Belgium has been characterised by coinciding linguistic, religious and economic cleavages and, at the time of our experiment, the tensions between the two main linguistic groups were at an historic high (Deschouwer 2012). The 2010 elections turned into an electoral victory for the nationalist/secessionist party in Flanders and resulted in a complete governmental stalemate for over one and a half years. During these 550 days, tensions kept rising and public opinion was completely polarised between the two groups.

Despite its deep division, the country has not known any violent outbursts since the 1960s–1970s. The political struggle is therefore more one of words than of deeds. This makes Belgium a divided society that stands out from other 'torn' polities, and the findings can thus not be generalised without caution. Nevertheless, Belgium does exhibit a number of characteristics that make it a very interesting case for studying the potential for deliberation. First of all, the country consists of 60 per cent Dutch-speakers and 40 per cent French-speakers and this language difference could impose a serious strain on citizen deliberation. After all, multilingualism constitutes a particular disincentive for deliberation, even though simultaneous translation could overcome some of the difficulties associated with the use of multiple languages (Doerr 2012).

Secondly, Belgium is generally considered to be the textbook example of a consociational democracy (Lijphart 1981), a type of democracy that stresses the central role of elites in the process of building bridges; and this comes at the expense of citizen participation. In a consociational system, citizens are required to remain politically passive because their active involvement would only deepen conflict and destabilise the political system. And this is particularly true in Belgium, where ethno-linguistic conflict management has continuously relied on elites (Deschouwer 2012).

Closely linked to this, we should also mention that the institutional infrastructure of Belgium aims at nothing more than to separate the two groups as much as possible. Whenever an issue generates tension, the elites resort to granting self-rule. Such a politics of separation radically opposes the deliberative assumption that citizens should sit together and talk through their differences (Dryzek 2005). The dismantlement of the federal state also meant that the possibilities and incentives for citizens to inform themselves about the viewpoints of the other side are very limited.

The linguistic divide between the north and the south of the country is further reinforced by split media and party systems. The split media system means that only unilingual media are followed on each side of the divide. This has led to a situation in which the media coverage is very one-sided and citizens have no idea what is going on in the other linguistic group. Moreover, Sinardet (2009) has shown that the Belgian media often use 'us versus them' rhetoric in order to increase their sales, which further deepens the conflict.

Also, the political party system is split along linguistic lines, with parties seeking votes only on their own side of the linguistic divide. This lack of nation-wide parties means that representatives don't rely on votes from the other linguistic group to get elected. The elites therefore have no incentive whatsoever to talk to voters on the other side. All lines of communication are closed and the best electoral strategy for parties is to radicalise their position at the expense of the other linguistic group (Deschouwer 2012).

All of these characteristics are evidence that the entire political and societal structure of Belgium is designed to prevent citizens from hearing the opinions of the other linguistic group. In light of the recent scholarship on deliberative systems, the Belgian case would thus score very poorly, which makes it all the more interesting as a counterfactual case for the viability of citizen deliberation.

Methodology

The absence of inter-group contacts in the population, which is the essence of the politics of containment in a divided society, makes it difficult to study the deliberative quality of communicative interactions between citizens. We therefore organised an experimental deliberative mini-public, which gathered a random selection of ordinary Belgian citizens with diverse and often radically opposed preferences on the future of the country. We asked them to discuss and reach decisions on the political and institutional issues that had polarised the political agenda for over 550 days. Because of the salience of these issues, and in order to raise the stakes for the participants, we told them that the results of the experiment would be communicated to the media and the political parties.

The experimental set-up had the additional benefit of allowing us to manipulate our treatment variables. Using a 3 x 3 factorial design, varying the group composition and the decision-making rule, we conducted nine deliberative experiments. With regard to the group compositions, the divided (bilingual) group was the treatment condition, whereas the homogeneous Dutch-speaking and homogeneous French-speaking groups were control conditions. For the decision-making rule, the majority-rule group was the control condition for determining the treatment effects of the two-thirds and unanimity rules.

In order to make strong causal inferences, we also kept some potential confounding variables constant. This is, first of all, the case for the number of participants per experiment. We sampled nine groups of ten persons, ensuring a gender balance and a balance between the linguistic groups in the divided experiments. Small groups ensure that exclusionary tendencies are not built into the design because large groups risk being dominated by those with the best communicative capacities (Young 2000). Moreover, we opted for a location which was not considered hostile territory by either side and which was near the Belgian and European parliaments, in order that the experiment gave a more serious impression. This ensured that the participants felt there was really something at stake in the discussions. We also chose a seating arrangement in which members of both groups were seated alternately (Gaertner *et al.* 1993: 12). Moreover, the participants received no background materials in advance since we did not want to disturb the natural flow of the group dynamics. The role of the moderator was also constant: he introduced the discussion and asked for a decision at the end. He did not interfere in the dynamics of the group by giving people the chance to speak, because this would have artificially boosted the level of participation and thus the discourse quality. Finally, the participants did not receive any rules of conduct at the beginning. They were not instructed to behave respectfully and give good arguments because this would have rendered our measurements of deliberative quality invalid.

Before the experiments took place, a pre-test questionnaire was sent out, based on which the participants were selected. This questionnaire was sent out to two random samples, drawn separately in Flanders and Wallonia to ensure the equal presence of both linguistic groups in the final pool. However, due to time and financial restrictions, these samples were drawn from an existing panel rather than from official census lists. Nevertheless, the panel of over 110,000 individuals closely resembled the socio-demographic composition of the Belgian population.[1]

---

1. Older age groups and non-active citizens are slightly overrepresented in the panel. This should not be a problem given the fact that these groups drop out in most surveys.

The participants were assigned to groups using block randomisation, which ensured that a wide diversity of perspectives and opinions was included in each group. Simple randomisation techniques would most likely have produced groups that were internally homogeneous because of the small number of participants in each group. The diversity of opinions was important because it would have been impossible to see whether division undermines deliberation if all participants in the group felt the same way. Through block randomisation, we divided our sample into several blocks based on a combination of their language, sex, age, preferences for the future of Belgium and out-group feelings; from each of these blocks, we randomly assigned the 90 participants to one of the nine groups in our experiment.

In order to improve the turnout, we sent multiple reminders and the participants received a participation fee to minimise dropping out.[2] The experiments began with a brief introduction stating the aims of the meeting, the fact that we wanted the participants to talk about 'the future of Belgium' and the rule by which they had to reach a decision.

The discussion took place in two rounds, each lasting about two hours; at the end of the each round, the moderator asked the participants to make a decision on the topics they had discussed. It was important to ask for a decision immediately after each round so that the participants would feel the institutional incentive of the decision-making rule. Finally, the experiments with the divided groups were simultaneously translated.

Measuring deliberative quality

After the deliberations took place, the recordings were transcribed word for word. The transcripts were partitioned into individual speech acts. This means that every time a participant made a statement, formulated a demand or took a position, this was considered a new unit of analysis. Each of these speech acts was subsequently coded using the Discourse Quality Index (DQI). This index was initially developed to determine the deliberative quality of parliamentary discourse (Steiner *et al.* 2004). It measures the crucial dimensions of the theoretical concept of deliberation, such as respect, justification, and inclusion.

However, the fact that the DQI was developed for analysing parliamentary discourse meant that its suitability for our purposes was somewhat limited. Parliamentary deliberation is, after all, characterised by certain limitations in speaking time and speaking order. Citizen discourse is much less bound by formal rules and its dynamics differ significantly. However, as Steenbergen and his colleagues (2003) argue themselves, the DQI is a flexible instrument and its items should be adapted to the necessities of the research setting. We therefore added respectful listening and respect for the in-group, as well as respect for the out-group.

---

2. This seems to have worked since 83 out of 90 invitees actually attended, despite the fact that the experiments were organised on a Saturday morning and in Brussels, a place with which most participants were not familiar.

Table 9.1: Absolute and relative frequency distribution for the Discourse Quality Items (N=1664 speech acts)

	N	%
A) Interruption		
1 Speaker interrupts another speaker	278	16.7
2 Regular speech act	1386	83.3
B) Respectful language		
1 Use of foul language to attack participants at a personal level	13	0.8
2 Use of foul language to attack participants' arguments without personal attacks	55	3.3
3 Neutral: no foul, nor explicitly respectful language	1427	85.8
4 Explicitly respectful language	169	10.2
C) Respectful listening		
1 The speaker ignores arguments and questions addressed to him or her by other participants	200	12.0
2 The speaker does not ignore arguments and questions addressed to him or her by other participants but distorts these arguments and questions	218	13.1
3 The speaker does not ignore arguments and questions addressed to him or her by other participants and engages these arguments and questions in a correct and undistorted way	1056	63.5
4 Missing: no arguments were formulated yet	190	11.4
D) Respect toward members of out-group		
1 No respect: only negative statements	62	3.7
2 Neutral: no positive nor negative statements	1577	94.8
3 Explicit respect: at least one positive statement	25	1.5
E) Respect toward members of in-group		
1 No respect: only negative statements	18	1.1
2 Neutral: no positive nor negative statements	1639	98.5
3 Explicit respect: at least one positive statement	7	0.4
F) Respect toward counter-arguments		
1 Counter-arguments are ignored	206	12.4
2 Counter-arguments are included but degraded	356	21.4
3 Counter-arguments are included in a neutral way	467	28.1
4 Counter-arguments are valued	400	24.0
5 Missing: no counter-arguments were formulated yet	235	14.1
G) Level of justification of arguments		
1 Speaker presents no arguments	216	13.0
2 Speaker says that something is a good or a bad idea	252	15.1
3 Speaker justifies position with illustrations	395	23.7
4 Speaker presents argument but no linkage is made why X will contribute to Y	179	10.8
5 Speaker presents one argument with explicit linkage	543	32.6
6 Speaker presents two or more arguments with explicit linkage	79	4.7

	N	%
H) Content of justification: common good		
1 Only references to group interests	54	3.2
2 Neutral: no reference to group interests, nor to common good	1498	90.0
3 Reference to common good in utilitarian terms	81	4.9
4 Reference to common good in terms of the difference principle	31	1.9
I) Content of justification: abstract principles		
1 Speaker does not refer to abstract principles	1523	91.5
2 Speaker refers to abstract principles	141	8.5
J) Constructive politics		
1 The speaker does not indicate a change in position and does not acknowledge the value of other positions heard	951	57.2
2 The speaker does not indicate a change in position but does acknowledge the value of other positions heard	691	41.5
3 The speaker indicates a change of position and does not acknowledge the value of other positions heard	10	0.6
4 The speaker indicates a change of position and gives as reason for change arguments heard	12	0.7

Table 9.1 lists all of these items but immediately it becomes evident that not all of them demonstrate strong variation. In particular, the respect accorded to the out-group and the in-group barely varies, which is an interesting finding. After all, we would have expected that inter-group deliberations would be full of disrespectful references to the out-group and explicitly respectful ways of acknowledging the superiority of some kind of the in-group. Equally unexpected is the fact that very few references were made to group interests or common interests during the deliberations. We expected that inter-group deliberations, which deal in essence with issues of identity and interests, would have contained more references to the fact that the interests of the groups were opposed.

The next step consists of determining whether these ten individual items constitute a genuine index for deliberative quality. This was tested statistically by means of a Mokken-scale analysis (Mokken 1997; Van Schuur 2011). Table 9.2 summarises the analysis of the DQI-items, and indicates a uni-dimensional solution with six items. The most 'easy' item is the level of justification of arguments, while a justification in terms of abstract principles poses a much higher threshold and is more 'difficult'. This means that speech acts that refer to abstract principles are also more likely to hold some elements of constructive politics; they are also associated with respectful listening and so on.

The analysis also provides an estimation of the scale consistency, rho (comparable to Cronbach's a). The closer rho is to one, the higher the consistency and reliability of the scale. In our case the DQI scale has a rho of .76, which can be considered as moderately consistent. On the basis of these results we construed a uni-dimensional DQI using six items. The resulting scale was standardised in order to have a minimum of zero and a maximum of hundred.

Table 9.2: Mokken-scale analysis on DQI-items: difficulty, homogeneity, Z-value and scale characteristics (N=1412 speech acts)

Items	Difficulty	i	Z
Content of justification: abstract principles	1.09	0.41	12.44
Constructive politics	1.49	0.45	22.74
Respectful listening	2.58	0.63	31.30
Respect towards the members of the out-group	2.75	0.57	32.00
Respectful language	3.06	0.49	19.09
Level of justification of arguments	3.54	0.47	28.56
Global homogeneity of the scale		0.52	(42.96)
Coefficient of reliability – rho		0.76	
Conventional Cronbach's *a*		0.75	

Results

Now that we have found that the individual items of the DQI can be combined into one reliable and valid scale, we will turn to the analysis of our experiments and determine to what extent group composition and decision-making rules affect the quality of the deliberation. We will do so by using a multilevel regression analysis. The primary unit of analysis is, after all, the speech act but each of these speech acts is nested in the individuals who are deliberating. As such, individuals in the deliberation process will be more likely to perform speech acts that have more in common than the speech acts of another participant will have with them. In order to adequately assess the impact of the independent variables, in the presence of nested data, we will use hierarchical linear models (Rodriguez 2008).

Before going into detail on the analysis, we should discuss the control variables we included. The first set of variables contains the socio-demographic characteristics of those who utter the speech act. We included gender, education and age. Gender was taken in because deliberation is argued to be stratified along the lines of gender (Sanders 1997). Since the more highly educated possess much more resources for deliberation in terms of political knowledge and verbal skills for formulating high-quality rational arguments (Hooghe 1999), we also included the educational level of participants. This variable distinguishes between four categories: lower secondary education, higher secondary education, higher non-university education and university education. The age of the speaker was also considered relevant because older generations were socialised in the turbulent post-war years, in which the relations between the linguistic groups were very uneasy. Moreover, those that grew up in the 1970s experienced severe political instability due to the inflamed tensions between the north and the south of the country, whereas the younger generations grew up in times of relative peace.

Besides socio-demographic variables, we also included self-reported out-group feelings, based on an eleven-point scale in the pre-test questionnaire.

People with negative feelings towards the out-group are more likely to behave less deliberatively when discussing an issue as controversial as the future of Belgium. Since this variable was not normally distributed, we re-coded it into a categorical variable distinguishing between four out-group feelings: negative, neutral, positive and very positive.

Our modelling strategy will concentrate on the impact of group composition and decision-making rules, controlling for potential confounding variables. In a first model we will test the crude impact of group composition (Model 1), whereas we control for the usual background suspects, such as gender, age, education and out-group feelings, in Model 2. In a subsequent Model 3 we look at the impact of decision-making rules, controlling for background in Model 4. A last model, however, looks at the simultaneous impact of group composition and rules, after controlling for the other relevant variables (Model 5).

Table 9.3 summarises the most relevant model parameters. The upper section provides the estimates for the different independent variables, as well as their statistical significance. The lower panel of the table provides the estimates of the variances at each level (individual speech act and individual speaker), the degree of clustering of speech acts in speakers (the intra-class correlation) and goodness-of-fit measures (-2 loglikelihood, but also R-squares at each level). Before estimating the five models we had to estimate an 'empty' model in order to assess the starting variances at both levels. The intra-class correlation – the clustering of variation on the level of the individuals – (r) amounts to 35.5 per cent. Put differently: 35 per cent of the differences in DQI between speech acts are attributable to differences between the individual speakers.

The most interesting model to start from is the fifth one. Its relatively high explained variance of 20.4 per cent means that the two experimental treatments under scrutiny are powerful predictors of deliberative quality. When compared to the preceding models, however, it is obvious that most of the variation can be accounted for by the decision-making rules. With an R-squared of 18.2 per cent, the rules prove to be a much more powerful predictor of deliberative quality than the group composition. Variation in deliberative quality will therefore much more likely be due to changes in decision-rule.

Despite this gap in explanatory power, group composition proves to be a significant predictor of deliberative quality. After all, a closer look at Table 9.3 reveals that both rules and composition are significantly related to deliberative quality in all of the models. Even after controlling for confounding variables, the effects remain statistically significant at the .01 level. Deliberative quality therefore does seem to be linked to the way in which groups are composed and required to make a decision.

The next question, then, relates to the strength and direction of these effects. The decision-making rules follow the hypotheses nicely: more stringent rules lead to significantly higher DQI scores. Both supermajorities have a strong positive impact on DQI, as is testified by the B-coefficients of 7.7 and 11.6 under two-thirds majority and unanimity respectively.

The effect of the group composition is more ambiguous. We hypothesised that group dividedness would undermine deliberative quality because citizens would activate prejudices and stereotypes rather than engage in a respectful and inclusive process of arguing back-and-forth. This argument is disconfirmed by our data. Even though the effect is relatively weak, divided groups do seem to exhibit higher-quality deliberation than homogeneous groups. As such, we find a first piece of evidence suggesting that the presence of the out-group does not necessarily induce resistance to respectful and rational interaction. Rather, putting opposed groups together seems to induce a more reasoned and open-minded spirit of argumentation.

As the control variables are entered in the analysis, and potential confounders identified, the effect of the experimental treatments weakens somewhat but they prove to be relatively robust and remain significant. This indicates that both experimental treatments are strongly related to the deliberative quality of the discussions.

Few of the control variables, however, seem to affect the DQI. There is a significant, yet weak, gender effect, in that the average DQI scores of women are lower than those of men. Moreover, speech acts formulated by the more highly educated demonstrate a significantly higher deliberative quality. The same cannot be said about the age variable. Moving up on the age ladder does not seem to leads to lower discourse quality and the language of the participant did not seem to affect the quality of the deliberation either. Finally, out-group feelings were not significantly related to the DQI. In part, this could be due to sampling biases. The drop-out rate in the days before the experiments was higher among those holding negative out-group feelings.[3] Those who had doubts about the trustworthiness of the out-group were somewhat outnumbered by those who felt more positively and might have yielded to 'the civilizing force of hypocrisy' (Elster 1998).

Both group composition and decision-making rules seem to determine the quality of discourse (Model 5 in Table 9.3) but both treatments could also interact with each other. The effect of rules on deliberative quality in homogenous groups could well prove to be different from heterogeneous groups. After having established the direct effects of both rules and composition on deliberative quality, we also took a look at possible interaction effects in a last model (Model 6 in Table 9.4). To this end, we constructed a new variable that combines each category of the group composition with the decision-making rule.

The parameter-estimates reveal a strong impact of the interaction categories between decision-making rules and group composition. The interaction terms are, moreover, somewhat stronger in divided settings than in the homogenous groups, with the notable exception of the interaction between heterogeneous group operating under a two-thirds majority-rule.

Including the interaction effect changes the patterns dramatically. In the divided groups, all the DQI scores, no matter what the required rule, move towards

---

3.   To be sure, participants with negative out-group feelings were represented in each group.

Table 9.3: Multilevel analysis: DQI-6 in function of composition and rules (N=1412 speech acts – N=83 speakers)

	Model 1		Model 2		Model 3		Model 4		Model 5	
	B	SE	B	SE	B	SE	B	SE	B	SE
Intercept	48.29	1.49	44.03	5.15	44.04	1.86	36.50	4.88	37.89	4.69
Composition: homogenous (ref.)										
Heterogeneous groups	7.14	2.56 **	6.96	2.45 **					6.68	2.10 **
Edu: at most lower secondary										
Edu: higher secondary			10.67	4.11 **			8.48	3.75 *	7.85	3.58 *
Edu: tertiary non-university			12.29	4.01 **			12.60	3.62 ***	10.47	3.53 **
Edu: university			14.45	4.06 ***			14.27	3.65 ***	12.48	3.53 ***
Age: younger than 30 (ref.)										
Age: 30-35			-1.42	3.31			0.24	2.89	-2.01	2.84
Age: 36-49			-4.04	2.86			-3.80	2.57	-3.27	2.45
Age: 50+			-4.91	3.55			-3.26	3.17	-4.93	3.06
Gender: male (ref.)										
Gender: female			-3.88	2.26			-3.16	2.00	-4.31	1.93 *
Language group: Dutch-speaking (ref.)										
Language group: French-speaking			-0.57	2.24			0.00	2.02	-0.53	1.93
Feelings towards out-groups: Negative (ref.)										

	Model 1		Model 2		Model 3		Model 4		Model 5	
	B	SE	B	SE	B	SE	B	SE	B	SE
Feelings out-groups: moderate			-3.94	3.54			-0.58	3.37	-0.55	3.22
Feelings out-groups: positive			-4.29	3.45			-0.10	3.10	-1.92	3.00
Feelings out-groups: very positive			-1.62	3.40			0.43	3.08	0.13	2.93
Rule: simple majority (ref.)										
Rule: supermajority 2/3					8.45	2.68 **	7.68	2.42 **	7.74	2.30 ***
Rule: unanimity					12.34	2.71 ***	11.68	2.34 ***	11.60	2.23 ***
Random part										
Variance level: speaker	103.74	18.67	72.22	13.77	84.46	15.71	55.32	11.07	48.46	9.95
Variance level: speech act	207.83	8.06	207.51	8.05	208.29	8.08	208.11	8.07	207.90	8.06
-2*loglikelihood:	11717		11690		11705		11676		11666	
Intra-class correlation (r)	33.3%		25.8%		28.9%		21.0%		13.9%	
R^2 2	9.2%		36.8%		26.1%		51.6%		57.6%	
R^2 1	0.0%		0.2%		-0.2%		-0.1%		0.0%	
R^2 total	3.3%		13.2%		9.1%		18.2%		20.4%	

Significance test (Type I -errors): ***: $a \leq 0.001$; **: $a \leq 0.01$; *: $a \leq 0.05$

Table 9.4: Multilevel analysis of interaction between group composition and rules on DQI-6 scale (N=1412 speech acts – N=83 speakers)

	Model 6	
	B	SE
Intercept	34.10	*4.23*
Edu: At most lower secondary		
Edu: higher secondary	7.08	*3.14* *
Edu: tertiary non-university	10.11	*3.15* ***
Edu: university	11.40	*3.15* ***
Age: younger than 30 (ref.)		
Age: 30–35	-3.10	*2.49*
Age: 36–49	-2.73	2.15
Age: 50+	-4.10	*2.68*
Gender: male (ref.)		
Gender: female	-3.93	*1.69* *
Language group: Dutch-speaking (ref.)		
Language group: French-speaking	-0.84	*1.68*
Feelings towards out-groups: negative (ref.)		
Feelings out-groups: moderate	-0.18	*2.84*
Feelings out-groups: positive	-1.06	*2.64*
Feelings out-groups: very positive	0.96	*2.55*
Interaction: homogenous group with simple majority (ref.)		
Interaction: homogenous group with supermajority (2/3)	14.74	*2.44* ***
Interaction: homogenous group with unanimity	16.48	*2.36* ***
Interaction: heterogenous group with simple majority (ref.)	17.83	*2.98* ***
Interaction: heterogenous group with supermajority (2/3)	12.90	*3.03* ***
Interaction: heterogenous group with unanimity	19.99	*3.01* ***
Random part		
Variance level: speaker	33.43	*7.52*
Variance level: speech act	207.99	*8.06*
-2*loglikelihood:	11645	
Intra-class correlation (*r*)	13.8%	
R^2 2	70.7%	
R^2 1	0.0%	
R^2 total	25.1%	

*Significance test (Type I): ***: a ≤ 0.001 ; **: a ≤ 0.01; *: a≤ 0.05*

one another. The differences between the three divided groups, all deciding under another rule, are therefore very limited. In the homogeneous groups, on the other hand, the decision-making rules have a much more noticeable effect: in those groups, there is a clear and distinctive pattern of deliberative quality according to whether the participants were asked to decide with a simple majority or with a supermajority.

Conclusion

This paper started from the generally held belief that democracy in divided societies can only be stable as long as the citizens remain passive subjects. Political alliances across divides can only come about by conscious efforts on behalf of the elites to accommodate inter-group conflicts, whereas grass-roots involvement will only deepen cleavages. The idea that respectful, rational and inclusive interaction across dividing lines is impossible figured not only in consociational theory. Deliberative democrats were also highly sceptical about the potential for inter-group deliberation. After all, in divided societies, the favourable conditions for deliberation, such as inter-group empathy and mutual trust, are missing or at least more difficult to attain.

However, another line of research on deliberation under different institutional incentives offered interesting perspectives for reversing the hypothesised negative relationship between group composition and deliberation. The implementation of different decision-making rules, this literature argued, could yield different deliberative dynamics. Institutional demands for a unanimous decision meant that the inclusion of all participants and their arguments and perspectives was necessary. As such, there would be more opportunity for thorough argumentation in a context of mutual respect and sincerity than under a simple majority rule.

The results from our Belgian experiments, however, had a mind of their own. The decision-making rules were significantly related to deliberative quality and in the direction proposed by the theory: but exclusively in the homogeneous groups. Only in those groups did supermajorities lead to high- and majority rule to low-quality deliberation. In the divided groups, the DQI scores tended to flock together, regardless of the decision-making rule.

The most interesting finding, however, was that group dividedness did not lead to lower but to higher quality deliberation. Even though the effect is not all-encompassing, citizens who differed fundamentally on highly contentious issues in Belgian politics were still able to act deliberatively and even to generate the same deliberative quality as homogeneous groups under the most stringent decision-making rule. Rather than undermining rational and inclusive decision-making, division seems to create openness towards others by confronting people with the radically different views from the other side. This lends some support to the contact hypothesis, which states that the perpetuation of conflict is reduced when groups are forced to sit together and work things out.

Despite the limitations of our experimental research design, these results offer good hopes for the potential of democratic deliberation between opposed groups. And even though the findings should be interpreted with caution, they do offer an alternative view of the role that citizens can play in the resolution of deep inter-group conflicts. Citizen activism on highly contentious issues will not necessarily undermine democratic stability, as consociationalists claim, and citizens can display some very accommodating and deliberative dispositions – albeit only under the right circumstances. Moreover, our findings suggest that reinforcing the segmentation of divided societies – through granting self-rule – might actually endanger democratic stability more than simply confronting the conflicting groups. After all, segmentation might create homogeneous blocs with ethnic groups caught up in a spiral of enclave deliberation and 'groupthink'.

There remain, however, blind spots in our understanding of the process. Despite the promising results, we agree that, in order to give the process of deliberation a viable chance, the participants should at least have a minimal common understanding or definition of the situation and of what is at stake. Language does not seem to be insuperable in the Belgian context but there are bound to be limits to the dissent deliberation can handle. Further research will therefore have to determine to what extent divided polities can tolerate citizen involvement under rather more adverse circumstances.

References

Allport, G.W. (1954) *The Nature of Prejudice*, Cambridge, MA: Perseus Books.

Austen-Smith, D. and Feddersen, T. J. (2006) 'Deliberation, preference uncertainty, and voting rules', *American Political Science Review* 100 (2): 209–17.

Baron, R. (2005) 'So right it's wrong: groupthink and the ubiquitous nature of polarized group decision making', *Advances in Experimental Social Psychology* 37: 219–53.

Bogaards, M. (1998) 'The favourable conditions for consociational democracy: a review', *European Journal of Political Research* 33: 475–96.

Davis, J. H., Kerr, N. L., Atkin, R. S., Holt, R. and Meek, D. (1975) 'The decision processes of 6- and 12-person mock juries assigned unanimous and two-thirds majority rules', *Journal of Personality and Social Psychology* 32 (1): 1–14.

Deschouwer, K. (2012) *The Politics of Belgium: Governing a divided society* 2nd edn, London: Palgrave.

Doerr, N. (2012) 'Translating democracy: how activists in the European Social Forum practice multilingual deliberation', *European Political Science Review* 4: 361–84.

Dovidio, J. F., Gaertner, S. L. and Kawakami, K. (2003) 'Inter-group contact: the past, present, and the future', *Group Processes and Inter-group Relations* 6 (1): 5–21.

Dryzek, J. S. (1990) *Discursive Democracy: Politics, policy, and political science*, Cambridge: Cambridge University Press.

— (2005) 'Deliberative democracy in divided societies: alternatives to agonism and analgesia', *Political Theory* 33 (2): 218–42.

Elster, J. (1998) 'Deliberation and constitution making', in J. Elster (ed.) *Deliberative Democracy*, Cambridge: Cambridge University Press.

Fishkin, J. S., Luskin, R. C., O'Flynn, I. and Russell, D. (2009) *Deliberating Across Deep Divides,* Stanford: Center for Deliberative Democracy.

Gaertner, S. L., Dovidio, J. F., Anastasio, P. A., Bachman, B. A. and Rust, M. C. (1993) 'The common in-group identity model: recategorization and the reduction of inter-group bias', *European Review of Social Psychology* 4: 1–26.

Gerardi, D. and Yariv, L. (2007) 'Deliberative voting', *Journal of Economic Theory* 134: 317–338.

Hastie, R., Penrod, S. D. and Pennington, N. (1983) *Inside the Jury*, Cambridge: Harvard University Press.

Hooghe, M. (1999) 'The rebuke of Thersites: deliberative democracy under conditions of inequality', *Acta Politica* 34: 287–301.

Lijphart, A. (1968) *Verzuiling, Pacificatie en Kentering in de Nederlandse Politiek,* Amsterdam: J. H. De Bussy.

— (1981) (ed.) *Conflict and Coexistence in Belgium: The dynamics of a culturally divided society*, Berkeley, CA: Institute of International Studies.

Lopes, D., Vala, J., Garcia-Marques, L. (2007) 'Social validation of everyday knowledge: heterogeneity and consensus functionality', *Group Dynamics: Theory, Research, and Practice* 11 (3): 223–39.

Luskin, R. C., O'Flynn, I., Fishkin, J. S. and Russell, D. (2012) 'Deliberating across deep divides', *Political Studies*, published online (doi: 10.1111/j.1467–9248.2012.01005.x)

McGraw, B. T. (2010) *Faith in Politics: Religion and liberal democracy,* Cambridge: Cambridge University Press.

Mansbridge, J. (1983) *Beyond Adversary Democracy,* Chicago, IL: University of Chicago Press.

Meirowitz, A. (2007) 'In defence of exclusionary deliberation: communication and voting with private beliefs and values', *Journal of Theoretical Politics* 19 (3): 301–27.

Mendelberg, T. (2002) 'The deliberative citizen: theory and evidence', *Political Decision Making, Deliberation and Participation* 6: 151–93.

Mill, J. S. (1991[orig. 1859]) 'Considerations on representative government', in J. Gray (ed.) *John Stuart Mill: On liberty and other essays,* Oxford: Oxford University Press.

Mokken, R. J. (1997) 'Nonparametric models for dichotomous responses', in W. J. van der Linden and R. K. Hambleton (eds) *Handbook of Modern Item Response Theory*, New York: Springer.

Morrell, M. (2010) *Empathy and Democracy: Feeling, thinking and deliberation,* University Park: Penn State University Press.

Mutz, D. (2006) *Hearing the Other Side: Deliberative vs. participatory democracy,* Cambridge: Cambridge University Press.

Nemeth, C. (1977) 'Interactions between jurors as a function of majority vs. unanimity decision rules', *Journal of Applied Social Psychology* 7: 38–56

O'Flynn, I. (2006) *Deliberative Democracy and Divided Societies*, Edinburgh: Edinburgh University Press.

Rodriguez, G. (2008) 'Multilevel generalized linear models', in J. de Leeuw and E. Meijer (eds) *Handbook of Multilevel Analysis*, New York, Springer.

Sanders, L. (1997) 'Against deliberation', *Political Theory* 25 (3): 347–76.

Saward, M. (1998) *The Terms of Democracy,* Cambridge: Polity Press.

Sinardet, D. (2009) 'Direct democracy as a tool to shape a united public opinion in a multilingual society? Some reflections based on the Belgian case' in M. Hooghe and D. Sinardet (eds) *Is Democracy Viable without a Unified Public Opinion?*, Brussels: Re-Bel Initiative.

Steenbergen, M. R., Bächtiger, A., Spörndli, M. and Steiner, J. (2003) 'Measuring political deliberation: a discourse quality index', *Comparative European Politics* 1: 21–48.

Steiner, J. (2009) 'In search of the consociational "Spirit of Accommodation"', in R. Taylor (ed.) *Consociational Theory: McGarry & O'Leary and the Northern Ireland conflict,* New York: Routledge.

Steiner, J., Bächtiger, A., Spörndli, M. and Steenbergen, M. R. (2004) *Deliberative Politics in Action: Analysing parliamentary discourse,* Cambridge: Cambridge University Press.

Sunstein, C. R. (2000) 'Deliberative trouble? Why groups go to extremes', *The Yale Law Journal* 110: 71–119.

Van Schuur, W. (2011) *Ordinal Item Response Theory: Mokken scale analysis,* Thousand Oaks, CA : Sage.

Young, I. M. (2000) *Inclusion and Democracy*, Oxford: Oxford University Press.

Chapter Ten

Participant Bias and Success in Deliberative Mini-Publics

Michael E. Morrell

Normative theory and empirical research

It has been over two decades since the first appearance of contemporary theories of deliberative democracy (*see*, for example, Bessette 1980; 1994; Dryzek 1990; Fishkin 1991). During the ensuing years, deliberative democracy has proved to be fertile ground for scholars engaged in empirical research solidly grounded in normative theory (for just a few examples among the many available, *see* Bächtiger and Hangartner 2010; Barabas 2004; Delli Carpini *et al.* 2004; Gastil 2004; Grönlund *et al.* 2010; Karpowitz and Mendelberg 2007; Karpowitz *et al.* 2012; Luskin *et al.* 2002; Mendelberg 2002; Morrell 2003; Mutz 2006; Neblo 2005; Parkinson 2006; Rosenberg 2005; Setälä *et al.* 2010; Trenél 2009; Walsh 2004; 2006; Warren and Pearse 2008). While some theorists have argued that deliberative democratic theory has now fully developed (for example, Chambers 2003), the empirical question of what contributes to successful deliberation is still open (*see* Mutz 2008 and Thompson 2008). One of the main difficulties in answering this question has arisen due to the very success of deliberative democratic theory. As more theorists have claimed or accepted the deliberative label, what counts as deliberative success has become more opaque; empirical researchers have not always recognised this dilemma. One of the first tasks one faces in delineating the conditions for successful deliberation is clarifying how the different theories might define success. On my reading of deliberative theory, there are three related, but different, possible definitions of deliberative success: a fully reflective public opinion; a democratically rational or reasonable decision; and an epistemically correct decision. While there may be some overlap among these three 'types' of deliberative success, their differences are sufficient to affect all attempts to institute and empirically study mini-public deliberation.

Once we understand what deliberative success means, it becomes easier to elucidate evidence on what might contribute to this success. While one might take several different approaches to this task, here I will concentrate on findings from social and political psychology. Evidence from these studies makes clear that some of the greatest threats to the success of mini-publics are various biases that participants bring to deliberation, including attribution bias, in-group/out-group bias and information-processing bias. These biases can impede reflective opinion, democratic rationality or epistemic correctness; although they do so for different reasons and in different ways, depending upon the normative and theoretical grounding of deliberation.

Understanding that participant biases pose threats to mini-public success is important but it is only helpful if we can determine ways to overcome those biases. On this point, we only have preliminary evidence. I suggest that the process of empathy is promising as a possible source of mitigation of the detrimental effects of these biases (Morrell 2007; 2010). Some studies indicate that both group composition and decision-making structures can affect mini-public success (Grönlund *et al.* 2010; Karpowitz and Mendelberg 2007; Karpowitz *et al.* 2012; Setälä *et al.* 2010). Another important issue is the role of facilitation or mediation but this area is currently underdeveloped, both theoretically and empirically (Trénel 2009; *see also*, Landwehr, Chapter Six in this volume). A final key issue in this area is whether mini-public participants ought to make group decisions. While such group decision-making is empowering, and thus might encourage further participation, it also might undermine other important goals in deliberation (Morrell 1999). Those who direct and study mini-public deliberation face a choice, therefore, between competing goals for deliberation. This demonstrates why it is important that scholars and practitioners ground the empirical study and practice of deliberative mini-publics in the normative theories that have been the impetus for their creation (Thompson 2008). Only with a solid normative theoretical foundation will we be able to ascertain empirically the conditions necessary for successful mini-public deliberation.

Different types of deliberation

One of the main difficulties with empirically testing theories of deliberative democracy, and this is a difficulty that arose in the earliest attempts to do so, is that there are significant differences among the various deliberative theories. In order to define success in deliberative mini-publics, we must understand the differences that exist between the different theories of deliberation. While I have previously argued for a two-fold division (Morrell 2010), as have other prominent theorists (Bächtiger *et al.* 2010), I believe that recent developments in deliberative theory have led to an additional strain of deliberative democracy. In defining deliberative success, the resulting three types of deliberative theory focus on 1) reflective opinion; 2) democratic rationality or reasonableness; and 3) epistemic correctness.

In one of the first attempts to classify deliberative theory of which I am aware, I argued that there are two main categories of deliberative democracy: Madisonian and Kantian (Morrell 2010: chapter two). Madisonian deliberation focuses on engaging citizens or members of Congress in reflective consideration of their own views; and I place theorists such as Joseph Bessette (1980; 1994) and James Fishkin (1991; 1995) in this camp. Kantian deliberation, in contrast, sees deliberation as providing some form of a rational or reasonable source for legitimate democratic decision-making. I argue that this strain includes Jürgen Habermas (1996a; 1996b),

John Rawls (1996) and the many theorists they influenced (for example, Bohman 1996; Chambers 1996; Dryzek 1990; 2000; Gutmann and Thompson 1996).

Appearing the same year as my work, André Bächtiger *et al.* (2010) provide an alternative typology of deliberative theories. Type I deliberation 'embodies the idea of rational discourse, focuses on deliberative intent and the related distinction between communicative and strategic action, and has a strong procedural component' (Bächtiger *et al.* 2010: 33). Type II deliberation 'generally involves more flexible forms of discourse, more emphasis on outcomes versus process, and more attention to overcoming 'real world' constraints on realizing normative ideals' (Bächtiger *et al.* 2010: 33). The Type I/Type II distinction does not appear to map well onto my own Madisonian/Kantian typology. Type I harkens back to Habermas's work in the *Theory of Communicative Action* (1984) and empirical attempts grounded in that work such as the Discourse Quality Index (DQI) (*see* Steenbergen *et al.* 2003). In contrast, Bächtiger *et al.* classify the scholarship of some influenced by Habermas (for example, Dryzek 2000) and Rawls (for example, Gutmann and Thompson 1996), and the work of Iris Marion Young (2002), as examples of Type II deliberation. They even see Habermas's work in *Between Facts and Norms* as moving toward Type II, although in the end it lands somewhere in between the two types. Bächtiger *et al.* also do not clearly indicate where Rawls, Fishkin, or Bessette might fit into their scheme, although it seems that Fishkin and Bessette could only be Type II, if they fit the typology at all. Where Rawls might fit remains unclear.

While I do not wish to debate the merits of these two typologies here, I offer them to demonstrate the substantial variety present in deliberative theories, even if we do not include what Mansbridge *et al.* (2010) describe as their 'newly reformulated' ideal of deliberation. If we look at both typologies, in addition to more recent theories of deliberation, there are three main categories of outcome that are important for mini-public deliberation, depending upon which deliberative theory scholars embrace: a democratically rational or reasonable decision; a fully reflective public opinion; and an epistemically correct decision.

Many of the earliest theories of deliberation focused mainly on the need for democratically rational or reasonable decisions. Bächtiger *et al.* posit '[r]ational consensus on validity claims' (2010: 36) as the outcome of Type I deliberation. This matches most of the theories I include under the label of 'Kantian' so, in addition to the early Habermas, I would include Rawls's deliberative theory of public reason as one of those theories that see a democratically rational or reasonable decision as the proper outcome of deliberation. Type II deliberation does not have to meet the strict criteria set out in Habermas's theory of communicative action for the kinds of utterances citizens can make or the types of arguments that might count in deliberation. Type II also does not require that citizens aim entirely at a rational consensus on validity claims. As such, Type II most closely matches my category of 'Madisonian' deliberation. Regarding the outcomes of Type II deliberation, Bächtiger *et al.* say that these are '[n]ot generally specified' but list three possibilities: preference structuration, meta-consensus and intersubjective rationality (2010: 36). These possible outcomes parallel those that Fishkin and his colleagues expect, including single-peaked preferences (*see*, for example, List *et al.* 2013). These outcomes – preference structuration, single-peaked preferences, meta-consensus and intersubjective rationality – reflect an expectation that deliberation can lead citizens toward a fuller reflection on their beliefs and preferences. A third outcome posited by recent deliberative theory that neither typology captures completely is epistemic correctness (*see*, for example, Estlund 2007; Martí 2006; Mercier and Landemore 2012). Deliberation focusing on epistemic correctness begins by assuming that 'there are better and worse answers to political questions' (Mercier and Landemore 2012: 244–5). To meet the expectations of epistemic deliberative theory, deliberation ought to lead citizens to better or more correct answers to factual, moral and political questions. While the concept of epistemic correctness has affinities with the other outcomes, I believe it is sufficiently different to warrant treating it separately. If my reading of deliberative theories is correct, therefore, deliberation ought to lead to a democratically rational or reasonable decision, a fully reflective public opinion or an epistemically correct decision, depending upon which theory or theories those studying and instituting deliberation embrace.

Biases and mini-public deliberation

Having established that different deliberative theories expect different outcomes, we are now in a position to examine what might help or hinder these different outcomes. One could look to many different sources to aid this investigation but here I have chosen to examine research from social psychology that suggests that people often have biases when evaluating others and the information they receive. While there may be many biases that people bring to the table, I am going to focus on three that political scientists and social psychologists have found that may have important implications for deliberation: attribution bias, in-group/out-group bias, and information-processing bias.

One possible barrier to successful mini-public deliberation is what social psychologists call *attribution bias*. Research suggests that people evaluate their own behaviour differently from how they evaluate the behaviour of others. Early research found that when people evaluate their own behaviour, they tend to attribute it to situational factors, while they attribute the behaviour of others to individual dispositions (for example, Nisbett *et al.* 1973). Later research distinguished between behaviour with negative and positive outcomes. People usually attribute their successes to their own personal dispositions but their failures to situational factors over which they have no control. They tend to make the opposite attributions to those they observe (*see*, for example, Sedikides *et al.* 1998; Streufert and Streufert 1969; Wolosin *et al.* 1973). Attribution bias could very likely lead to misunderstandings that would undermine the exchange of reasons central to successful mini-public deliberation.

Another form of bias that may inhibit good deliberative outcomes is *in-group/out-group bias*. People are usually positively disposed toward those they see as like themselves or those they like (in-group), and have a more negative view of those they view as unlike themselves or that they dislike (out-group) (*see*, for example, Judd *et al.* 2005; Mackie and Ahn 1998; Ratliff and Nosek 2011). Over time, people generate affective tallies that lead them, pre-cognitively, to have either positive or affective reactions to these others. The problem for deliberative theory is that such automatic affective reactions by citizens may have deleterious consequences. Citizens will often react to political stimuli with bias (Redlawsk 2002), and this will likely undermine the reciprocity that deliberative democracy requires. Not only could such reactions create out-group bias; it may also lead to polarisation. This is especially true for citizens with strong attitudes and holds true even for citizens trying to be 'impartial'. Since all human beings engage in affectively directed reasoning, many citizens will likely fall prey during deliberation to biases against those whom they consider to be part of an out-group.

Closely related to, but clearly distinct from, in-group/out-group bias is a group of attitudes that I will call *information-processing bias*. One form of this bias is *confirmation bias*, where people tend to confirm their prior beliefs and disconfirm competing beliefs when faced with evidence and arguments (Mercier and Landemore 2012). People 'are apt to see congruent arguments as inherently stronger than those which are attitudinally incongruent; they spend time and cognitive resources counterarguing the points that challenge their priors; they seek to insulate themselves from challenging information by actively searching out congruent information' (Lodge and Taber 2005: 456). Such biases can arise even when people consciously try to eliminate them. 'Even when motivated to be even-handed, "to leave their feelings aside" ,people find it near impossible to view political policy arguments dispassionately (on gun control, affirmative action, federal support for the arts, etc.)' (Lodge and Taber 2005: 476). Not only can confirmation bias undermine the processing of information and arguments necessary for successful deliberation, Sunstein (2002) has even provided evidence that deliberation can increase these biases in a way that leads to polarisation. Polarisation occurs when interlocutors actually move in a more radical direction from what one would predict, even given their prior beliefs. A second form of information-processing bias is the *common-knowledge effect*. Whenever groups get together to discuss an issue, the participants tend to focus on information that is 'known by all group members before discussion begins and overvalue such information in their decision-making' (Myers 2012: 1). It is almost too obvious to mention but, clearly, biases in information processing could have serious deleterious effects on successful mini-public deliberation.

While all three forms of bias ought to concern those who research and institute deliberative mini-publics, the biases that are most important depend to a great degree on the outcomes of deliberation discussed earlier. In Table 10.1, I present a classification of the threats of these biases based upon the different outcomes of deliberation. I classify the threat to deliberative outcome as either low, medium or high.

Attribution bias poses the greatest threat to theories of deliberative democracy that aim at democratically rational or reasonable decisions. These theories rely upon a strong sense of reciprocity and the willingness to listen to and mutually respect others, among deliberators. It also requires, if not complete consensus, at

Table 10.1: Threat of participant bias to deliberative outcomes

	Form of Bias		
Deliberative outcome	attribution bias	in-group/out-group bias	information-processing bias
Democratically rational or reasonable decision	high	high	high
Reflective public opinion: preference structuration	low	low	high
Reflective public opinion: meta-consensus	medium	medium	high
Reflective public opinion: intersubjective rationality	low	low	high
Epistemic correctness	medium	low	High

least a tendency for most citizens to come to an agreement on the reasons for a democratic decision. People who cannot even agree on the sources of behavioural successes and failures are highly unlikely to be able to agree on the reasons for or against a decision. Imagine, for example, a situation in which wealthy people think that their success arose from their own hard work and that the failure of poorer people is because those people are simply lazy. Poorer people, on the other hand, might attribute their failures to the system or their bad luck and the success of the wealthy to their good luck or background. In such a situation, there would be little reciprocity or mutual respect between these groups, let alone the ability to agree on the reasons for a decision affecting social welfare programmes. If we want a democratically rational or reasonable decision, something must exist that helps reduce the effects of attribution bias.

For all other the other deliberative outcomes, however, attribution bias is less important; it poses little threat to either preference structuration or intersubjective rationality. One could have clearly structured, single-peaked preferences even if one views the sources of behaviour of oneself and others differently. Intersubjective rationality, that is the consistency across deliberators of a link between beliefs and preferences, is also possible even in the face of attribution bias. For example, taking the scenario I just described, all of the wealthy might have consistent and similar preferences on social welfare programmes, while all of the poor could as well, even though the two groups had very different assessments of the reasons for poverty and wealth. Since intersubjective rationality does not require that the groups agree with one another, only within their group, attribution bias poses little threat.

For epistemic correctness and meta-consensus, attribution bias also seems to be of less concern, although in both cases there are caveats that raise the concern to a medium rather than a low level. For epistemic correctness, if there is a correct answer regarding the sources of behavioural success or failure, then attribution bias could pose a greater than minimal threat, although certainly less of a threat than information-processing biases. Given this possibility, I have posited the threat of attribution bias to epistemic correctness as medium. The threat to meta-consensus is also medium. Meta-consensus requires citizens to come to some agreement on the issues at stake and the various beliefs involved in deliberation. The threat posed by attribution bias depends upon how strong this agreement must be. Using the example of the wealthy and poor again, both groups may agree that the issue of social welfare depends upon, among other things, questions of the sources of wealth and poverty, even if they have different beliefs about those sources. It is possible to conceive of a situation, however, where attribution biases become so strong that people cannot even agree on the issues and beliefs that are a legitimate part of the discussion. For this reason, I classify the threat of attribution bias to meta-consensus as medium.

The threats from in-group/out-group bias are very similar to those from attribution bias. This bias poses the greatest threat to deliberation aimed at making a democratically reasonable or rational decision. By undermining the reciprocity and mutual respect required of such deliberation, in-group/out-group bias would likely interfere with the ability of participants to reach decisions upon which they can agree. Jürgen Habermas, for example, argues that deliberation is a process of reciprocal recognition, implied by the very nature of politics itself, wherein individuals who compose society come together to do good for everyone (1996b: 21). Contrary to a marketplace of ideas, Habermas contends, 'the paradigm is not the market, but dialogue' (1996b: 23). In deliberating, citizens do not simply put ideas on display but actually have reciprocal discussions among themselves. For Rawls, being reasonable, and therefore good Rawlsian deliberative democrats, necessitates that citizens adhere to the criterion of reciprocity. This criterion 'requires that when those terms are proposed as the most reasonable terms of fair cooperation, those proposing them must also think it at least reasonable for others to accept them, as free and equal citizens, and not as dominated or manipulated, or under the pressure of inferior political or social position' (Rawls [1997] 2005: 446). The criterion of reciprocity excludes domination, manipulation or pressure exerted on those in inferior social or political positions and asks deliberators to offer the most reasonable terms of fair co-operation that they believe it reasonable for others to accept. In-group/out-group bias would clearly undermine the possibility of any of these processes taking place during mini-public deliberation.

As with attribution bias, in-group/out-group bias would also pose a medium threat to meta-consensus. For deliberators to reach meta-consensus, they should agree 'about the nature of the issue at hand, not necessarily on the actual outcome' (Niemeyer and Dryzek 2007: 500). In-group/out-group bias is likely to make such agreement less probable. This becomes even more clear when we see that Niemeyer and Dryzek argue that meta-consensus 'occurs because deliberation requires that individuals transcend private concerns and that they engage with competing views, taking them into account as part of their evaluations' (2007: 500). While this requirement may not be as exacting as those found in Habermas and Rawls, it is significant enough to raise the threat of in-group/out-group bias to the medium level.

With regard to preference structuration, intersubjective rationality and epistemic correctness, in-group/out-group bias poses a minimal threat. It is possible that such biases would interfere with citizens' views of the issue at hand and the evidence regarding those views and, as such, it might cause people to defend preferences that are not coherent or single-peaked. This problem might lead those who agree on basic beliefs and values to disagree on preferred outcomes if crosscutting cleavages exist that divide them into in-groups and out-groups; this would undermine intersubjective rationality. It is possible that interlocutors will dismiss evidence if it comes from a member of an out-group and this might lead to less epistemically correct decisions. These are all possible effects but, since they are only outside possibilities, not central to or inherent in these theories of democracy, and in some ways overlap and meld with what I am calling information-processing bias, I categorise these threats as low.

With regard to information-processing biases, I contend that these present a high level of threat to all possible deliberative outcomes. Problems such as confirmation bias and the common-knowledge effect will undermine the process of deliberation regardless of whether we aim at a democratically rational or reasonable decision, reflective public opinion, or epistemic correctness. I think epistemic correctness is the outcome for which this kind of bias represents the clearest and most direct threat. Researchers who have looked at these biases have often done so within the context of epistemic correctness (*see*, for example, Mercier and Landemore 2012; Myers 2012). If the goal of deliberation is getting the correct answer, anything that interferes with information processing should cause us concern. Yet while this is the clearest threat, information-processing bias would also undermine the other possible outcomes of deliberation. Testing validity claims under Habermasian deliberation or engaging in the use of public reason within Rawlsian deliberation both rely upon not just reciprocity and mutual respect but also upon the condition that participants pay close attention to arguments and reasons. Arguments and reasons, in turn, depend upon accurate information that information-processing bias can undermine. Reflective public opinion – whether characterised by preference structuration, meta-consensus, or intersubjective rationality – also depends upon accurate information and the ability to adjust one's preferences and beliefs when confronted with new information. Confirmation bias and the common-knowledge effect will both decrease the likelihood of this occurring. Since it would likely have deleterious effects on rational or reasonable decision-making, reflective public opinion or epistemic correctness, I have classified information-processing bias as a strong threat to all possible deliberative outcomes.

Participant biases can pose threats to successful deliberation but what I have tried to demonstrate is that these threats vary depending upon the outcomes important to the particular theory of deliberative democracy chosen by those who plan and investigate mini-public deliberation. Attribution bias poses a high threat to those interested in rational or reasonable decisions, a moderate threat to those interested in meta-consensus or epistemic correctness and only a low threat to those interested in preference structuration and intersubjective rationality. The risk presented by in-group/out-group bias is high when trying to reach democratically rational or reasonable decisions, moderate when aiming at meta-consensus but only low when preference structuration, intersubjective rationality or epistemic correctness is the goal. Finally, information-processing bias presents a high level of threat to all possible outcomes of successful deliberation. Understanding the nature of these threats allows us to examine what those who design mini-public deliberation can do to diminish them.

Reducing bias in deliberation

As David Redlawsk so aptly put it: '[W]e cannot really hope to avoid every bias affect brings. At best, by understanding the nature of these biases we can devise ways to correct for them' (Redlawsk 2002: 1041). While we still need more research in this area, several studies give preliminary indications of actions we can take to decrease the threat of biases in mini-public deliberation. Before discussing this research, I want to point out that, if we think about democracy in general, there is some positive news for deliberation. As Mercier and Landemore (2012) point out, when we think of the effects of biases on mini-public deliberation, we must think about the alternative: no deliberation. Biases will exist whether citizens participate in face-to-face deliberation or not; and they will likely have more negative consequences in the absence of face-to-face deliberation than in its presence. There is the possibility that face-to-face deliberation might lead to further entrenchment and polarisation, so biases are still important but, in many ways, face-to-face deliberation offers a greater possibility of mitigating these biases than relying upon citizens to work against them on their own. Yet even in face-to-face deliberation we must work at mitigating these biases and there is good preliminary evidence of what might reduce their effects.

In my own research, I have examined the effects of empathy on deliberation, and there is intriguing evidence that empathy might provide a way to correct for biases so that mini-publics can lead to the outcomes expected by deliberative theories, especially democratically rational and reasonable decisions (*see* Morrell 2010). Several studies indicate that empathy tends to reduce behavioural attribution bias; inducing observers to empathise affectively with a target leads them to make similar attributions for the target's behaviour as they do for their own (*see*, for example, Archer *et al.* 1979; Betancourt 1990; Galper 1976; Regan and Totten 1975; Wegner and Finstuen 1977). Gould and Sigall (1977) also indicate that subjects induced to feel affective empathy for a target tend to make attributions for the target's successful and unsuccessful behaviour similar to those they make about their own behaviour. As Davis summarises, affective role-taking instructions 'lead observers to offer causal attributions which resemble those typically found among actors' (1994: 96). Melburg *et al.* (1984) argue that complete role-playing, a combination of affect and cognition, can lead to changes in observers' attributions of others' behaviour. Increasing empathy, therefore, appears to be one promising way to overcome attribution bias.

Further research indicates that empathy can have a positive effect on decreasing out-group biases. Researchers have found that predispositions to empathy, measured with a multi-dimensional scale, can lead to a decreased likelihood of evaluating an out-group negatively (Underwood and Briggs, cited in Davis 1994: 102). Some sense of belonging to a common group leads to more emotional and behavioural reactions to the plight of others who seem at first glance to be very alien (Yzerbyt *et al.* 2003). Inducing perspective-taking increases the likelihood that observers who interpret the actions of out-groups in abstract terms will empathise with and help both non-stigmatised and stigmatised others (Levy *et al.* 2002). In the one study specifically connecting empathy to deliberation, Diana Mutz argues that

> among those high in perspective-taking ability, mean levels of tolerance were higher when subjects were exposed to rationales for dissonant views. However, among those low in perspective-taking ability, tolerance levels were lower when subjects were exposed to dissonant views, although the higher variance among this group makes this a suggestive, though not significant difference (Mutz 2002: 121).

These studies indicate the strong probability that empathy can buttress deliberative outcomes by affecting out-group evaluations.[1] By decreasing out-group bias, empathy is also likely to decrease polarisation. As I have hypothesised elsewhere, this is another reason to see empathy as important in fighting bias (Morrell 2010: 135). Redlawsk argues that some people attenuate the biases arising from their automatic affective responses because they do not make final evaluations until they have to make decisions (2002: 1040–1); they are more likely to incorporate information contrary to their initial reactions into their final judgements. While there is no empirical evidence yet directly connecting empathy to memory processors, the similarity between the evidence Redlawsk finds and that cited earlier on attribution biases and out-group evaluations suggests that citizens who empathise are more likely to make judgements in a way that attenuates the biasing effects of their immediate affective reactions. They are thus less likely to polarise during deliberation and more likely to exhibit reciprocity.

Thus, because empathy is likely to decrease attribution and in-group/out-group biases, and moderate the chances of polarisation, those who design mini-public deliberation ought to pay attention to things such as the instructions and information they give participants. Participants often receive an information packet that gives arguments for both sides of an issue but, if empathy is as important as the evidence indicates, it is also important to include items that are likely to induce participants to empathise. For example, it would be helpful to include stories of the effects of the various policy options on specific persons. Alternatively, if the mini-public deliberation includes a question and answer session, having only 'experts' as part of the panel might not create a good environment for empathy to flourish. It

---

1. A possible objection to this general conclusion is the evidence from Batson *et al.* (1995) that empathy can harm the common good. Their conclusion, however, derives from evidence of what happens when people empathise with some, but not all, others.

would be important to allow people whom the policy will affect to speak as well. More research could help us discover which of these strategies is the most likely to increase empathy and thereby decrease the negative effects of biases on mini-public deliberation; but the preliminary evidence indicates that inducing empathy is likely to be important for success in mini-public deliberation.

Beyond empathy, several studies have demonstrated the importance of the composition of the group in preventing biases from undermining mini-public deliberation. Some studies demonstrate the need for deliberative groups to have varied, and even conflicting, interests. For example, Mercier and Landemore argue that '[g]roup polarization will mostly happen when people share an opinion to begin with' (2012: 252). In other words, having a group with a diverse set of interests is most likely to prevent polarisation that arises from information-processing biases. C. Daniel Myers makes a similar case with regard to the common-knowledge effect; while his evidence is only preliminary, he maintains that, in his studies, he finds 'no evidence that commonly known information is more influential over either attitudes or decisions than uncommonly known information' (2012: 25). The most important factor to ensure that this occurs is that there is interest conflict during deliberation. As he concludes, 'Given the ubiquitousness of interest conflict in political deliberation, this finding suggests that the [common-knowledge effect] is at worst a minor barrier to deliberative democracy' (Myers 2012: 25). Finally, Christopher Karpowitz, Tali Mendelberg and Lee Shaker have focused not on the opinion or interest diversity in a group but on its gender diversity (Karpowitz and Mendelberg 2007; Karpowitz *et al.* 2012). With regard to group composition, they point out that there is a 'substantial gender gap in voice and authority', depending upon the group composition and decision-rule (Karpowitz *et al.* 2012: 533). While I will discuss decision-making structures shortly, here I want to note that gender composition was important in the success of the deliberation studied by Karpowitz, Mendelberg and Shaker. The important point to take away from these studies for those who design mini-public deliberation is that groups should be diverse in terms of both opinions and interests if they want to reduce the likelihood of biases undermining deliberative outcomes, especially those outcomes that rely upon the absence of information-processing bias. They must also pay attention to the effects that gender composition might have on achieving deliberative success. While the evidence here is only preliminary and we need further studies to refine our understanding of the relationships among different group compositions and participant biases, it seems clear that these relationships are highly important.

In addition to group composition, several studies have also determined that decision-making structures can have important effects, although we again need even further study linking these to participant biases. As noted above, Karpowitz, Mendelberg and Shaker found that decision-making structures had important interactive effects with gender composition. They argue that the gender gap in voice 'disappears under unanimous rule and few women, or under majority rule and many women' (Karpowitz *et al.* 2012: 533). This demonstrates the complexity of the relationship between decision-making structures and outcomes. If designers of mini-publics want to avoid the possibility of bias, especially gender bias, it appears that their choice of group composition will depend upon their choice of decision rule. If the deliberation will aim at unanimity, then it would be better to have a lower percentage of women in each group; if there is majority rule, however, then women need to be a larger presence in each group. A similar distinction in decision rules appears in the work of Maija Setälä, Kimmo Grönlund and Kaisa Herne. They compare the differences between decisions made by secret ballot majority rule with those made by formulating a common statement. While they do not address biases directly, they do find that knowledge increased more among those who formulated a common statement, giving indirect evidence that this procedure better overcame information-processing biases and led to better epistemic decisions (Setälä *et al.* 2010). In a second set of results, they also indicate that the common-statement procedure had positive effects on political trust and readiness for collective action (Grönlund *et al.* 2010). These findings provide indirect evidence that the common-statement procedure may have reduced in-group/out-group biases. A final study, however, finds something slightly different. In my own research, I discovered that those who participate in unstructured, consensus-oriented procedures were less likely to accept collective decisions and enjoy their deliberative experience than those who participate in more structured, majority-rule procedures (Morrell 1999). The problem, therefore, is that the evidence on decision-making procedures we have is mixed but the one thing that does seem correct is that they do have important effects. If we want to mitigate bias, we need better evidence that will help demonstrate what those who design mini-public deliberation can do when choosing a decision-making structure.

Conclusion: Deliberative theories, deliberative designs and deliberative success

I have made the case that the biases that participants bring to mini-public deliberation pose a threat to deliberative success. Those who study and design mini-public deliberation must be aware of these biases and how their choices about the information they give participants, the composition of deliberative groups and the structures of decision-making can exacerbate or alleviate the problems those biases can cause. Whether or not they are conscious of the specific biases I have named, I believe that most conveners of mini-public deliberation are aware of the basic concerns they raise. Mini-public deliberation usually provides balanced information, occurs in groups that represent diverse views, includes input from experts and stakeholders and avoids forcing a consensus that does not exist. Yet what designers often fail to recognise, I believe, is that there are trade-offs when making these institutional design decisions.

If there is one major point I want the readers of this chapter to recognise, it is that the importance of the effects of biases on deliberation is intricately linked to the theory of deliberation, and thus the definition of deliberative success, that drives those who study and design mini-public deliberation. In this, I concur with several of the arguments made by Dennis F. Thompson. I agree that '[e]mpirical researchers do not have to agree on a single concept of deliberation' (Thompson

2008: 501), and I would extend this argument by positing that those who design mini-publics do not have to agree on a single concept of deliberation either. Yet those who design and study mini-public deliberation 'must be clear about what practice they are investigating' (Thompson 2008: 501). Empirical researchers and designers must return to the theories of deliberation, even to what Mark Warren (2007) has called 'middle level' theory, when they discuss the purposes of the specific instantiation of mini-public deliberation they are studying or running. Such a return to theory must guide mini-public deliberation practice and research, I would argue, especially when we discuss the success, or lack thereof, of deliberation. While Thompson focuses on 'the core problem of deliberation' (2008: 501), I have here tried to focus instead on the different outcomes different theories of deliberation expect. The problems that participants' biases pose will vary depending upon the theoretical underpinnings of the practice of deliberation.

To illustrate my point: by way of example, take the issue of opinion change after deliberation. Many might argue that if mini-public deliberation does not lead to opinion change, then we cannot define the deliberation as a success. On its surface, this claim would make sense. Yet if we look more closely at the various deliberative theories, it becomes clear that not all opinion change indicates successful deliberation. If our goal is a democratically rational or reasonable decision, for example, then the only people who should change their opinions through deliberation are those whose prior beliefs are not rationally valid or consistent with public reason. We can make similar conclusions regarding the outcomes of reflective public opinion and epistemic correctness. We should only expect change from those participants whose prior beliefs are not reflective or not epistemically correct.

If we apply this kind of basic observation to the issue of biases and deliberative success, we can see the importance of theoretical grounding. Studying or designing mini-public deliberation that aims at reaching a democratically rational or reasonable decision requires being sensitive to all three forms of bias I highlight –attribution, in-group/out-group, and information-processing – yet because of the kind of reciprocity required by this kind of deliberation, attribution and in-group/out-group biases should be of particular concern. In such cases, trying to induce empathy as I have suggested might be especially important, as might insuring a decrease in the gender gap in voice highlighted by Karpowitz, Mendelberg and Shaker (2012). Aiming at epistemic correctness as the proper outcome of deliberative theory, however, may not require the same emphasis on empathy or the gender gap, even if they still might be of some importance. Epistemic correctness might instead require more focus on institutionalising mechanisms that most mini-public deliberation eschews. For example, it might require placing people in the deliberative groups whose specific goal is to be a 'devil's advocate' (see, for example, Schweiger et al. 1986; Schweiger et al. 1989). Mercier and Landemore even recognise a devil's advocate as a possible necessity in deliberation aimed at epistemic correctness (2012: 254); it may be the best way to overcome the specific types of biases that most threaten this type of deliberation. Defining deliberative success as reflective public opinion is even more complicated. Preference structuration and intersubjective rationality are likely the most sensitive to biases in information processing, while meta-consensus is likely also sensitive to attribution and in-group/out-group bias.

These considerations, I believe, demonstrate that deliberative theories define success differently and these differences are important for those who wish to empirically investigate and actually institute mini-public deliberation. Before engaging in either activity, people should define the theory of deliberation that is most important to them; this will help them decide how to structure deliberation and how they should empirically measure deliberative success. It will also, as I have tried to make most clear, give them a good indication of what biases are the most likely to hinder deliberative success. Yet we need more research in this area to determine the best ways to overcome those biases. Only with this further research, whatever theory we choose, will we be able to confidently define success in mini-public deliberation.

References

Archer, R. L., Foushee, H. C., Davis, M. H. and Aderman, D. (1979) 'Emotional empathy in a courtroom simulation: a person–situation interaction', *Journal of Applied Social Psychology* 9 (3): 275–91.

Bächtiger, A. and Hangartner, D. (2010) 'When deliberative theory meets empirical political science: theoretical and methodological challenges in political deliberation', *Political Studies* 58 (4): 688–714.

Bächtiger, A., Niemeyer, S., Neblo, M. A. *et al.* (2010) 'Disentangling diversity in deliberative democracy', *Journal of Political Philosophy* 18 (1): 32–63.

Barabas, J. (2004) 'How deliberation affects policy opinions', *American Political Science Review* 98 (4): 687–701.

Batson, C. D., Batson, J. G., Todd, R. M., Brummett, B. H., Shaw, L. L. and Aldeguer, C. M. R. (1995) 'Empathy and the collective good: caring for one of the others in a social dilemma', *Journal of Personality and Social Psychology* 68 (4): 619–31.

Bessette, J. M. (1980) 'Deliberative democracy: The majority principle in republican government', in R. A. Goldwin and W. A. Schambra (eds) *How Democratic Is the Constitution*, Washington, DC: American Enterprise Institute.

— (1994) *The Mild Voice of Reason*, Chicago, IL: The University of Chicago Press.

Betancourt, H. (1990) 'An attribution-empathy model of helping behavior: behavioral intentions and judgement of help-giving', *Personality and Social Psychology Bulletin* 16 (3): 573–91.

Bohman, J. (1996) *Public Deliberation: Pluralism, complexity, and democracy*, Cambridge, MA: MIT Press.

Chambers, S. (1996) *Reasonable Democracy*, Ithaca, NY: Cornell University Press.

— (2003) 'Deliberative democratic theory', *Annual Review of Political Science*, 6 (1): 307–26.

Davis, M. H. (1994) *Empathy: A social psychological approach*, Madison, WI: Brown and Benchmark Publishers.

Delli Carpini, M. X., Cook, F. L. and Jacobs, L. R. (2004) 'Public deliberation, discursive participation, and citizen engagement: a review of the empirical literature', *Annual Review of Political Science* 7: 315–44.

Dryzek, J. S. (1990) *Discursive Democracy: Politics, policy, and political science*, Cambridge: Cambridge University Press.

— (2000) *Deliberative Democracy and Beyond*, Oxford: Oxford University Press.

Estlund, D. (2007) *Democratic Authority: A philosophical framework*, Princeton, NJ: Princeton University Press.

Fishkin, J. S. (1991) *Democracy and Deliberation*, New Haven, CT: Yale University Press.

— (1995) *The Voice of the People: Public opinion and democracy*, New Haven, CT: Yale University Press.

Galper, R. E. (1976) 'Turning observers into actors: differential causal attributions as a function of "empathy"', *Journal of Research in Personality* 10 (3): 328–335.

Gastil, J. (2004) 'Adult civic education through the national issues forums: developing democratic habits and dispositions through public deliberation', *Adult Education Quarterly* 54 (4): 308–28.

Gould, R. and Sigall, H. (1977) 'The effects of empathy and outcome on attribution: an examination of the divergent-perspective hypothesis', *Journal of Experimental Social Psychology* 13 (5): 480–91.

Grönlund, K, Setälä, M. and Herne, K. (2010) 'Deliberation and civic virtue: lessons from a citizen deliberation experiment', *European Political Science Review* 2: 95–117.

Gutmann, A. and Thompson, D. (1996) *Democracy and Disagreement*, Cambridge, MA: Belknap Press of Harvard University Press.

Habermas, J. (1984) *The Theory of Communicative Action I: Reason and rationalization of society*, Boston: Beacon.

— (1996a) *Between Facts and Norms: Contributions to a discourse theory of law and democracy*, Cambridge, MA: The MIT Press.

— (1996b) 'Three normative models of democracy', in S. Benhabib (ed.) *Democracy and Difference: Contesting the boundaries of the political*, Princeton, NJ: Princeton University Press.

Judd, C. M., Park, B., Yzerbyt, V., Gordijn, E. H. and Muller, D. (2005) 'Attributions of intergroup bias and out-group homogeneity to in-group and out-group others', *European Journal of Social Psychology* 35 (6): 677–704.

Karpowitz, C. F. and Mendelberg, T. (2007) 'Groups and deliberation', *Swiss Political Science Review* 13 (4): 645–62.

Karpowitz, C. F., Mendelberg, T. and Shaker, L. (2012) 'Gender inequality in deliberative participation', *American Political Science Review* 106 (3): 533–47.

Levy, S. R., Freitas, A. L. and Salovey, P. (2002) 'Constructing action abstractly and blurring social distinctions: implications for perceiving homogeneity among, but also emphasizing with and helping others', *Journal of Personality and Social Psychology* 83 (5): 1224–38.

List, C., Luskin, R. C., Fishkin, J. S. and McLean, I. (2013) 'Deliberation, single-peakedness, and the possibility of meaningful democracy: evidence from Deliberative Polls', *Journal of Politics* 75 (1): 80–95.

Luskin, R. C., Fishkin J. S. and Jowell, R. (2002) 'Considered opinions: Deliberative Polling in Britain', *British Journal of Political Science* 32: 455–87.

Lodge, M. and Taber, C. S. (2005) 'The automaticity of affect for political leaders, groups, and issues: an experimental test of the hot cognition hypothesis', *Political Psychology* 26 (3): 455–82.

Mackie, D. M. and Ahn, M. N. (1998) 'In-group and out-group inferences: when in-group bias overwhelms outcome bias', *European Journal of Social Psychology* 28 (3): 343–60.

Mansbridge, J., Bohman, J., Chambers, S., Estlund, D., Føllesdal, A., Fung, A., Lafont, C., Manin, B. and Martí, J. L. (2010) 'The place of self-interest and the role of power in deliberative democracy', *Journal of Political Philosophy* 18 (1): 64–100.

Martí, J. L. (2006) 'The epistemic conception of deliberative democracy defended', in S. Besson and J. L. Martí (ed.) *Deliberative Democracy and Its Discontents*, Burlington, VT: Ashgate.

Melburg, V., Rosenfeld, P., Riess, M., and Tedeschi, J. T. (1984) 'A reexamination of the empathic observers paradigm for the study of divergent attributions', *Journal of Social Psychology* 124 (2): 201–08.

Mendelberg, T. (2002) 'The deliberative citizen: theory and evidence', in M. X. Delli Carpini, L. Huddy and R. Y. Shapiro (eds) *Political Decision Making, Deliberation and Participation*, Oxford: Elsevier Press.

Mercier, H. and Landemore, H. (2012) 'Reasoning is for arguing: understanding the successes and failures of deliberation', *Political Psychology* 33 (2): 243–58.

Morrell, M. E. (1999) 'Citizens' evaluations of participatory democratic procedures: normative theory meets empirical science', *Political Research Quarterly* 52 (2): 293–322.

— (2003) 'Survey and experimental evidence for a reliable and valid measure of internal political efficacy', *Public Opinion Quarterly* 67 (4): 589–602.

— (2007) 'Empathy and democratic education', *Public Affairs Quarterly* 21 (4): 381–403.

— (2010) *Empathy and Democracy: Feeling, thinking and deliberation*, University Park: Pennsylvania State University Press.

Mutz, D. C. (2002) 'Cross-cutting social networks: testing democratic theory in practice', *American Political Science Review* 96 (1): 111–26.

— (2006) *Hearing the Other Side*, New York: Cambridge University Press.

— (2008) 'Is deliberative democracy a falsifiable theory?', *Annual Review of Political Science* 11: 521–38.

Myers, C. D. 'Political deliberation, interest conflict, and the common knowledge effect', paper presented at the Annual Meeting of the American Political Science Association, New Orleans, LA, 2012.

Neblo, M. A. 'Deliberative breakdown: how and why deliberation succeeds and fails', paper presented at the Annual Meeting of the International Society of Political Psychology, Toronto, 2005.

Niemeyer, S. and Dryzek, J. S. (2007) 'The ends of deliberation: meta-consensus and inter-subjective rationality as ideal outcomes', *Swiss Political Science Review* 13 (4): 497–526.

Nisbett, R. E., Caputo, C., Legant, P. and Marecek, J. (1973) 'Behavior as seen by the actor and as seen by the observer', *Journal of Personality and Social Psychology* 27 (2): 154–64.

Parkinson, J. (2006) *Deliberating in the Real World*, Oxford: Oxford University Press.

Ratliff, K. A. and Nosek, B. A. (2011) 'Negativity and out-group biases in attitude formation and transfer', *Personality and Social Psychology Bulletin* 37 (12): 1692–703.

Rawls, J. (1996) *Political Liberalism*, (Paperback edition) New York: Columbia University Press.

— (2005) *Political Liberalism: Expanded Edition*, New York: Columbia University Press.

Redlawsk, D. P. (2002) 'Hot cognition or cool consideration? Testing the effects of motivated reasoning on political decision-making', *Journal of Politics* 64 (4): 1021–44.

Regan, D. T. and Totten, J. (1975) 'Empathy and attribution: turning observers into actors', *Journal of Personality and Social Psychology* 32(5): 850–56.

Rosenberg, S. 'Types of political discourse and the democracy of deliberation: evidence from a field experiment in California', paper presented at the Annual Meeting of the American Political Science Association, Washington, DC, 2005.

Schweiger, D. M., Sandberg, W. M. and Ragan, J. W. (1986) 'Group approaches for improving strategic decision making: a comparative analysis of dialectical inquiry, devil's advocacy, and consensus', *Academy of Management Journal* 29 (1): 51–71.

Schweiger, D. M., Sandberg, W. R. and Rechner, P. L. (1989) 'Experiential effects of dialectical inquiry, devil's advocacy, and consensus approaches to strategic decision making', *Academy of Management Journal* 32 (4): 745–72.

Sedikides, C., Campbell, W. K., Reeder, G. D. and Elliot A. E. (1998) 'The self-serving bias in relational context', *Journal of Personality and Social Psychology* 74 (2): 378–86..

Setälä, M., Grönlund, K. and Herne, K. (2010) 'Citizen deliberation on nuclear power: a comparison of two decision-making methods', *Political Studies*, 688–714.

Steenbergen, M. R., Bächtiger, A., Spörndli, M. and Steiner, J. (2003) 'Measuring political deliberation: a discourse quality index', *Comparative European Politics*, 1: 21–48.

Streufert, S. and Streufert, S. C. (1969) 'Effects of conceptual structure, failure, and success in attribution of causality and interpersonal attitudes', *Journal of Personality and Social Psychology* 11 (2): 138–47.

Sunstein, C. (2002) 'The law of group polarization', *The Journal of Political Philosophy* 10 (2): 175–195.

Thompson, D. F. (2008) 'Deliberative democratic theory and empirical political science', *Annual Review of Political Science* 11: 497–520.

Trénel, M. (2009) 'Facilitation and inclusive deliberation', in T. Davies and S. P. Gangadharan, *Online Deliberation: Design, research, and practice*, CSLI Publications.

Walsh, K. C. 'Deliberation and difference: The contributions of civic dialogue', paper presented at the Annual Meeting of the American Political Science Association, Chicago, 2004.

—   (2006) 'Communities, race, and talk: an analysis of the occurrence of civic intergroup dialogue programs', *Journal of Politics* 68 (1): 22–33.

Warren, M. E. (2007) 'Institutionalizing deliberative democracy', in S. Rosenberg (ed.) *Deliberation, Participation and Democracy: Can the people govern?*, London: Palgrave-Macmillan.

Warren, M. E. and Pearse, H. (eds) (2008) *Designing Deliberative Democracy: The British Columbia citizens' assembly*, Cambridge: Cambridge University Press.

Wegner, D. M. and Finstuen, K. (1977) 'Observers' focus of attention in the simulation of self-perception', *Journal of Personality and Social Psychology* 35 (1): 56–62.

Wolosin, R. J., Sherman, S. J. and Till, A. (1973) 'Effects of cooperation and competition on responsibility attribution after success and failure', *Journal of Experimental Social Psychology* 9 (3): 220–35.

Young, I. M. (2002) *Inclusion and Democracy*, Oxford: Oxford University Press.

Yzerbyt, V., Dumont, M., Wigboldus, D. and Gordijn, E. (2003) 'I feel for us: the impact of categorization and identification on emotions and action tendencies', *British Journal of Social Psychology* 42 (4): 533–49.

Chapter Eleven

Scaling Up Deliberation to Mass Publics: Harnessing Mini-Publics in a Deliberative System

Simon Niemeyer

Introduction

Deliberative democracy did not begin as a field of political thought with mini-publics at the core of its institutional dimension. Yet, for better or worse, mini-publics have become a dominant feature at the interface between theory and practice, at least in terms of citizen deliberation. Their use grows in many constituencies, although the manner varies greatly (Goodin and Dryzek 2006). And while such growth might indicate success, this popularity has also highlighted weaknesses. Issues such as quality control; their potential misuse as a 'fig leaf' of legitimation for predetermined outcomes; and, in extreme cases, the possibility of outright manipulation of mini-publics all threaten to undermine their role in real-world settings (Parkinson 2006). Moreover, the relatively small number of participants restricts the inclusiveness and, consequently, the democratic potential of mini-publics (Pateman 2012; Parkinson 2006). This restriction, in particular, means that, while mini-publics can represent democratic deliberation – in some cases, at least – they do not, and cannot, claim to be instances of deliberative democracy in the service of the masses (Chambers 2009; Dryzek 2009).

It should go without saying that deliberative democracy should seek to include the wider public beyond mini-publics, ideally including all those affected by political decisions. But achieving widespread deliberation is challenging (*see*, for example, Goodin 2000). The more recent, and very important, 'systemic turn' in deliberative democracy (Parkinson and Mansbridge 2012) potentially gets around both the scale and quality issues. Here, deliberative quality is an emergent property of the system as a whole, rather than the sum of individual deliberative moments across all possible sites. In short, systems-thinking emphasises the deliberative democratic qualities of complex (political) systems, which 'entails a set of distinguishable, differentiated, but to some degree, interdependent parts, often with distributed functions and a division of labor, connected in such a way as to form a complex whole' (Mansbridge *et al.* 2012: 4).

Mini-publics are compatible with the deliberative system. However, apart from Mackenzie and Warren (2012), there is thus far a tendency to treat them as relatively discrete entities, more connected to decision-making than they are to mass publics (for example, Bohman 2012; Chambers 2012). This is ostensibly consistent with the idea of a deliberative system, as advanced in the Parkinson and Mansbridge volume (2012), which advocates the specification of deliberation among different sites and actors, with different qualities. Some sites (including mini-publics) may be more deliberative than others but it is the deliberative and democratic qualities of the system as a whole that is of primary importance.

However, while specialisation is inherent in the idea of a deliberative system, it has its limits. Chambers (2012), for one, rejects specialisation to the extent that mass participation can be entirely cleaved from the deliberative function: the system is improved to the extent that all sites are deliberative. Specialisation does not mean accepting that deliberative quality is no longer a goal for all sites, including mass-publics. To the extent that all actors can become 'more deliberative', this can surely only enhance the quality of the system as a whole.

Can mini-publics play a role in improving the deliberative system? In her earlier work, Chambers laments the dominance of mini-publics, which has crowded out the democratic (mass-public) dimension of deliberative democracy (Chambers 2009). This is true enough in terms of the institutional dimension. However, mini-publics can still make an important contribution as we move toward systems-thinking, despite the limitations of so doing that Thompson (2008) identifies. It might be true that the conditions achieved within mini-publics are different from what is possible, or even desirable, beyond them (Mansbridge 1999; Hendriks 2006; Habermas 1998).[1] However, as Thompson also recognises, mini-publics play a role in developing an understanding of the conditions under which deliberation is possible, including in mass-public settings.

Here, I hope to extend the current understanding of deliberation in mini-publics and recast it in broader systemic terms, highlighting the conditions that mini-publics can create within the system, rather than as discrete deliberative entities. In doing so, I argue that mini-publics can contribute to our understanding of how a deliberative system might work and how deliberation might be scaled up. The term 'scaling up' here refers specifically to the task of achieving in 'mass democracy'[2] the same effect as deliberation observed in idealised mini-public settings. I am not concerned with finding a way to make mini-publics more inclusive or even to replicate the process of deliberation that they can facilitate (cf., Menkel-Meadow 2011). Rather, here I am looking for the antecedents and mechanisms that lead to give rise to the same outcomes as what we might call 'deliberation' – which I define here in terms of both the propagation of, and reflection upon discourses – in wider, everyday, political settings. I am also interested in the potential contribution of mini-publics to improving the prospect of deliberation in mass settings.

In this chapter, I present a case for a twofold role for mini-publics in deliberative systems. Firstly, rather than for *decision-making* as proxies for mass publics, mini-

---

1.   Thanks to Nicole Curato for pointing this out.
2.   The term 'mass democracy' is used by Simone Chambers (2012) to contrast with forms of democracy that restrict participation in decision-making.

publics can be used for *deliberation-making* in mass publics. Mini-publics can distil, constrain and synthesise relevant discourses to be transmitted to the wider public in a manner that is not possible via mass media, or likely through electoral representatives. The idea is similar to the 'trust-based' role of mini-publics as information providers (MacKenzie and Warren 2012), although I would stress a slightly more discursive mechanism than information transmission. Secondly, mini-publics can be used for *capacity-building*, by improving the deliberative abilities of citizens, as deliberative exemplars in a manner similar to that proposed by Rosenberg (2007). To the extent that scaling-up mini-public deliberation is possible, it is hoped that the public sphere as a whole might be nudged in a more deliberative direction.

The following discussion considers current thinking around the idea of the deliberative system and where it might go. It proceeds by (very tentatively) comparing the current state of knowledge in the field to systems-thinking in economics. The chapter then moves on to consider the components of the system –particularly as they relate to a potential role for mini-publics. The discussion draws on the literature as well as experience from observation of mini-publics to examine what the system components might look like and how one part of the system might affect another. Finally mechanisms whereby mini-publics can contribute to improving the quality of mass public deliberation are considered.

A systems view of scaling-up

When looking at deliberation in any setting (mini-public, mass, parliamentary and so on) it is important both to ask what is desirable and what is possible and that this thinking be informed by deliberative theory (Steiner 2008). At its core, deliberative democracy is concerned with authentic reasoning in deciding what course of action should be taken (Chambers 2012: 57; citing Cohen 2007: 222), which Dryzek (2009) formulates in terms of deliberation being deliberative, inclusive and consequential.

As Dryzek (2009) notes, a systems view opens up a number of possibilities in terms of what might count as authentic deliberation but it also requires that such claims be assessed through some form of systems-based model. The task is complex because it is not a straightforward matter of judgeing deliberation as a good without considering its causes and consequences as it interacts with other parts of the system.

Take for example, at the micro-deliberative level, the proposition that deliberation can be liberated from the limitation of scale by considering it an internal process of 'deliberation within' (Goodin 2000) rather than a dialogical process among citizens. On its own terms, the prospect seems promising. The assumption here is that individuals are capable of, and motivated to, engagement in this kind of internal reflection. Clearly, there is a good deal of variation in these tendencies among citizens. But there might be qualities within the system that overcome (or perhaps render unproblematic) the barriers to individual reflection, despite a purported indelible link between cognition and dialogue (Mercier and

Landemore 2012). One possible mechanism for increasing motivation to engage in deliberation could occur where the system emulates what can be observed in mini-public deliberation, in which participants engage with information more thoroughly in anticipation of having to defend their positions (Goodin and Niemeyer 2003).[3]

My main point here is that it is not possible to think about the kind of deliberation we seek, or the role of mini-publics in a deliberative system, without first accounting for the features of the rest of the system. There are a number of ways in which the idea of a deliberative system can be conceptualised. One approach is to view the system primarily in terms of distributed deliberation across different sites (for example, Mansbridge, Bohman *et al.* 2012).[4] Here, I wish to consider the deliberative system in a slightly different way, not just in terms of the sites of deliberation but also: what specific deliberative encounters are supposed to achieve (intermediate outcome); via what procedure; the assumptions we can reasonably make about the possibilities for deliberation, given the capabilities and predispositions of citizens; and the institutional settings that frame, regulate and facilitate deliberation. These elements work together to describe the system as a whole.

I cannot possibly do justice to each of these components here. In any case, there is still a good deal to be worked through. Systems-thinking is not new to democratic theory (take, for example, the idea of checks and balances), but deliberative-systems-thinking opens up a slightly different way of conceptualising it. Yet the idea of the deliberative system is at its infancy. It might, and perhaps should, take a good deal of time before the contours of the system are more clearly explicated, as our understanding of democratic systems is updated by examining its components through the lens of deliberative democracy.

Compare the concept of the deliberative system to the much more developed idea of the economic system – something that has developed over 200 years since Adam Smith.[5] Table 11.1 outlines the main elements comprising economic systems as described by economic theory. The system has a clearly identified goal (maximise utility or material happiness), from which established procedures (market exchange) produce intermediate outcomes (efficient pricing). The operation of the system is founded on particular assumptions, especially in relation to how the individual behaves in that system (economic person) as well as a set of institutions that bound or regulate the behaviour of individuals.

---

3. There are other possible mechanisms but I do not want to pre-empt the discussion about the deliberative person, below.

4. Mansbridge *et al.*, describe the deliberative as consisting of four 'arenas' (binding decisions of the state; related activities; informal talk related to binding decisions; talk not intended for binding decisions) and three functions (epistemic, ethical, democratic) (Mansbridge *et al.* 2012: 9–19).

5. I want to be careful not to overplay the comparison to economic systems. I do not concur with the sometimes excessive abstraction deployed by some areas of economics, nor with the historically grotesque interpretation of human motivation (although this is improving, as it becomes more evidence-based). However, the elegance of the theory is alluring and it provides a potential template for thinking about deliberative systems.

Table 11.1: System components (economics and deliberative democracy)

GOAL	PROCEDURE	INTERMEDIATE OUTCOMES	ASSUMPTION	INSTITUTIONS
		Economics/Economic System		
Maximise Utility	• Market Exchange • Bargaining	• Efficient pricing	• Individual (economic person) • Utility maximising behaviour (instrumental rationality) • Perfect Information	• Property Rights • Markets
(Material 'Happiness')			Other Assumptions • Divisible Goods • Excludability	
		Deliberative Democracy/Deliberative System		
Political Legitimacy	• Discussion *vs* Information? • Deliberation within?	• 'Reasoned' Preferences (choices reflect underlying 'will')?	• Individual (deliberative person) • Discursive Psychology Other Assumptions • Issue characteristics?	• Minipublics? (Scaling up) – Division of labour? – Minipublic trust? – Agenda setting?
(Political 'Happiness')	• Ideal Speech? • Rhetoric? • Contestation?	• Emancipated preferences?	Individual • Inquisitiveness? • Self-interest?/Other-regarding interest?	• Demoi? • Online deliberation? • Parliaments?

By comparison, there is (rightly) a good deal of contestation when it comes to the corresponding components of the deliberative system, shown in the lower half of Table 11.1.[6] This makes it difficult to pin down definitively what role a mini-public should play in the system; but it is possible to sketch out possibilities in light of what is known. The list of possibilities shown in Table 11.1 is not exhaustive. The intention is merely to indicate how much has to be sorted through and to flag some of the components that I will consider below.

Attributes of the system

The following discussion covers each of the elements described in Table 11.1, with a view to sketching out what might be possible and desirable in terms of mass deliberation in the deliberative system – informed in part from observation from mini-publics – and the potential role for mini-publics themselves. In doing so I recognise that, beyond the broad goal of legitimacy, there is considerable debate regarding what deliberation and deliberative democracy should look like. But it is possible to focus on some possibilities and sketch a broadly construed outline of how a system should work. Here, I focus specifically on those parts that are related to the potential role of mini-publics, drawing both from the literature and empirical evidence.[7]

---

6. I have argued elsewhere in more detail for the need to develop a systemic view of deliberative systems, including the need for a foundational idea of the deliberative person (Niemeyer 2012b). However, economics merely provides an example of a systemic approach, rather than an exemplar of how a system should operate in practice.

7. The evidence is drawn from the analysis of 14 mini-public events over a period of 10 years, varying from small-scale citizens' juries (N=12) to 21st Century Town Meetings® (N=400). For

System goal

Of the elements described in Table 11.1, the system goal for deliberative democracy should be least controversial. However, as Mansbridge *et al.* (2012: 10–12) point out, even here, there is some disagreement. For them, a deliberative system can accommodate a number of goals, including an epistemic function (producing opinions and so on informed by facts and logic); an ethical function (producing respect among citizens); and a democratic function (promoting an inclusive political process in terms of equality). These goals are hard to disagree with in terms of the broad aims of the system but I am not sure that they constitute first-order goals in the same sense that maximising utility drives thinking about the economic system. Rather, I suggest that they are second-order goals – or perhaps even third-order, behind Dryzek's (2009) deliberativeness, inclusiveness and consequentiality – that shape the rest of the system. Epistemic function shapes the way we assess intermediate outcomes; ethical functions shape the procedural ideals; and the democratic function shapes both institutions and procedure.

This still begs the question whether there *is* an overarching goal, or 'good'? There is much consensus that deliberative democracy is primarily oriented toward producing legitimate political outcomes (Manin 1987; Cohen 1997). There is nothing particular about deliberative democracy in this sense. Just as there are competing accounts within economics regarding how material happiness is maximised, there are competing accounts of legitimacy in political theory.[8] To put it simply: in a deliberative system, legitimation is maximised to the extent that citizens get to decide, in light of reasons, what should be done (Chambers 2012: 57; citing Cohen 2007: 222). It is from this premise that Dryzek's (2009) elements of deliberative capacity follow. How this capacity is best achieved in practice is, in part, a question of process.

The process of deliberation

There is a diversity of positions regarding the procedure that deliberation should ideally follow. This has been captured by Bächtiger *et al.* (2010), who distinguish between Type I (Habermasian, formal) and Type II (open, less formal) deliberation. Whether or not we accept a Type I or Type II account, observation of mini-public deliberation suggest that the key process is reasoning (consistent with Rawls 1997). In short, deliberation should involve some form of reasoning, during which individuals genuinely engage with different perspectives (for example, Goodin 2005), which may result in transformed preferences (*see* Intermediate outcomes, below).

---

an overview of these mini-publics and the methodologies used to assess them, *see* Niemeyer (2012a).

8. Liberal democrats might argue that a system that emphasises selection of representatives via voting is the best way to achieve legitimation, or political 'happiness'. Deliberative democrats may not disagree outright but they do point to failures with this approach and emphasise greater inclusion and deliberation in order to determine the best possible outcomes on the basis of deliberation and reasoning by all those affected.

Demand and supply in deliberative exchanges

For the purposes of scaling up, I will assume that more open forms of deliberation may at least be admissible, even desirable. However, I do so with qualification. When discussing the process of deliberation, most deliberative democrats focus on the propagation of claims, contentions and discourses in relation to political issues – or on the 'supply' of arguments, to extend the economics metaphor

However, there is much more to deliberation than speech acts. As well as *propagation* (supply), there is the 'consumption' (demand) of these arguments, involving a process of *reflection*: interrogating and judgeing claims and, if necessary, synthesising the content with existing beliefs and adjusting positions. Demand-side thinking accepts that individuals are not only deliberative 'makers'; they are also deliberative 'takers' in deciding what to accept as a legitimate argument (Dryzek and Niemeyer 2006). The reflective/demand side of deliberation is well understood by Goodin (2002). His argument for 'deliberation within' harnesses the internal-reflective capacities of citizens. Bächtiger also recognises the reflective side in his discussion of contestatory modes of deliberation (Bächtiger 2011; *see also* Curato *et al.* 2013).

Intermediate outcomes

Whether deliberation is necessarily a group process or whether it is possible to deliberate alone depends to some extent on what deliberation is supposed to achieve. The notion of an ideal intermediate outcome has received relatively less consideration than ideas about deliberative process. The most common refrain is that deliberation should transform preferences. Some have also gone on to explain why this occurs (Barabas 2004). But transformation by itself is surely a poor indicator of deliberativeness. All sorts of perverse outcomes might be possible, perhaps due to poor design. Thus, it is important to identify how, or even when, deliberation should transform preferences. This is not to suggest that there is a 'correct' preference for any given political issue. What is of interest is the nature of preferences and the way in which they relate to a process of deliberative reasoning (Niemeyer and Dryzek 2007).

The most promising form of deliberative outcome that speaks to the legitimacy question is Manin's (1987) argument that deliberation should produce a situation in which reflection aligns inner reasons – made salient during deliberation –with appropriate political choices. As it turns out, this effect can be observed in mini-public deliberation. Before deliberation, the preferences of citizens may be unduly influenced by strategic arguments deployed in politics specifically to confound the public will – a phenomenon that is nicely captured by the idea of 'symbolic politics' (Edelman 1985). Deliberation results in the identification of these symbolic arguments and, where they cannot be sustained in the face of deliberative scrutiny, their rejection (Niemeyer 2011a). This effect, combined with reflection on wider facets of the issue, is made possible, in part, by the rejection of distorting symbols, resulting in a stronger alignment between will and preference.[9]

---

9.   Emancipation through dissolving symbolic/manipulatory influences on public opinion is unlikely

The process that contributes to this dissipation of symbolic arguments can be compared to what cognitive social psychologists refer to as a move from peripheral thinking (involving short cuts) to central processing in cognition (Petty and Cacioppo 1984; Petty and Cacioppo 1986) and the overlapping concepts of memory versus online reasoning (Hastie and Park 1986) and, more recently, System I (fast) thinking and System II (slow, considered) thinking (Kahneman 2011). Peripheral thinking resonates to some extent with Rosenberg's (2002) account of linearity in every day political reasoning.

Elsewhere I have considered how (high-quality) group deliberation invokes more intensive central (slow, intensive) cognition, when participants have engaged in demand-side reflection, which results in a more coherent position in relation to the issue at hand (Niemeyer 2004; 2011a). Although I recognise the practical limits in mass settings, I have (with Dryzek) suggested that this reflection produces a situation in which there is intersubjective agreement on the relevant dimensions of the issue (meta-consensus) without this necessarily producing straightforward consensus (Dryzek and Niemeyer 2006). This outcome, along with intersubjective consistency – which captures one form of meta-consensus, in the way that inner states map on to preferences (Niemeyer and Dryzek 2007) – can only result from a situation in which there has been an attempt to grapple with all the relevant arguments at some level, as opposed to taking cognitive shortcuts and choosing outcomes by satisficing intuitive, biased predispositions (*see* discussion on deliberative pathologies, below).

Thus, overall, deliberative transformation can be thought of in terms of outcomes that reflect a measure of (intersubjective) reasoning (Niemeyer 2011c; Niemeyer and Dryzek 2007), in which preferences (or political choices) come to reflect the inner reasons that Manin refers to. These inner reasons are themselves subject to deliberative scrutiny as individuals develop a shared meta-consensus about the important dimensions pertaining to the issue.[10] This effect has been repeatedly observed in high-quality mini-public deliberation (Niemeyer 2011a, b). However, there is a question regarding the extent to which the processes (described above) contributing to this outcome can be replicated on a larger scale. The possibilities are dependent, in part, on the capabilities of citizens and the demands that this kind of transformation makes of them, as well as on the settings that might induce deliberative behaviour.

---

to be the only kind of desired outcome of either mini-public or wider public-sphere deliberation. At least two other kinds of effects have been observed: construction and reconstruction of public will. However, here I focus on the emancipatory impact for the purposes of demonstrating how mini-public might be scaled up.

10. Ideally there is also agreement on what values and beliefs are legitimate and relevant to the issue (meta-consensus) and what sort of values and beliefs map onto what sort of preference (*see* discussion in relation to assumptions about the individual below). In other words, there is intersubjective agreement on the process of reasoning, in a manner not dissimilar to that described by pragmadialectics (Eemeren and Grootendorst 1984).

Assumptions about the individual

There are conflicting views on the deliberative capacity of many ordinary citizens in the literature:[11] some positive (Dahl 1993; Page and Shapiro 1992); some sanguine (Tetlock 1998; Rosenberg 2002); and others profoundly negative (Schumpeter 1976[1943]); Somin 1998).[12] Evidence from mini-publics suggests that, under the right circumstances, individual-level capacity to engage in the kind of deliberation described above does exist among many ordinary citizens; or at least that there is considerable potential for achieving improved outcomes from a deliberative perspective.

In principle, the effect of mini-public deliberation should be scalable in a broad sense. Although there are undoubtedly issues with self-selection, we are talking about the roughly same population in mass-publics, with the same capabilities as those observed in mini-publics.[13] The question then becomes whether there are individual traits that might explain the difference between mini-public and mass deliberation and whether there are features of mini-publics that can be harnessed to achieve something approaching deliberative behaviour in wider settings.

The deliberative truth-seeker

If the deliberative person can be characterised by 'truth-seeking' behaviour (as opposed to utility-maximising in economics) then regulation of the supply-side of deliberation may be less important. In economics, the need for consumer-protection is mitigated to some extent by our ability to be discerning in our consumption choices. In the case of deliberation, the strategic use of rhetoric is less problematic if the individual is attuned to what the interlocutor is trying to communicate: whether they are attempting to manipulate the audience or to use rhetoric to build conceptual bridges in ways that serve to illuminate the issue (Dryzek 2010).

The inquisitive truth-seeker is also 'truth-sensitive' insofar as she actively seeks, and takes into account, the best available reasons. This is more straightforward when we think of scientific evidence (including social-scientific evidence), where the best available evidence is defined by *status quaestionis* or 'state of the investigation', that is, the scholarly consensus (Christiano 2012: 31).

---

11. The term deliberative capacity is used in a different, but overlapping, manner from Dryzek (2009). Here, I refer to the specific willingness and capability of citizens to engage in deliberative reasoning, which is related to Dryzek's 'deliberativeness' as a component of overall deliberative capacity.

12. The conclusions here depend heavily on assumptions about what is desirable in respect to citizens as political agents. These assumptions vary considerably among these authors, including preference-stability, epistemic quality and reason-giving.

13. There is some, albeit conflicting, evidence that the average (US) citizen is indeed less likely to engage in mini-public deliberation (Hibbing and Theiss-Morse 2002; Morrell 2005; Neblo *et al.* 2010). This may be true but it is also the case that those who do turn up for deliberation improve their reasoning via mechanisms that ought to be possible to scale up to the wider population.

However, when it comes to complex issues such as climate change, where even an individual expert is unlikely to encompass all the relevant knowledge in the field, the truth-seeking citizen must accept a lack of resources and, to some extent rely on specialisation within the system in the form of experts.

The nature of truth-seeking

Specialisation in the production of knowledge does not abrogate the requirement of judgement by the citizen. At the very least, there is a need to avoid the kind of heuristics and biases to which citizens can be subject; this applies, for example, when citizens come across information that merely endorses their prior beliefs (confirmation bias: Nickerson 1998) or wilfully refuse to concede an otherwise valid argument that they have accessed (Redlawsk 2002). And the deliberative person is ideally open to accepting the (likely) imperfect nature of their reasoning and open to updating in light of new reasons. Truth-seeking can assist citizens to form judgements about the relationship between a claim and their interests because the assessment is made based on actively matching the two, as well as considering higher-level goals that the citizen is seeking to fulfil (more of which below). The closest things in social psychology to what I refer to as truth-seeking are the related concepts of 'need to evaluate', or form an opinion (Bizer *et al.* 2002), and the 'need for cognition', to work through cognitively challenging tasks (Cacioppo and Petty 1982). Both seem highly commensurate with desirable deliberative characteristics but there is still a need for openness to re-evaluation – or Socratic humility, conceding that the truth might be at least temporarily beyond the individual's grasp – as part of the truth-seeking process.

Multiple truths, multiple selves

For those deliberative democrats who do not subscribe to the idea of complete rational consensus (which I think is most), the idea of 'truth' does not capture the whole story. For a start there is also a need to consider the volitional aspect of deliberation, or the ultimate (non-instrumental) goal that we are trying to achieve. But here the problem starts to get messy, even when it comes to the self.

Manin (1987) recognised that individuals embody multiple and sometimes competing positions. This recurring idea is articulated by discursive psychologists (Harré *et al.* 2009) as different discourses, or storylines, that are both constructed and evoked in the context of real-world discourse. For Manin, deliberation is directed at making these contradictions salient, along with all other relevant arguments, and engaging in dialogue (both internal and external) in order for individuals to realise which 'true' preference reflects their inner state.

According to discursive psychology, individuals are constantly reproducing and developing discourses via social processes, which may involve multiple competing perspectives. However, unlike deliberative democracy, which is goal-oriented, discursive psychology is phenomenological/descriptive and makes no claim regarding the quality of outcomes, although it is nonetheless useful in helping to understand deliberative encounters (O'Doherty and Davidson 2010).

While I draw on ideas from discursive (as well as cognitive) psychology, I also side with Manin and other deliberative democrats (such as Cohen 2007: 222) to the extent that deliberation is primarily goal-oriented: deciding 'what to do' in light of reasons. The deliberative person, then, ideally, interrogates their own and others' reasoning with a view to finding the 'best' way forward – even where the truth of the situation is that it is not possible to produce a definitive argument for any particular course of action. They are aware of and accept the different perspectives that are collectively deemed legitimate – a form of meta-consensus (Dryzek and Niemeyer 2006) – even those that might simultaneously exist in tension with each other. These competing arguments might even be internal to the individual.

Take, for example, the classic tension between a citizen and a consumer perspective regularly cited in the literature, particularly in relation to environmental issues such as climate change (Sagoff 1988; Miller 1992; Keat 1994). However, rather than being a predetermined consumer–citizen frame, for discursive psychologists, these kinds of orientation are formed in context. Although observable discourses may well reflect consumer–citizen dimensions, these 'positions' are ultimately discursively constructed. But, importantly, they can also be reconstructed (and reframed) during deliberative encounters.

The effect of truth-seeking

When viewed through the lens of these psychological processes, deliberation should, and indeed appears to, involve: a) the acknowledgement of relevant issue dimensions (meta-consensus); b) the reconciliation and/or synthesis of competing discourses, as far as possible; c) the (active) exercise of choice pertaining to important goals and epistemic foundations for a decision; and d) the intersubjective translation of these discourses/inner states into coherent and consistent preference positions that are open to updating in light of further information and/or reflection (Niemeyer and Dryzek 2007).

Not all tensions between discourses are reconcilable (Davies and Harré 1990); for example, one cannot always simultaneously reconcile self-interest with the common good. But both can, and do, co-exist: the utility-maximiser keeps an eye on the price of bananas, while the citizen simultaneously questions the fairness of the trading conditions under which the bananas were exported from the developing country of origin and, indeed, whether these considerations are important. However, it is important, from a deliberative point of view, to be explicitly aware of these tensions and make a conscious choice between them (Elster 1983: 17–18). The exercise conforms to Manin's ideal of deliberative legitimacy as well as to a deeper form of free agency (Watson 1975). To be sure, there are limits to what will be possible, or even necessary, in terms of truth-seeking, depending on the context and conditions of a particular decision.

The conditions for truth-seeking: individual or group deliberation?

Goodin (2000) suggests that the reflective component of deliberation offers a way around the problem of scale in deliberative democracy. The experimental evidence is very mixed (Goodin and Niemeyer 2003; Eveland and Thomson 2006; Muhlberger and Weber 2006), as is the case with many questions relating to deliberative democracy, precisely because there are so many factors that interact to contribute to a particular outcome: hence the need for systems-thinking. However, it is quite probable that the tendency of participants to reflect on political issues as observed in mini-public deliberation is much more difficult to achieve in the wider public context. On balance, while it certainly seems that deliberative forms of reflection by isolated individuals that would be acceptable to Goodin are possible, it does seem much more likely to happen within the group (*see* Niemeyer 2012a).

An important condition for truth-seeking involves the motivation to reflect on what is the best course of action. Where does this motivation come from? Mini-publics can create conditions in which the deliberating group develops these truth-seeking norms as a common cause (Batalha *et al.* 2012). [14] Goodin and Niemeyer (2003) concede that, although deliberation might begin before formal talk, it is the prospect of group discussion – along with the group norm – that provides the motivation for reflection. There is, then, a question about the extent that it is possible to develop these norms in mass settings, at least on a short time-scale.

Truth-seeking and scarce cognitive resources

And even with the best will in the world, the ideal of the truth-seeking deliberative person may be difficult to find beyond specific settings – although, so, too, is the ultimate rational utility-maximiser described by economic theory (for example, Kahneman *et al.* 1982). Both the economic person and the deliberative person face limitations due to scarce resources. [15] The average consumer cannot acquire all relevant 'perfect information', just as the average citizen cannot devote the time and attention needed to achieve a thorough comprehension of many issues (Warren 1996; Bohman 1999, cited in MacKenzie and Warren 2012: 97). [16]

---

14. Moreover, there does appear to be something very liberating about the experience, with the vast majority of participants expressing considerable pleasure in having been involved. Although in some cases, depending on design, there is a danger that mini-publics, can fail to move beyond the motivational stage and stop short of actually engaging in deep reflection, thus turning into a large 'group hug' (Curato and Niemeyer 2012).

15. The scarcity question is one taken seriously by Mackenzie and Warren (2012) in their formulation of the role mini-publics could play in deliberative systems – a theme to which I will return.

16. The challenge is notionally greater for the deliberative person because the strategy of consumer satisficing is not available. Because the deliberative decision also involves recognition of discourses that involve different ends, the problem is not simply one of optimisation; there is a need to consider ethical dimensions, such as justice, in discursively framing the nature of the issue and determining the best course of action.

Cognitive scarcity can be reduced to the extent that there are trusted sources of information available to citizens to enable them to act 'as if they had all the available information' (Page and Shapiro 1992; *see also* Lupia 1994). There may even be mechanisms that help citizens to decide when they need to deploy more resources to the issue at hand (MacKenzie and Warren 2012). This approach, which is consistent with the idea of division of labour in deliberative systems (Christiano 2012; Chambers 2012), is also consistent with the idea of the truth-seeking deliberative person making these higher-order judgements.

And the deliberative person does not need to be 'rational' in the classical sense. There is a role for emotions in decision-making, particularly in respect of political decisions in which there is a normative component (Etzioni 1988). And emotions can be relied on under certain conditions (Scherer 2011). The important thing is that the truth-seeking deliberative person judges the information that is becoming available with an open mind; rather than passively inducting information that comfortably fits with their pre-existing position, biases and fears, which could contribute to the possibility of pathologies of deliberation (Stokes 1998).

Context and the deliberative person

The role of context in influencing the way in which individuals make decisions, and their emotional foundations, is well established in economics and is also well known to social psychologists (for example, Schwartz 1977). This is also true in respect to discursive psychology, where the very formation of meaning can be contextual (Harré, Moghaddam *et al.* 2009; Davies and Harré 1990). The behaviour invoked within a facilitated mini-public will be very different to other political situations. Thus, a model of the deliberative person must take into account the role of context and whether maintaining deliberative quality is possible when moving from one context to the other.

I have already mentioned the context of the group as an important feature of mini-public deliberation, which appears to help produce a deliberative group norm (Batalha, Niemeyer *et al.* 2012). This does not appear to be the case for online discussion, which could well provide the counter-example to a context in which good deliberation can be achieved. While the internet is inclusive, and increases the capacity to access arguments (for example, Deuze 2006), the overall effect is to exacerbate deliberative pathologies. The mechanisms include information-overload; a tendency to short-cut deliberation by seeking out information reaffirming an existing position via confirmation bias (Kaye and Johnson 2002; Kim 2009) and partisan selective exposure (Stroud 2010) or enclave thinking (Sunstein 2007). This effect is exacerbated by the nature of the internet, which is populated by dissociated, anonymous individuals, communicating (at best) in sequence (Noveck 2009; Coleman and Blumler 2009).[17] There is a case for

---

17. Although the robust nature of online debate may, arguably, reflect the necessarily frank nature of political discourse (Papacharissi 2004), there is less evidence that the propagation of arguments

harnessing the inclusive power of online participation in a deliberative system, and its information delivery, but not for its deliberative quality, given the nature of the online experience.

In the non-online world, the role of context in the form of 'space' in democratic functioning is well described by Parkinson (2012). Bearing in mind an understanding of the other features of the deliberative system and the deliberative person, achieving scaling-up can be, in part, a matter of providing forums that promote meaningful citizen deliberation. The physical nature of this space is beyond the scope of this chapter but it does relate to a wider institutional question of the incentives that structure the political behaviour of citizens and the possibilities for mass deliberation.

Institutions

There has already been a good deal written about mini-publics and institutionalising deliberation, most notably by Smith (2001; 2009) and Fung (2003). But from a systems perspective the question goes well beyond mini-publics, to include established laws and practices that directly or indirectly facilitate scaling up. These settings can influence the kind of deliberative (or truth-seeking) behaviour described above in mass-publics and the potential role for mini-publics in scaling up.

Certainly the institutional context seems to count when it comes to public deliberation – along with culture (Bächtiger and Hangartner 2011); Sass and Dryzek forthcoming (2014)). For example, it seems more likely to motivate deliberation in settings where there are high levels of social interaction and social capital – such as in regional northern areas in Italy (Putnam *et al.* 1993). This contrasts with Australia, where the very idea of a citizens' assembly to address climate change was widely ridiculed. A good part of the reason for this is the dominance of the idea of representative democracy and of the political role of citizens being limited to voting (Boswell *et al.* 2013). By contrast, the very idea of a small-scale deliberative event in the Valsamoggia region near Bologna, Italy – where there is a strong connection between politics and the community – captured the public imagination (Niemeyer *et al.* 2012).

There are all kinds of possible links between institutional settings and both the deliberative behaviour of citizens and the wider qualities of the deliberative system, as well as internal feedbacks. One is between the quality of parliamentary debate – which is related to the structure of the parliament (Steiner *et al.* 2004) – and wider public discourse.[18] Although it needs to be investigated, the relationship probably goes in both directions, involving feedback, where better public debate improves parliamentary debate and visa versa. A similar interaction occurs with

---

is translating into reflection regarding competing perspectives (Black *et al.* 2011).

18. For example, in Australia a link has been suggested between the parliamentary debate on climate change and the public debate (Niemeyer 2013; Boswell *et al.* 2013).

mass media, where the market meets public demand for quality journalism. This improves the provision of a trusted (and trustworthy) source of information and, in turn, the deliberativeness of the system (Moy and Gastil 2006).

This observation strongly suggests that the potential for scaling up deliberation depends, at least in part, on institutional, cultural (and indeed technological) settings that take some time to develop. It is highly unlikely that the commissioning of a few isolated mini-publics in a particular constituency is going to produce any significant – or, perhaps even – effect on public discussion, let alone facilitate the development of deliberative capacity, particularly where existing institutional settings are hostile to the idea. But, given the right circumstances – such as a concerted effort to institutionalise the use of mini-publics so that the rest of the public takes them seriously – they might be harnessed as deliberation-making and capacity-building machines. How these circumstances come about is beyond the scope of this discussion but it is possible to ascribe some tentative modes of scaling up and the role of mini-publics in this process, albeit with caution.

Implications for scaling up: What can mini-publics contribute?

In terms of what is both desirable and possible for public deliberation, I have argued that it should, ideally, result in a situation in which citizens are aware of the relevant dimensions of an issue and of their own underlying interests and beliefs as well as potential internal conflicts and biases. While truth-seeking behaviour has been idealised, at a minimum they are able to deal with manipulative arguments that potentially play into their bias, even against their own interest. The deliberative system can involve specialisation in the production and synthesis of knowledge but it should at least enable the citizen to make decisions 'as if they had all the relevant information'. And, ideally, the system is characterised by institutional settings that provide incentives, or at least the conditions, for engaging in deliberative truth-seeking.

On the face of it, scaling up appears to pose a considerable challenge. However, there is some wiggle room, particularly when we accept a more constructive role for cognitive short-cuts under certain conditions and we break the process of deliberation into a supply-side and a demand-side.

In terms of the supply (propagation) side, mini-publics can play a role in the market of ideas, 'laundering' arguments for consumption by the wider public, with a corresponding impact on laundering the resulting preferences, albeit via a different mechanism to Goodin's (1986). On the demand (reflective) side, while deliberation does work best in groups, it is at least possible to achieve in a distributed system under the right circumstances (Mercier and Landemore 2012). At the very least, deliberativeness *can* be improved. It is also possible, over a longer period, to improve truth-seeking by creating the incentives to do so or at least reducing the 'transaction costs' associated with acquiring trustworthy information/accessing discourses. Below I explore how mini-publics might contribute to this process.

Mini-publics as deliberative nodes: Propagating and regulating the supply of arguments

The possibilities for scaling up are clearer in terms of the propagation perspective than that for reflection. It is much easier to regulate or facilitate the reproduction of discourses in the public sphere. This is precisely what already occurs in the political system via mass media, interest-group representation and so on.[19] This mechanism would potentially facilitate the outcomes observed in deliberation, via exposure to new arguments.

However, there are two problems with viewing the challenge of a deliberative system primarily through the lens of a 'market of ideas'. The observation of confutation during mini-public deliberation demonstrates that exposure to arguments alone – even a diversity of arguments (*cf.,* Sunstein 2000) – does not ensure deliberative outcomes, particularly where the demands on cognition are high: there will always be alluring arguments that are intuitively or emotionally appealing but misrepresentative of what the individual might really want.

Mini-publics as argument-regulators

From a supply-side point of view, it might be possible to find ways to regulate manipulatory (symbolic) arguments, possibly by subjecting them to thorough scrutiny at source. However, if anything, there is a decreasing capacity in the public sphere to regulate arguments, particularly via media outlets (Kovach and Rosenstiel 2001).

Can mini-publics play a role in regulating the propagation of arguments? One tantalising possibility is Mackenzie and Warren's (2012) 'trust-based' vehicle for inducing public-sphere transformation, in which mini-publics act as trusted information proxies. Their hypothesis, which is built on evidence from the British Columbia Citizens' Assembly, suggests the public will trust fellow citizens who have participated in deliberation and confer legitimacy on them because they are people 'like them'. The emphasis in this example is in trust on the outcomes and information. By contrast, I do not emphasise information *per se*. More important are the resulting arguments (or discourses involving both affective and factual components) – much as jurisprudence emphasises the reasons offered by judges for rulings in law, but with greater transparency in relation to the volitional component (Niemeyer 2011a).

Mini-publics can act as a regulator of information in the public sphere by doing the hard work of sorting through arguments and providing reasons for the resulting positions to the remainder of the public – and in terms understood by them. Because mini-publics, ideally, reflect the greater population, both the underlying reasoning and the transmitted values are more likely to reflect 'community values' than those specific to a particular profession (such as journalism) or interest group. Moreover,

---

19. Indeed, one emphasis of (an early version of) deliberative systems appears to be on this very process of bringing arguments to bear on important public issues (Mansbridge *et al.* 2011).

mini-publics can help to publicise views that do not ordinarily find a voice among the principal political actors, thus contributing to discursive legitimacy (Dryzek 2001) by making public those arguments that have been identified by their peers.

Mini-publics as knowledge-shapers

These arguments that are transmitted by mini-publics will sometimes include the synthesis of highly specialised knowledge. Unlike most citizens, mini-public participants (ideally) have the time, resources and incentive to work closely with experts in sifting the 'wheat from the chaff' when it comes to relevant information and can broker that knowledge to their peers (*see also* MacKenzie and Warren 2012). The process can also have a long-term benefit for the system of production of knowledge in a manner similar to that identified by Christiano (2012), where interaction with citizens in mini-publics can help shape a sense of what is important for the scientific agenda in a manner not possible via mass-publics, as well as improving the skills of experts as public communicators of science. The way in which knowledge-production is shaped should be more responsive to the wider public, improving the overall deliberative quality of the system via the provision of improved, trustworthy and accessible, information.

Mini-publics as myth-avoiders and myth-busters

A deliberative system that utilises mini-publics to distil, synthesise and shape information for public consumption is particularly important when issues are at their early stages – they can act as an 'anticipatory public' (MacKenzie and Warren 2012). Doing so could forestall the most manipulative uses of public discourse, as described earlier under the rubric of 'symbolic politics'. But for those issues where the public will has been distorted, mini-publics can play a role of confutation, by exposing and dispelling symbolically powerful myths that subvert democratic will-formation (Niemeyer 2011a).

Limits to supply-side thinking

The supply (and acceptance) of arguments to the public sphere gets us part-way to scaling up, but is of little use where non-truth-seeking modes of thinking continue to operate. The propagative (supply-side) role of mini-publics would still need to operate alongside other existing avenues of information and argumentation in the public sphere. No deliberative democrat would advocate a Soviet-style censorship, no matter how well intended. Citizens would thus need to exercise some form of truth-seeking as part of any deliberative system, even if mini-publics effectively reduce the cost of accessing all the relevant arguments.

Mini-publics as capacity-building nodes: Developing the deliberative citizen

The reflective (demand) side of public deliberation is far more difficult to modify than the supply-side. And it is a longer-term goal, involving the process of human development in social (and political context) (Doheny and O'Neill 2010; Griffin 2011). However, there are ways in which it is conceivable that mini-publics could play a role in developing individual-level deliberative capacity.

Griffin (2011) cites Vygotsky's account of childhood development to suggest a mechanism for the development of deliberative minds in which the 'best characteristics' of contemporary culture are held up and exemplified. If mini-publics are an exemplar of deliberation in contemporary politics, then it is plausible that increasing their formal status in political systems will have longer-term developmental implications. Moreover, there is an argument that experiencing mini-public deliberation first hand has an impact beyond the event itself (Doheny and O'Neill 2010; Gastil *et al.* 2008) although, the evidence is somewhat mixed, which is not surprising in light of the above discussion about the role of context.

In a similar way to how our everyday experience with the market teaches us to be attentive to value in our consumption choices and move toward an approximation of the ideal of the economic person in that particular context, exposure to the requisites for good mini-public deliberation (such as truth-seeking and avoiding *ad hominem* attacks) could help citizens to better approximate deliberative behaviour in a wider political context. Moreover, a deliberative system that inculcates these norms in political behaviour is also one that is more likely to avoid the subversion of the public will. Just as good consumers are wary of being duped by dodgy vendors, good deliberative citizens avoid being duped by manipulative arguments.

However, the consumer has a built-in incentive to find the best way to use limited resources, whereas the political citizen – at least putatively – does not (Downs 1957). And the problem is even greater as the scale of the democratic system increases. In both cases, demand can be 'manufactured': in economics to induce consumption (Galbraith 1979) and, more positively, in deliberation to promote truth-seeking behaviour. One possibility is that widespread participation in mini-publics can have a long-term effect in improving the civic skills of participants, (Hall *et al.* 2011) although (yet again) the evidence is mixed due to context of the deliberative experience in terms of duration, facilitation, issue topic and so on.

The role of status of mini-publics in scaling up

However, for any of these mechanisms to work, mini-publics would need to achieve considerable democratic status, well beyond what is ordinarily the case thus far (Goodin and Dryzek 2006; Dryzek *et al.* 2009). When given such status, provided that they are applied at an early stage of an issue, mini-publics can potentially play a constructive role in building public discourses that facilitate, rather than manipulate the development of the public will. However, there is, of course, a risk that raising the stakes of mini-publics also invites greater corruption in the way that they are used –for example, they could be commissioned to endorse and legitimise a predetermined decision. Thus, the way in which mini-publics are institutionalised is critically important and I have already discussed the need to not treat them as single-shot affairs but rather to conduct multiple events on the same or overlapping issues.

Thus, the success of mini-publics in contributing to scaling up is not certain, dependent as it is on a wide variety of factors, including they way they are encountered in the prevailing set of political circumstances. However it is just possible that, given a chance and in the right settings, mini-publics might play a role that approximates authentic deliberation. In doing so, mini-publics might help to nudge politics in a more deliberative direction (*cf.,* John *et al.* 2009).

Conclusion

Achieving a deliberative system that enhances citizens' exposure to a diversity of arguments as well as developing their capacity to work through those arguments and arrive at positions that reflect their underlying will (truth-seeking) is an important, if challenging, task. The observation of mini-public deliberation suggests that mini-publics can play a role in transforming the public sphere in a deliberative direction. On the supply side, mini-publics can help to sort the 'wheat from the chaff' and identify legitimate arguments. On the demand side, it is ultimately up to citizens whether to take the lead from mini-publics. Under the right conditions, in the right institutional and cultural context and when mini-publics are thought of as exemplary forms of political reasoning by their peers, they have the potential to contribute to a longer-term transformation of mass public deliberation. It is a relatively open question whether this would actually happen, but it is certainly worth exploring further.

References

Bächtiger, A. 'Contestatory deliberation', paper presented at Epistemic Democracy Conference, Yale University, 2011.

Bächtiger, A. and Hangartner, D. 'Institutions, culture, and deliberative ideals: A theoretical and empirical inquiry', paper presented at Annual Meeting of the American Political Science Association, Chicago, 2011.

Bächtiger, A., Niemeyer, S., Neblo, M., Steenbergen, M. R. and Steiner, J. (2010) 'Disentangling diversity in deliberative democracy: competing theories, their empirical blind-spots, and complementarities', *Journal of Political Philosophy* 18 (1): 32–63.

Barabas, J. (2004) 'How deliberation affects policy opinions', *American Political Science Review* 98(4): 687–701.

Batalha, L., Niemeyer, S. J., Curato, N. and Dryzek, J. S. (2012)'Group dynamics and deliberative processes: affective and cognitive aspects', paper presented at Annual Scientific Meeting of the International Society of Political Psychology, Chicago, IL, 6–9 July 2012.

Bizer, G. Y., Krosnick, J. A., Holbrook, A. L., Wheeler, S. C., Rucker, D. D. and Petty, R. E. (2002) 'The impact of personality on cognitive, behavioral, and affective political processes: the effects of need to evaluate', *Journal of Personality* 72 (5): 995–1027.

Black, L. W., Welser, H. T., Cosley, D. and DeGroot, J. M. (2011) 'Self-governance through group discussion in Wikipedia: measuring deliberation in online groups', *Small Group Research* 42 (5): 595–634.

Bohman, J. (1999) 'Democracy as inquiry, inquiry as democratic: pragmatism, social science, and the cognitive division of labor', *American Journal of Political Science* 43 (2): 590–607.

— (2012) 'Representation in the deliberative system', in J. Parkinson and J. J. Mansbridge (eds), *Deliberative Systems: Deliberative democracy at the large scale*, Cambridge: Cambridge University Press, pp. 72–94.

Boswell, J., Niemeyer, S. J. and Hendricks, C. M. (2013) 'Julia Gillard's citizens' assembly proposal for Australia: a deliberative democratic analysis', *Australian Journal of Political Science* 48 (2): 164–78.

Cacioppo, J. T. and Petty, R. E. (1982) 'The need for cognition', *Journal of Personality and Social Psychology* 42 (1): 116–31.

Chambers, S. (2009) 'Rhetoric and the public sphere: has deliberative democracy abandoned mass democracy?', *Political Theory* 20 (3): 323–50.

— (2012) 'Deliberation and mass democracy', in J. Parkinson and J. J. Mansbridge (eds), *Deliberative Systems: Deliberative democracy at the large scale*, Cambridge: Cambridge University Press, pp. 52–71.

Christiano, T. (2012) 'Deliberation among experts and citizens', in J. Parkinson and J. J. Mansbridge (eds), *Deliberative Systems: Deliberative democracy at the large scale*, Cambridge: Cambridge University Press, pp. 27–51.

Cohen, J. (1997) 'Deliberation and democratic legitimacy', in J. Bohman and W. Rehg (eds), *Deliberative Democracy: Essays on reason and politics*, Cambridge, MA: MIT Press.

—   (2007) 'Deliberative democracy', in S. W. Rosenberg (ed.), *Deliberation, Participation and Democracy: Can the people govern?*, Basingstoke: Palgrave Macmillan.

Coleman, S. and Blumler, J. G. (2009) *The Internet and Democratic Citizenship: Theory, practice and policy*, Cambridge and New York: Cambridge University Press.

Curato, N. and Niemeyer, S. J. 'Appreciative and contestatory inquiry in deliberative forums: can group hugs be dangerous?' paper presented at the conference Deliberative Democracy in Action, Åbo Akademi University, June 2012.

Curato, N., Niemeyer, S. J. and Dryzek, J. S. (2013) 'Appreciative and contestatory inquiry in deliberative forums: can group hugs be dangerous?', *Critical Policy Studies* 7 (1): 1–17.

Dahl, R. A. (1993) 'Finding competent citizens: Improving democracy', *Current* (351): 23–30.

Davies, B. and Harré, R. (1990) 'Positioning: the discursive production of selves', *Journal for the Theory of Social Behaviour* 20 (1): 43–63.

Deuze, M. (2006) 'Ethnic media, community media and participatory culture', *Journalism* 7: 262–80.

Doheny, S. and O'Neill, C. (2010) 'Becoming deliberative citizens: the moral learning process of the citizen juror', *Political Studies* 58 (4): 630–48.

Downs, A. (1957) *An Economic Theory of Democracy*, New York: Harper & Row.

Dryzek, J. S. (2001) 'Legitimacy and economy in deliberative democracy', *Political Theory* 29 (5): 651–69.

—   (2009) 'Democratization as deliberative capacity building', *Comparative Political Studies* 42 (11): 1379–402.

—   (2010) 'Rhetoric in democracy: a systematic appreciation', *Political Theory* 38 (3): 319–39.

Dryzek, J. S., Goodin, R. E., Tucker, A. and Reber, B. (2009) 'Promethean elites encounter precautionary publics: the case of GM foods', *Science, Technology and Human Values* 34 (3): 263–88.

Dryzek, J. S. and Niemeyer, S. J. (2006) 'Reconciling pluralism and consensus as political ideals', *American Journal of Political Science* 50(3): 634–49.

Edelman, M. J. (1985) *The Symbolic Uses of Politics*, Urbana: Univ. of Ill. Press.

Eemeren, F. H. v. and Grootendorst, R. (1984) *Speech Acts in Argumentative Discussions: A theoretical model for the analysis of discussions directed towards solving conflicts of opinion*, Dordrecht, Holland; Cinnaminson, USA: Foris Publications.

Elster, J. (1983) *Sour Grapes: Studies in the subversion of rationality*, Cambridge: Cambridge University Press.

Etzioni, A. (1988) 'Normative-affective factors: toward a new decision-making model', *Journal of Economic Psychology* 9 (2): 125–50.

Eveland, W. P. and Thomson, T. (2006) 'Is it talking, thinking, or both? A lagged dependent variable model of discussion effects on political knowledge', *Journal of Communication* 56 (3): 523–42.

Fung, A. (2003) 'Recipes for public spheres: eight institutional design choices and their consequences', *Journal of Political Philosophy* 11 (3): 338–67.

Galbraith, J. K. (1979) *The New Industrial State*, Boston: Houghton Mifflin.

Gastil, J., Black, L. W., Deess, E. P. and Leighter, J. (2008) 'From group member to democratic citizen: how deliberating with fellow jurors reshapes civic attitudes', *Human Communication Research* 34: 137–69.

Goodin, R. E. (1986) 'Laundering preferences', in J. Elster and A. Hylland (eds), *Foundations of Social Choice Theory*, Cambridge: Cambridge University Press, pp. 75–102.

— (2000) 'Democratic deliberation within', *Philosophy and Public Affairs* 29 (1): 81–109.

— (2002) *Reflective Democracy*, Oxford: Oxford University Press.

— (2005) 'Sequencing deliberative moments', *Acta Politica* 40 (2): 182–96.

Goodin, R. E. and Dryzek, J. S. (2006) 'Deliberative impacts: the macro-political uptake of mini-publics', *Politics & Society* 34: 219–44.

Goodin, R. E. and Niemeyer, S. J. (2003) 'When does deliberation begin? Internal reflection versus public discussion in deliberative democracy', *Political Studies* 51 (4): 627–49.

Griffin, M. (2011) 'Developing deliberative minds: Piaget, Vygotsky and the deliberative democratic citizen', *Journal of Public Deliberation* 7 (1): article 2.

Habermas, J. (1998) 'What is universal pragmatics?', in M. Cooke (ed.), *On the Pragmatics of Communication*, Massachusetts: MIT Press.

Hall, T. E., Wilsony, P. and Newman, J. (2011) 'Evaluating the short- and long-term effects of a modified Deliberative Poll on Idahoans' attitudes and civic engagement related to energy options', *Journal of Public Deliberation* 7 (1): article 6.

Harré, R., Moghaddam, F. M., Cairnie, T. P., Rothbart, D. and Sabat, S. R. (2009) 'Recent advances in positioning theory', *Theory & Psychology* 19 (1): 5–31.

Hastie, R. and Park, B. (1986) 'The relationship between memory and judgement depends on whether the judgement task is memory-based or on-line', *Psychological Review* 93 (3): 258–68.

Hendriks, C. M. (2006) 'Integrated deliberation: reconciling civil society's dual role in deliberative democracy', *Political Studies* 54: 486–508.

Hibbing, J. R. and Theiss-Morse, E. (2002) *Stealth Democracy: Americans' beliefs about how government should work*, New York and Cambridge: Cambridge University Press.

John, P., Smith, G. and Stoker, G. (2009) 'Nudge nudge, think think: two strategies for changing civic behaviour', *Political Quarterly* 80 (3): 361–70.

Kahneman, D. (2011) *Thinking Fast and Slow*, London: Allen Lane.

Kahneman, D., Slovic, P. and Tversky, A. (1982) *Judgement under Uncertainty: Heuristics and biases*, Cambridge and New York: Cambridge University Press.

Kaye, B. K. and Johnson, T. J. (2002) 'Online and in the know: uses and gratifications of the web for political information', *Journal of Broadcasting & Electronic Media* 46 (1): 54–71.

Keat, R. (1994) 'Citizens, consumers and the environment: reflections on "The Economy of the Earth"', *Environmental Values* 2: 333–49.

Kim, Y. M. (2009) 'Issue publics in the new information environment: selectivity, domain specificity, and extremity', *Communication Research* 36 (2): 254–84.

Kovach, B. and Rosenstiel, T. (2001) *The Elements of Journalism: What newspeople should know and the public should expect*, New York: Three Rivers Press.

Lupia, A. (1994) 'Shortcuts versus encyclopedias: information and voting behaviour in California insurance reform elections', *American Political Science Review* 88 (1): 63–76.

MacKenzie, M. K. and Warren, M. E. (2012) 'Two trust-based uses of mini-publics in democratic systems', in J. Parkinson and J. J. Mansbridge (eds), *Deliberative Systems: Deliberative democracy at the large scale*, Cambridge: Cambridge University Press, pp. 95–124.

Manin, B. (1987) 'On legitimacy and political deliberation', *Political Theory* 15 (3): 338–68.

Mansbridge, J. J. (1999) 'Everyday talk in the deliberative system', in S. Macedo (ed.), *Deliberative Politics: Essays on democracy and disagreement*, New York: Oxford University Press, pp. 211–39.

Mansbridge, J., Bohman, J., Chambers, C., Christiano, T., Fung, A., Parkinson, J., Thompson, D. and Warren, M. 'A systemic approach to deliberative democracy', paper presented in workshop Frontiers in Deliberative Democracy at ECPR Joint Sessions, St Gallen, 2011.

Mansbridge, J. J., Bohman, J., Chambers, S., Fung, A., Parkinson, J., Thompson, D. and Warren, M. (2012) 'A systemic approach to deliberative democracy', in J. Parkinson and J. J. Mansbridge (eds), *Deliberative Systems: Deliberative democracy at the large scale*, Cambridge: Cambridge University Press, pp. 1–26.

Menkel-Meadow, C. (2011) 'Scaling up deliberative democracy as dispute resolution in healthcare reform: a work in progress', *Law and Contemporary Problems* 74 (1): 1–30.

Mercier, H. and Landemore, H. E. (2012) 'Reasoning is for arguing: understanding the successes and failures of deliberation', *Political Psychology* 33 (2): 243–58.

Miller, D. Y. (1992) 'Deliberative democracy and social choice', *Political Studies* 40 (special issue): 54–67.

Morrell, M. E. (2005) 'Deliberation, democratic decision-making and internal political efficacy', *Political Behavior* 27 (1): 49–69.

Moy, P. and Gastil, J. (2006) 'Predicting deliberative conversation: the impact of discussion networks, media use, and political cognitions', *Political Communication* 23 (4): 443–60.

Muhlberger, P. and Weber, L. M. (2006) 'Lessons from the Virtual Agora project: the effects of agency, identity, information, and deliberation on political knowledge', *Journal of Public Deliberation* 2 (1): 1–37.

Neblo, M. A., Esterling, K. M., Kennedy, R. P., Lazer, D. M. L. and Sokhey, A. E. (2010) 'Who wants to deliberate—and why?', *American Political Science Review* 104: 566–83.

Nickerson, R. S. (1998) 'Confirmation bias: a ubiquitous phenomenon in many guises', *Review of General Psychology* 2 (2): 175–220.

Niemeyer, S. J. (2004) 'Deliberation in the wilderness: displacing symbolic politics', *Environmental Politics* 13 (2): 347–72.

— (2011a) 'The emancipatory effect of deliberation: empirical lessons from mini-publics', *Politics and Society* 39 (1): 103–40.

— (2011b) 'Intersubjective consistency in deliberative outcomes', in J. Font, D. della Porta and Y. Sintomer (eds) *Methodological Challenges in Participation Research*, Cordoba.

— (2011c) 'Intersubjective reasoning and the formation of metaconsensus', in J. Yearwood and A. Stranieri (eds), *Technologies for Supporting Reasoning Communities and Collaborative Decision Making: Cooperative approaches*, Hershey, PA: IGI Global, pp. 18–37.

— (2012a) 'Building a deliberative system for earth systems governance: lessons from and possibilities for mini-publics', paper presented at the Lund Conference on Earth Systems Governance, Lund, 2012.

— (2012b) 'Building the foundations of deliberative democracy: the deliberative person', working paper, Centre for Deliberative Democracy and Global Governance, The Australian National University, Canberra.

— (2013) 'Democracy and climate change: what can deliberative democracy contribute?', *Australian Journal of Politics and History* 59 (3): 430–49.

Niemeyer, S. J. and Dryzek, J. S. (2007) 'The ends of deliberation: metaconsensus and intersubjective rationality as deliberative ideals', *Swiss Political Science Review* 13 (4): 497–526.

Niemeyer, S. J., Felicetti, A. and Ruggero, O. D (2012) 'Preliminary Report: Valsamoggia Citizens Initiative Review', Centre for Deliberative Democracy and Global Governance, The Australian National University, Canberra.

Noveck, B. S. (2009) *Wiki Government: How technology can make government better democracy stronger and citizens more powerful*, Washington, DC: Brookings Institution Press.

O'Doherty, K. C. and Davidson, H. J. (2010) 'Subject positioning and deliberative democracy: understanding social processes underlying deliberation', *Journal for the Theory of Social Behaviour* 40 (2): 224–45.

Page, B. I. and Shapiro, R. Y. (1992) 'The rational public: fifty years of trends in Americans' policy preferences', *American Politics and Political Economy Series*, Chicago, University of Chicago Press.

Papacharissi, Z. (2004) 'Democracy online: civility, politeness, and the democratic potential of online political discussion groups', *New Media & Society* 6 (2): 259–83.

Parkinson, J. (2006) *Deliberating in the Real World: Problems of legitimacy in democracy*, Oxford: Oxford University Press.

—   (2012) *Democracy and Public Space: The physical sites of democratic performance*, Oxford: Oxford University Press.

Parkinson, J. and Mansbridge, J. J. (2012) *Deliberative Systems: Deliberative democracy at the large scale*, Cambridge: Cambridge University Press.

Pateman, C. (2012) 'Participatory democracy revisited', *Perspectives on Politics* 10 (1): 7–19.

Petty, R. E. and Cacioppo, J. T. (1984) 'The effects of involvement on responses to argument quantity and quality: central and peripheral routes to persuasion', *Journal of Personality and Social Psychology* 46: 69–81.

—   (1986) *Communication and Persuasion: Central and peripheral routes to attitude change*, New York: Springer-Verlag.

Putnam, R. D., Leonardi, R. and Nanetti, R. (1993) *Making Democracy Work: Civic traditions in modern Italy'*, Princeton, NJ: Princeton University Press.

Rawls, J. (1997) 'The idea of public reason revisited', *University of Chicago Law Review* 94: 765–807.

Redlawsk, D. P. (2002) 'Hot cognition or cool consideration? Testing the effects of motivated reasoning on political decision making', *The Journal of Politics* 64: 1021–44.

Rosenberg, S. W. (2002) *The Not So Common Sense: Differences in how people judge social and political life*, New Haven, CT and London: Yale University Press.

—   (2007) 'Rethinking democratic deliberation: the limits and potential of citizen participation', *Polity* 39: 335–60.

Sagoff, M. (1988) *The Economy of the Earth: Philosophy, law and the environment*, Cambridge: Cambridge University Press.

Sass, J. and Dryzek, J. S. (forthcoming 2014) 'Deliberative cultures', *Political Theory.*

Scherer, K. R. (2011) 'On the rationality of emotions: or, when are emotions rational?', *Social Science Information* 50 (3–4): 330–50.

Schumpeter, J. (1976[1943]) *Capitalism, Socialism and Democracy*, London: Allen and Unwin.

Schwartz, S. H. (1977) 'Normative influences on altruism', *Advances in Experimental Psychology*, 10: 221–75.

Smith, G. (2001) 'Taking deliberation seriously: institutional design and green politics', *Environmental Politics* 10 (3): 72–93.

—   (2009) *Democratic Innovations: Designing institutions for citizen participation*, Cambridge: Cambridge University Press.

Somin, I. (1998) 'Voter ignorance and the democratic ideal', *Critical Review* 12 (4): 413–58.

Steiner, J. (2008) 'Concept stretching: the case of deliberation', *European Political Science* 7 (2): 186–90.

Steiner, J., Bächtiger, A., Spörndli, M. and Steenbergen, M. R. (2004) *Deliberative Politics in Action: Analyzing parliamentary discourse*, Cambridge, UK and New York: Cambridge University Press.

Stokes, S. C. (1998) 'Pathologies of deliberation', in J. Elster, *Deliberative Democracy*, London and New York: Cambridge University Press, pp., 123–39.

Stroud, N. J. (2010) 'Polarization and partisan selective exposure', *Journal of Communication* 60 (3): 556–76.

Sunstein, C. R. (2000) 'Deliberative trouble? Why groups go to extremes', *Yale Law Journal* 110 (1): 71–119.

—— (2007) *Republic.com 2.0*, Princeton: Princeton University Press.

Tetlock, P. E. (1998) 'The ever-shifting psychological foundations of democratic theory: do citizens have the right stuff?', *Critical Review* 12 (4): 545.

Thompson, D. F. (2008) 'Deliberative democratic theory and empirical political science', *Annual Review of Political Science* 11: 497–520.

Warren, M. E. (1996) 'Deliberative democracy and authority', *American Political Science Review* 90 (1): 46–60.

Watson, G. (1975) 'Free agency', *The Journal of Philosophy* 62(8): 205–20.

Chapter Twelve

Deliberative Democracy and Framing Effects: Why Frames are a Problem and How Deliberative Mini-Publics Might Overcome Them

Aubin Calvert and Mark E. Warren

When democracies channel decision-making into democratically-structured deliberation, they will tend to produce decisions that are epistemically better, more ethically robust and politically more legitimate than decisions made without the benefit of deliberation. These effects follow intrinsically from deliberation, just because what defines deliberation is influence that works through reference to facts, norms and interests refined through self-reflection and justification. At least, this is the ideal that is theorised in deliberative democratic theory. The quality of deliberation in actually existing democracies, however, remains a challenge. Public discourse about important issues – from healthcare reform to crime, from abortion to climate change, from financial regulation to income inequality and from immigration to aging populations – often suffers from polarisation, inattention to evidence, thin menus of alternatives, name-calling, scapegoating and – too often – racist, ethnocentric, or other forms of speech that erode the very conditions of deliberation. Of course, to the extent that public discourse is *political*, we should expect it to have a rough-and-tumble quality. And if, however rough-and-tumble, public discourse works within deliberative systems so that the excesses of some kinds of speech are resisted, complemented or corrected by other kinds of speech, then deliberative democrats should have little cause to worry (Mansbridge *et al.* 2012).

But much public discourse may not be self-correcting – and, indeed, may undermine deliberative influence through what political psychologists call *framing effects*. Frames organise cognition by bundling claims into a framework, such that any particular claim brings with it unreflective judgements about other claims. Insofar as they are *pre-reflective*, frames undermine the autonomy of individual judgement. Insofar as they include *pre-judgements* about others, they risk undermining the status of individuals as beings who can be moved by persuasion. Both effects compromise deliberation.

Yet framing is an inevitable part of politics – deliberative or otherwise – for two reasons. First, frames make up the cognitive structures through which people can understand issues, form preferences and share a common set of references for discussing them with others. Frames are inevitable: we need them to talk and think. Second, many democratic institutions are structured in ways that incentivise frames, just because democracies crowd much conflict into speech and then structure speech competitively – into campaigns, soundbites, legislative debates, advocacy and media market appeal. Under these circumstances, adversaries will seek favourable framing effects wherever they can and use increasingly sophisticated techniques, such as focus-group testing, to find strategically effective frames.

We make two arguments in this chapter. First, by specifying the nature of framing effects from the perspective of deliberative ideals, we can separate out the generic functions of framing (which are inevitable) from three more specific kinds of framing that are problematic (and which are not inevitable). We refer to these problematic frames as *dominant, polarising* and *group-based*. Second, by specifying the kinds of threats each of these frames poses to deliberation, we can identify institutional responses. Empirical research suggests that cross-cutting conversations and exposure to heterogeneous frames reduce their effects, through a combination of frames cancelling each other out and prompting more careful reflection (Chong and Druckman 2007b: 113). Institutions that build on this finding should be able to push back against the anti-deliberative effects of frames. We focus on one institution in particular: deliberative mini-publics. Mini-publics open up possibilities for institutional design by structuring deliberation through learning, sequencing of stages, and facilitation in ways that can mitigate the anti-deliberative influence of problematic frames. If mini-publics are credibly designed, organised and publicised, their results could, at least in principle, feed back into public discourse, helping to avoid the harmful influences of problematic frames.

We proceed as follows. In the first section, we elaborate the epistemic and ethical problems frames pose for deliberative democracy. Second, we identify three kinds of frames that should be cause for concern – dominant, polarising and group-based frames – and distinguish them from more generic kinds of framing. In the third section, we ask what features of mini-publics enable them to overcome the anti-deliberative effects of framing. Fourth, we look at what mini-publics need to accomplish for each frame type and how variation in the institutional features of mini-publics might enable them to achieve these goals. We conclude with another research agenda that follows from our argument: we need to understand how mini-publics might counter the anti-deliberative effects of framing within broader deliberative systems.

The problem

Frames can be understood as 'a speaker's emphasis on a subset of potentially relevant considerations in ways that cause individuals to focus on these considerations when constructing their opinions' (Druckman 2001: 1042). Frames build on metaphors, analogies, symbols and narratives that audiences find comprehensible (Gamson and Modigliani 1989; Nelson and Kinder 1996). To some extent, frames are inevitable as a part of political strategy. For social movements, frames perform the essential tasks of identifying a problematic condition, attributions of blame, articulating alternatives and urging others to act (Benford and Snow 2000: 615). Likewise, organised interests have incentives to ensure that issues are framed in ways that support their interests and they strategically deploy soundbites, slogans, analogies and imagery to that end (Nelson *et al.* 1997). When faced with incentives to get third parties on-side with an issue, political actors use frames to ensure that the issue is interpreted in way that favour their interests. The time and resources devoted to determining the kinds of language and frames that will resonate with audiences is evidence of what political strategists know well: frames are powerful sources of influence.

Frames work 'by making new beliefs available about an issue, making certain available beliefs accessible, or making beliefs applicable or "strong" in people's evaluations' (Chong and Druckman 2007b: 111). Frames alter the weight given to different considerations (Nelson *et al.* 1997: 226) and they connect core values with decisions (Brewer 2001: 46–7). The availability, accessibility and applicability of particular beliefs influence both individual judgement and interpersonal deliberation. Brewer and Gross (2005) find, for example, that frames not only affect the direction of opinion shift but also how people construct their responses to questions: if a frame introduces a value as pertinent, participants are more likely to invoke that value in describing their own thoughts. On the one hand, they argue, this kind of effect might provide opponents with a shared frame of reference for discussing an issue. On the other hand, it may render public deliberation less rich and diverse by limiting the range of considerations likely to be introduced (Brewer and Gross 2005: 944). Frames affect not only how people *respond* to reasons but also how they formulate them. Such findings highlight the status of frames as forms of talk-based influence that operate prior to the *deliberative* influence generated by giving and responding to reasons. And, indeed, many empirical studies of framing effects are motivated by worries about their implications for citizens' ability to think and talk about policy issues and to make good choices.

We take these arguments as our starting point. We consider framing in light of the conviction in deliberative democratic theory that holds that deliberative venues have the potential to produce decisions that are better, more ethically robust, and more legitimate than those produced without deliberation. These effects follow, according to the theory, from references to facts, norms and interests embedded in claims and which are (in principle) available to participants for discursive testing for their truth, rightness and truthfulness (or sincerity) in relation to the contexts they reference. The normatively desirable effects of deliberation depend, however, upon two conditions. The first is *autonomy*: in order for persuasion to be a normatively desirable form of influence, actors should be able to give reasons for their claims that reflect their considered judgements. They should be able to justify their claims to others, based on reasons that they 'own' in the sense that they could defend them with considered reasons, in contrast (say) to repeating arguments unreflectively acquired from authorities or the media. This deliberative requirement is primarily *epistemic* – having to do with the range of considerations that can be introduced into deliberation, the weight they are given and the depth of reflection on claims. The second condition of these good deliberative effects is that participants must be *recognised* in their capacity as speakers – as potential contributors of meaningful reasons. To respond to a claim is to enact recognition of another, insofar as they are sources of claims that demand response (Warren 2006). In very much this spirit, Rawls refers to persons as 'self-authenticating sources of value claims' (Rawls 1993: 72). This requirement is primarily *ethical* – deliberative democratic ideals depend upon conditions that enable the recognitions of others as speakers, such that participants might persuade and be persuaded by one another.

Framing effects can and often do compromise these epistemic and ethical conditions for deliberation, deliberative democratic ideals. Frames affect the ways arguments are weighed. They limit the range of competing considerations actors draw on in their reasoning processes. When frames are embedded in arguments – whether through slogans, images, symbols or metaphors – they influence how claims are received and they tend to do so pre-discursively, without the benefit of reflection. In this way they compromise the *epistemic* value of deliberation. And to the extent that frames embed pre-judgements that violate mutual recognition – *prejudices* – they damage the *ethical* conditions for deliberation.

At the same time, frames are inevitable – we could not think or deliberate without them. Frames are not just an unfortunate part of political strategy; they can be an essential and inevitable part of persuasion. According to Nelson and Kinder, frames 'teach ordinary citizens how to think about and understand complex social policy problems' (1996: 1058). They 'constitute the cognitive structures by which thinking on matters of policy is organised within the minds of individual citizens' (Nelson and Kinder 1996: 1073). In this sense, frames are necessarily prior to opinion-formation on an issue or policy: they enable people to understand the problem and form preferences because, although people may not have an opinion on a specific issue or policy, they are likely to have opinions on general types of solutions to which it is linked or compared (Lau and Schlesinger 2005). Moreover, the presence of a frame in a discourse may enable deliberation. A frame that links an issue to a specific value such as equality, freedom, or compassion, for example, can provide people with common terms of reference for meaningful conversation (Brewer and Gross 2005).

So to the extent that deliberative democracy requires autonomous opinion-formation under conditions of mutual respect, we need to be able to distinguish the deliberation-supportive functions of frames from those that undermine its conditions. There are, of course, values, beliefs, facts and other potential referents of claims that are independent of frames but, as soon as they are organised into opinions and judgements, framing effects are at work. Frames may range from relatively benign aspects of cognition to outright manipulation, with most working somewhere in between. Whether strategically deployed with attention to goals, or taken up from conversation as cognitive short-cuts, frames are essential features of the discursive landscape within which deliberation takes place.

Problematic frames: Dominant, polarising and group-based

Frames are inevitable and, in many cases, indispensable elements of communication and persuasion. At the same time, they can be pathological for deliberation, either directly, by enabling strategic actors to manipulate the judgement of individuals, or indirectly, by undermining the ethical conditions for deliberation. So a key task for a theory of democratic deliberation seeking to account for frames is to establish *when* and *how* they become problematic. In order to understand the particular problems frames pose for deliberation and democratic autonomy, it is useful to return to the theory of communication that underwrites much of deliberative democratic theory. Of particular importance is the notion that an exchange of reasons can carry with it a normatively desirable form of influence – what Habermas calls 'the force of the better argument' (1984: 25).

To understand this kind of influence in a way that helps elucidate its relationship to frames takes us – like Habermas – into the pragmatics of language use. For our purposes, an especially relevant account can be found in the work of Robert Brandom (1998). Brandom's key insight is that when people use language, they make assertions (or claims to validity) that form webs of interpersonal commitments and entitlements. These webs are comprised, in part, of conditional and normative inferential relationships embedded in claims. Following this understanding of the pragmatic sources of communicative influence, we can think about the influence of frames in terms of inferential structures within which claims to validity are embedded – in particular, the conditional 'if/then' and 'should/shall' relationships that make up theoretical and practical reasoning. We can then conceive of frames as 'bundling' validity claims, such that signing on to one part of a frame – perhaps the more obviously acceptable part – *commits the hearer to a number of other beliefs and commitments and excludes still others, by virtue of its inferential structure* – that is, the set of commitment-preserving and entitlement-preserving conditional and normative relationships embedded in the frame. By virtue of their implicit status within the frame, these commitments are subject neither to competing validity claims nor to the reflexive judgement that should follow. In short, they function to bypass the testing of validity claims that enables deliberative democracy to structure influence through 'the force of the better argument.'

In the remainder of this section, we identify three types of frames, all of which undermine deliberation owing to the ways their inferential structure cause individuals to adopt commitments as a consequence of their implicit inferential structures, thus sheltering those commitments from deliberative consideration. We are, of course, ideal-typing these frames in order to highlight those features that are likely to undermine the epistemic and ethical conditions for deliberation.

Dominant frames

A dominant frame is one that functions to produce a pre-deliberative consensus, usually defining a problem as being solely of one type, or admitting only one possible solution. Regardless of the particular topic, dominant frames work primarily by committing people to a range of associated claims and excluding alternative considerations or unfamiliar solutions. In their discussion of policy metaphors, Lau and Schlesinger (2005) argue that information environments consisting of a single interpretation are likely to lead to shallow processing. In these cases, people are likely to be influenced more by the interpretation provided by the frame than by their own beliefs, since the frame tends to block them from engaging their own beliefs. By contrast, in environments with multiple interpretations, people are likely to employ more complex information-processing strategies (Lau and Schlesinger 2005).

Dominant frames are problematic for deliberation primarily for epistemic reasons. The epistemic argument for deliberation holds that deliberative judgements are better because they incorporate an expanded pool of reasons and information, draw on broader range of perspectives and involve reflection and justification (Bohman 2006; Estlund 1997). Dominant frames will tend to limit the availability, accessibility or weight of contravening reasons, thereby lending a claim more influence than it would merit were it to be tested and justified. By limiting these deliberative resources, dominant frames short-circuit the processes by which actors attend to the validity of claims. Moreover, the influence of argument is only normatively desirable to the extent that it relies on actors' freedom to accept or reject the validity claims as more or less convincing. But by implicitly making some considerations more salient, a dominant frame 'induces choice' (Barker 2005: 375). In Canada, for example, debates over public healthcare delivery often follow the model of dominant frames. In the Canadian case, the dominant frame paints any compromise of the system's current principles as an inevitable step towards American-style 'privatisation', embedding an implicit claim – that is, a claim not explicitly argued or evidenced – that millions would be left without access to healthcare. At the same, this dominant frame affirms (implicitly) the universal accessibility and quality of the existing system, while framing away alternative sets of policies or comparisons to other, higher-performing universal healthcare systems.

Polarising frames

The second type of frame that should be troubling to democratic theorists are polarising frames – frames partisans use to induce oppositional judgement between themselves and their issues and their opponents. Like all frames, polarising frames cause opponents to draw from different (and polarised) sets of considerations to define problems. In addition, not only do these frames define problems in competing ways but, like all frames, each has a set of inferential entailments, perhaps laying responsibility on certain actors or limiting the range of acceptable solutions that follow from the problem definition.

The damage wrought by polarising frames is both epistemic and ethical, although the ethical damage is largely a result of epistemic damage. Epistemically, deliberation cannot do its work if people are talking past one another because their cognitive pathways and the inferences that follow are locked into opposing frames. Brewer (2001), for example, argues that in 1990s welfare reform debates in the US, both sides initially tried to link their arguments to the core value of compassion. It turned out, however, that each side had a different conception of compassion and each subsequently accused the other of attempting to redefine the meaning of compassion (Brewer 2001). Moreover, in these kinds of situations, individuals' commitments to frames with polarising characteristics are likely driven, at least in part, by opposition to individuals or groups who hold other frames. Under these circumstances, frames inferentially link with an individual's assumptions about the problem's causes and consequences; they establish attitudes towards the relative importance of different considerations; and they orient towards potential solutions. An individual's evaluation of the merit of competing solutions to a problem depends on the causes they associate with the problem which, in turn, shapes how they weigh the consequences of various courses of action (or inaction). But polarising frames ensure that arguments cannot be fully tested because claims *within* a frame provide their own validity conditions and because the *polarisation* – knowing the other frame to be wrong – is part of the commitment. Owing to these two features, any discursive challenge from an opponent defines, rather than disrupts, the internal inferential commitments of the frame.

The harmful effects of polarising frames are epistemic in the first instance but ethical harms tend to follow. Frames create difficulties because actors speak past one another. But they may also create disincentives to speak at all by creating an environment of epistemic 'discounting', in which any argument that appears to be grounded in a competing frame, regardless of its content, is given less weight. Ascribing to others beliefs associated with a polarising frame may lead to situations in which speakers view one another as incapable of being moved by arguments – as ideological, closed-minded, or dogmatic – which, in turn, damages the ethical recognition and respect of others *as claim-makers*.

Debates that pit 'the environment' against 'the economy' or 'jobs' tend to be characterised by polarising frames. Although both sets of considerations matter in most such frames the relative weight given to these considerations can vary dramatically according to the frame. Such polarisation makes it difficult if not impossible, for actors to agree on anything without endorsing other aspects of the frame: the nature, sources and culprits of the problem and the likely consequences of various courses of action. As a consequence, the 'force of the better argument' cannot take hold. The presence of strong polarising frames makes arguments 'slippery', in the sense that arguments grounded in one frame have no purchase on the commitment structures bounded by another. In such situations, influence will tend to follow from the pre-discursive appeal of a frame that follows from a dominant tradition, culture or discourse. Or, more troublingly, influence will follow from the capacity of a partisan actor – such as a group or a party to test, repeat and magnify a message or code word that triggers a polarising frame – what commentators often describe as a 'dog whistle' – as is often the case in highly partisan political campaigns.

Group-based frames

Frames often trigger people's views about groups, leading them to substitute their prejudices about groups – and particularly the moral qualifications of the intended beneficiaries of a policy – for their judgements about a policy (Nelson and Kinder 1996: 1071). The result is that assumptions about groups are packaged into arguments about a political decision. While both dominant and polarising frames may involve group prejudices, what distinguishes group-based frames as a distinct type is the way they link judgements about groups of people to decisions that affect those people. Group-based frames may also be dominant or polarising but treating them as a separate ideal type allows us to consider the distinctive risks they pose to the normative goals of deliberative democracy.

Group-based frames bring many of the same epistemic concerns as other types of frames: they have the ability to induce choice by bypassing active reflection, because they embed the salience, weight, accessibility or emotive features of inferential structures that influence judgement. To a greater extent than dominating and polarising frames, however, the harms of group-based frames are *ethical*, since they function to deny group members status as speakers who might influence others and be influenced by the validity of claims. Group-based stereotypes or prejudgments embedded in frames may perpetuate status inequalities in ways that make deliberation difficult or impossible because they undermine mutual recognition and respect (Warren 2006: 163). This type of frame casts people as objects rather than subjects of deliberation, thereby undermining reciprocity in the exchange of reasons. Such frames function to devalue the interests, perspectives, claims and arguments of a group. Groups subjected to such frames will feel misjudged, stereotyped and insulted. Group-based frames tend to exclude responses among and between individuals, in favour of tit-for-tat prejudicial judgements. Because they feel unreasonably judged, any efforts towards deliberation by other group members will be viewed as naïve or misplaced, while even good-faith efforts by members of dominant groups will be interpreted as cynically strategic.

Nelson and Kinder (1996) highlight a number of instances in which beliefs about groups function as heuristics to reduce judgement of a policy to judgement of a group. Attitudes towards welfare programmes tend to turn on whether 'typical' recipients deserve aid (1996: 1056) or on general predispositions about whether members of such groups are responsible for their own situations (Gross and D'Ambrosio 2004: 11). In the United States, 'welfare' is often a frame-based code for Black, thus associating 'undeserving,' (and often other implicit signifiers, including promiscuous, drug-using and so on) with race. In this way, the frame-based stereotype of the welfare mother not only pre-empts considerations of facts, contexts and contingencies – the frame closes the case – but strips the objects of the frame of their ethical status as the authors of claims. What Nelson and Kinder (1996: 1061) call 'the freeloader frame' for welfare denies anyone identified as part of this groups the recognition necessary to influence others through claims – thus disenabling deliberation.

We summarise these ideal types of problematic frames in Table 12.1. Some frames may fall into multiple categories. For instance, the frame of the welfare freeloader, in addition to inducing group-based judgements, might also be considered a dominant frame, in the sense that it is well known, frequently invoked and seemingly immovable. Similarly, polarising frames may include judgements about groups. Nevertheless, the three ideal types serve to specify different sets of anti-deliberative effects and thus to distinguish among frames in terms of their harms. This said, the distinctions are idealised: empirically-existing frames are likely to generate harmful effects across types, functioning to promote a limited set of considerations at the expense of others; to downgrade considerations connected to a competing frame; or to implicate judgements about people in judgements about claims in a way that undermines the deliberative status of some subjects. By specifying *how* a problematic frame is harmful in terms of its influence and consequences, however, the three ideal types identify those features of frames that should be balanced or complemented in order to underwrite deliberative goods while also taking full measure of their necessary cognitive functions.

Table 12.1: Framing effects that undermine deliberation

Frame type	Characteristics relevant to deliberation	Damages to deliberation
Dominant	Shallow cognitive processing Insufficient testing of reasons	*Primarily epistemic:* Dominant frames circumvent processes of opinion and will-formation by limiting range of considerations and thus undermining communicative freedom to take yes/no positions on validity claims on the basis of reasons.
Polarising	People talk past one another	*Epistemic:* Polarising frames make it difficult to weigh individual claims apart from frames within which they are embedded. *Ethical:* Polarising frames lead to discounting or dismissing opinions of opponents in their entirety, undermining their status as speakers.
Group-based	Prejudicial dismissal of claims and arguments	*Primarily ethical:* Group-based frames embed pre-judgements of individuals, undermining mutual respect, reciprocity and trust necessary for them to respond to one another as speakers.

Deliberative mini-publics

Can we design institutions that respond to these problematic frames? Our analysis so far tells us what an institution must accomplish if it is to combat problematic frames. While there are many institutional arrangements that might counter problematic frames, here we focus here on deliberative mini-publics – that is, deliberative bodies whose members are selected to represent descriptively some public relevant to an issue. In this section, we examine how five key design features of mini-publics might limit the impact of problematic frames: (1) the method of participant selection; (2) the agenda, issue, or problem; (3) opportunities for trust-building and learning; (4) the quality of facilitation; and (5) the range of potential institutional outputs, including binding decisions, recommendations directed at agencies or governments, agendas for future processes, mission statements for official stances for institutions, or individual, post-deliberation surveys. There are a number of general reasons why these features help to counter problematic framing effects, which we detail below. In subsequent sections we relate features of institutional design to each type of problematic frame.

First, the ways participants are selected for deliberative mini-publics should limit incentives for using problematic frames. Mini-public bodies are *selected* for descriptively representative purposes – to resemble relevant publics – rather than *elected* or *self-selected*. Selection might take a number of forms, depending upon the issue, including random or near-random selection or stratified sampling. While there are a variety of reasons to prefer selection of this kind (Warren 2008), three are especially important. (1) Members of the body are free from pressures of competitive re-election that incentivise problematic frames. (2) The body avoids the effects of self-selection, which will often bias participation toward those who are heavily invested in positions that come with problematic frames attached. And (3) representative cross-sections of publics are more likely to multiply frames and dilute opportunities for frame-based coalitions.

Second, agendas can be important to avoiding problematic frames. Mini-publics tend to be formed around specific problems or issues, as opposed to (say) around ideologies and platforms as are political parties and advocacy groups. It is often the case that problem-driven agendas cut across received frames and so decrease the psychological utility of received frames. This feature of their design also affects the selection process itself: the pool from which participants are selected should, ideally, encompass the constituency of those most affected by a problem, which should, in turn, result in incentives to focus on the problem rather than the frame. In practice, of course, agenda-setting is rarely ideal and highly contingent on the incentives and capacities of existing jurisdictions and organisations (Warren 2009).

Third, because mini-publics are constructed, they can be designed and facilitated in ways that encourage trust-building among participants. For issues to be deliberated – especially divisive ones – participants must recognise others as willing and capable of committing to what they assert and argue, while trusting others to do the same. Frame-based fears that others are insincere, manipulative, hiding their meanings and the like, make it difficult for participants to respond to claims. Likewise, participants must trust one another enough to ask, probe and evoke in good faith. Trust of this kind can be encouraged by trained facilitators even across divides of race, ethnicity and class – often by focusing on trust-building before attempting deliberation.

Fourth, mini-publics are likely to underwrite the epistemic goals of deliberation, even against frames, in two ways. One is learning: frames often become less compelling the more individuals learn about the relevant universes of facts, the positions of others and so on. Thus, mini-public designs that do more to incorporate not only learning materials but also testimony from advocates, experts and others who can add information, complexity and nuance are more likely to undermine problematic frames. The second feature of design involves, simply, deliberation itself, encouraged by trained facilitators. As we argued above, the pragmatic account of language underwriting much of deliberative democracy – the notion that actors raise, test and accept or reject validity claims in order to co-ordinate action – suggests that problematic frames work because they 'bundle' validity claims. When people sign on to one compelling claim within a frame, they both commit themselves to a range of other claims and exclude other alternatives from consideration. This feature of frames suggests that, at minimum, breaking pre-reflective linkages will involve disaggregating the range of claims embedded in frames, so that each can be subjected to reflective judgement – to reordering, re-prioritising and re-imagining the relative importance and implications of considerations other than those embedded in the received frame. 'Disaggregating' does not mean that each claim stands or falls separately: any universe of claims is likely to be logically and practically interconnected. Rather the idea is that making a range of claims explicit (Brandom 1998) should enhance autonomous judgement and to combat what Robert Goodin (1980: 96) calls 'smuggling in the goods' – a form of manipulation he associates with rhetorical questions that commit audiences to premises or implications that would be rejected if they were expressed explicitly. As with trust-building, the capacities of mini-publics to 'make it explicit' can often be increased by trained facilitators.

Finally, it is important that mini-publics have a task that is linked to the problem or purpose, whether it is setting a new agenda, providing a new form of input into public opinion, advising an agency or legislative body, or making decisions. This feature of design complements the initial problem or issue that provides the body with a reason for its existence and is likely to keep participants on task, focused on achievable tasks and goals, which, in turn, will often cross-cut and undermine problematic frames.

Frame-specific considerations

These are, however, general considerations. We can also theorise other mini-public design considerations that are relevant to each kind of problematic frame.

Dominant frames

A basic insight from the empirical literature on framing is that exposure to counter-frames moderates the effects of each frame, whether by prompting careful reflection or simply because the influence of one frame is cancelled out by others (Druckman 2004). But is this strategy sufficient to counter dominant frames? Chong and Druckman (2007a) find that strong frames will trump weaker frames even when the latter are frequently repeated. Owing to this effect, organisers of mini-publics should be attentive to the risk that merely exposing people to alternative views of an issue may not be sufficient to dislodge dominant frames. Dominant frames produce something like selective hearing: although audiences may be exposed to multiple frames and act on the ones they find persuasive, this persuasiveness depends as much on how well the frame resonates with already-held core values and world views as it does on a careful weighing of its assumptions and implications (Barker 2005). In cases of highly dominant frames, then, it may not be enough to expose people to competing frames by introducing alternative viewpoints to the conversation, either because these competing frames are not strong enough or because the dominant frame has become so embedded that nothing else resonates quite as strongly.

In these kinds of cases, how might an institution induce people to challenge their assumptions, to examine information excluded by the dominant frame and to think in new ways about the problem and potential solutions? One of the key institutional aims for all problematic frames is to reduce incentives to fall back on familiar problem definitions and solutions – that is, familiar frames. Focusing the agenda on a specific practical problem is one such technique. When organisers have some control over the agenda, they can disaggregate issues, which not only reduces the cognitive demands on participants but also focuses questions in ways that enable relevant forms of information to be brought to bear. Focusing on specific questions – for instance, asking how hospitals should be funded, rather than debating the merits of public and private healthcare delivery – can often free up space for people to think creatively, while reducing the sense of risky uncertainty for participants when asked to weigh in on a complex policy area. Another technique involves choosing speakers and developing educational materials that introduce alternatives not typically present in discourse and which prompt creative responses. However, organisers should be conscious of the risks that the event itself can carry frames that will prime reactions. Framing an event around a need to challenge a dominant frame, for example, can risk failing to recognise aspects of the dominant frame that remain persuasive and valuable to participants, even when challenged. Facilitators with patronising views of dominant frames, or who issue 'politically correct' directives to 'educate' participants, risk de-legitimising the process, undermining deliberation and, perhaps, even strengthening the dominant frame. This said, in combination with careful facilitation focused on tracking and moderating the effects of the dominant frame, this technique can, ideally, enable mini-publics to generate new agendas that break with dominant frames.

Polarising frames

Polarising frames pose challenges different than from those of dominant frames. Polarising frames involve two or more competing positions, in which proponents of each frame have already been exposed to (and dismissed) opposing frames. Polarising frames affect not only our judgements but also our abilities to have conversations in which we weigh the validity of arguments – our abilities to draw on an exchange of reasons and engage in deliberative judgement. Polarizing frames pose challenges for facilitators that are different than those posed by dominant frames. Frames are constituted, at least in part, by uses of concepts or persuasive definitions that carry implicit assumptions and consequences (Macagno and Walton 2008: 204). Challenging polarising frames means rendering these explicit so that people can communicate about them. But often different frames are carried within the same words or terms, leaving conflicts of meaning implicit, in essence burying the conflict and making it more difficult for participants to discuss. If the conflict in interpretation remains implicit, deliberation will replicate frustrations and further distance competing positions, undermining the depolarising aims of mini-public design. Thus, processes that merely expose participants to competing frames – a tactic that is appropriate to moderating dominant frames – run the risk of reinforcing polarisation.

Beyond the basic goal of disaggregating elements of polarising frames, then, strategies should function in ways that make explicit the inferences embedded in differing uses of symbols, persuasive definitions and other features of frames, with the aim of enabling participants to understand the inferential connections among the beliefs that are embedded in the frames. These goals can be organised into mini-publics by ensuring that people have the space to weigh individual claims without feeling that they have to endorse (or reject) an entire set of interpretations and beliefs that frame an issue. As with dominant frames, these effects can be achieved, at least in part, by setting an agenda focused on a specific, actionable problem.

The impact of participant selection on these effects, however, is more complicated. On the one hand, the trend in mini-public design has been towards random or stratified sampling as a way of selecting participants – a method that should help to ensure that diverse perspectives are present, while avoiding the over-representation of people who are strategically invested in particular outcomes, as is typical of self-selected and elected bodies. To the extent that it produces a body with a representative array of participants subscribing to a variety of frames held with varying degrees of intensity, random selection may be adequate for dealing with polarising frames. Particularly on prominent issues, random selection is likely to generate such a distribution. However, the problem of polarising frames might sometimes require selection that produces a representative sample of frames, both to ensure that the mini-public *is* representing the kinds of polarising frames in the broader public and to enable participants to learn from those whose thinking is framed in different ways (*see*, for example, Dryzek and Niemeyer 2008).

Issues characterised by polarising frames suggest additional design considerations with respect to learning and trust-building. The 'weighting' account of framing (Nelson *et al.* 1997) is useful here: frames structure how people think about an issue by telling them how to weigh and thus prioritise the range of considerations that are involved in every political issue:

> Both supporters and opponents of nuclear power may agree on the potential economic benefits of nuclear energy, but they may disagree strongly on the importance of such benefits relative to the risks of a major accident involving a nuclear power plant […] this is the setting in which frames operate. Frames tell people how to weight the often conflicting considerations that enter into everyday political deliberation. Frames may supply no new information about an issue, yet their influence on our opinions may be decisive through their effect on the perceived relevance of alternative considerations (Nelson *et al.* 1997: 226).

One goal of learning and deliberation within mini-public contexts is to provide opportunities to discuss these kinds of prioritisation in ways that make them explicit, reducing the prejudgements embedded in frames. In situations with polarising frames, it is likely that people will express judgements that, loosely speaking, reflect the extent to which a frame resonated with their pre-existing priorities. But if deliberation is working, these connections between weighted priorities and judgements will have been made explicit and subjected to testing. Potentially, the process of making these connections explicit will reveal commonalities with perceived opponents. In addition, new information introduced into a deliberative process may bridge, or at least unsettle, polarised frames. This said, it may sometimes be preferable to focus learning on small issues around which agreements can be built, producing the trust necessary to talk about the more divisive issues that define polarising frames. Such agreements may, in turn, enable participants to see those who they might have previously dismissed as dogmatic as open to persuasion, correcting for one of the major ethical harms of polarising frames. Without such corrections, however, conversations with those from opposing points of view risk merely reinforcing polarising frames.

Group-based frames

If we imagine a mini-public on any issue that crosses divides of class or race, we can see that the initial problem will be to mitigate the effects of group frames. Participants in deliberation face a general obligation to justify their beliefs and practical commitments in terms of reasons and considerations others might accept. Deliberating within the context of group-based frames, however, risks placing burdens on some participants that preclude the very possibility of deliberation. Group-based frames will cast participants as representatives of a group and place them in the position of having to answer for ascribed group characteristics. These kinds of group ascriptions are obstacles to recognising others as deliberators who can persuade and be persuaded.

The key task of a mini-public should be to structure conversations so as to lower the costs of entry for participants who are likely to be subject to these kinds of discourse-undermining judgements, by working to eliminate these surplus burdens. These effects are likely to be difficult to build into issue-based deliberation itself. It is more likely that they will be achieved through learning and trust-building that works prior to and alongside deliberation. The problem is one of structuring conversations in such as way that members of stereotyped groups can disclose their perspectives and experiences without being forced by stereotypes either to defend against ascriptions or to argue for their status as individual speakers. The most effective way of avoiding these effects of group-based frames seems to be through informal personal interactions through which participants can become acquainted with one another as people. So a key part of the organiser's task will involve structuring mini-publics in such as way that informal interactions can build the commitments that subsequently underwrite mutually respectful deliberation. It is for this reason that National Issues Forums in the United States will often spend months developing trust among (say) Black and White participants, usually in closed, quasi-therapeutic settings and always prior to deliberating the topics of the forums themselves (National Issues Forum 2000; Warren 2006: 169).

In comparing the three kinds of frames with respect to the techniques most likely to overcome their anti-deliberative effects, those aimed at group-based frames concern deliberation itself least directly. The challenge that is specific to group-based frames is that they affect not just the beliefs of people, but also their deliberative status. Conversations around group-based frames must incorporate many of the same considerations as polarising and dominant frames but with the additional consideration of correcting for status-based harms. Thus, the aim of conversations structured to correct for group-based frames is primarily to create the necessary conditions for subsequent deliberation. Pre-deliberative learning about other participants and building trust are key. Beyond these pre-deliberative tasks, the correctives to group frames are much like those above, involving deliberative techniques that break down frames into their constituent inferential parts. Facilitators should encourage participants to distinguish judgements about groups from judgements about policy decisions. Agenda-setting considerations are also important to undermining the harmful effects of group-based frames: if deliberation remains problem-focused, participants have fewer opportunities to fall back on familiar recommendations.

In sum, although framing effects pose significant challenges to deliberative ideals, their effects might be mitigated with well considered institutional design. Mini-publics provide particularly good examples of the kinds of designs that push back against problematic frames. Of course, most design choices involve trade-

Table 12.2: Designing mini-publics to counter problematic framing effects

Mini-public features	Types of problematic frames		
	Dominant	**Polarising**	**Group-based**
Design goals	Disaggregate claims. Induce people to think and talk outside the frame.	Break down frames, extract assumptions, discuss priorities apart from frame-linked positions. Build trust.	Equalise status so participants can respond to the content of claims and arguments. Build trust.
Design features that address goals			
Agenda-setting	Constrained; focused so problem exceeds dominant frame.	Constrained; focused so that problems cross-cut frames.	Constrained; focused on problems shared by groups.
Participant selection	Random or stratified, increasing chances alternative frames will be represented.	Random or stratified, increasing diversity of frames represented.	Stratified sampling to represent relevant groups.
Trust-building	Less important.	Pre-deliberation phase focused on trust-building.	Pre-deliberation phase focused on trust-building.
Learning	Participants learn about alternatives or information challenges or undermines dominant frame.	Discovering what two sides have in common. Discovering priorities *apart* from influence of frames. Expert testimony may add neutral or bridging information.	Learning, especially through narrative and personal testimony.
Facilitation	Facilitators seek to bring alternative frames into deliberation.	Facilitators seek to enhance norms of respect, reciprocity and attentiveness to facts, as well as help to make assumptions explicit.	Facilitators seek to enhance norms of respect and reciprocity.
Defining outcomes	Constrained and focused, so specific outcomes exceed frames.	Constrained and focused agendas or recommendations that cross-cut polarising frames.	Problem-focused agendas or recommendations that cross-cut group identities.

offs. Limiting the agenda might reduce incentives to rely on problematic frames, while also limiting the scope of the information it can provide or recommendations it can issue. Likewise, in order to push back against frames, mini-publics might set agendas that result in a range of recommendations rather than offering consensus results. Broad agendas, however, may also reduce participants' motivation to learn and deliberate carefully – or may make it easier for decision-makers and publics to ignore the results. Such trade-offs are likely to be inevitable wherever problematic frames are operating. Trade-offs should be made, however, with the aim of underwriting and maximizing deliberative influence. Table 12.2 summarises the kinds of design considerations that can and should be taken into account.

To the extent that a process is intended as a corrective to a problematic frame, design choices should be governed primarily in terms of whether they achieve the design goals identified in Table 12.2 and only secondarily in terms of their implications for the other potential goods a mini-public might advance.

Conclusion

It is one thing to mitigate the effects of anti-deliberative frames within the controlled, small-scale context of a mini-public. Broader public discourse, within which anti-deliberative frames are common and often effective, are not susceptible to similar kinds of institutional design choices. But we can ask whether mini-publics designed to mitigate problematic frames might have also have these effects within broader publics. The question of how to scale up these effects would involve answering a complex set of questions around how and where mini-publics might be positioned in relation to other elements of a deliberative system, in order to have effects beyond participants themselves. Because this set of questions is so complex, we are not able to address it here (cf. Parkinson and Mansbridge 2012).

We conclude, instead, by noting that the problem is probably not, strictly speaking, one of 'scaling up' mini-publics into broader publics. The kind of work participants accomplish within mini-publics – trust-building, learning about particular issues in depth, deliberating in good faith with a few others – cannot be replicated in mass-publics. The scale, contingencies, incentives, contexts and agents are necessarily different. So instead we shall need to think about how mini-publics might be integrated into broader publics, by identifying their roles in the public division of discursive labour as well as their relationships to existing political institutions, such as legislatures, agencies and advocacy groups. We shall need to conceptualise and study their potential roles within a *deliberative system* – that is, within the context of all talk-based approaches to conflict-resolution and political decision-making. Building on our analysis here, we will want to focus especially on the question of how the advantages of mini-publics in mitigating the anti-deliberative impacts of frames might be captured within the broader system. For example, if mini-publics come to be judged by broader publics as democratically legitimate, they might take on roles as new kinds of trusted information proxies (Cutler and Johnson 2008; Mackenzie and Warren 2012), alongside more traditional proxies, such as political parties, advocacy groups, unions, networks and like-minded friends. In this way, mini-publics might signal new ways of defining and discussing issues that would compete with those kinds of forums and bodies that are more subject to the anti-deliberative effects of framing.

We can also think of the systematic roles of mini-publics from an institutional perspective: how do they add new deliberative and representative depth to administrative agencies and legislatures? Indeed, a great deal of mini-public activity has centred on administrative agencies seeking public mandates in areas where political directives are absent or ambiguous (Warren 2009). Legislatures, a second potential channel for mini-public influence, might resort (and in a few cases have resorted) to deliberative mini-publics in the face of legislative impasse on a particularly intractable problem or in situations in which there is no popular choice (Lang and Warren 2012). Of course, each institution will have issue-specific limits in its capacity to address problematic frames, since such institutions are defined by high levels of politicisation. Thus, administrative agencies will usually tread carefully, so as not to appear to wade into 'politics,' although they can often accomplish good deliberative work within the contexts of carefully defined policy problems (Warren 2009). Legislatures may have more incentives to use mini-publics but probably only on issues on which elected politicians can see no political gain from invoking problematic frames. Such issues may be few and far between, as politicians are often elected just because they successfully deploy these very frames. That said, some electoral and legislative systems – many proportional representation systems and some systems of separated powers – incentivise deliberation, which may then provide opportunities for mini-public-like contexts (Steiner *et al.* 2004). Most political realities, however, will dictate that much of the innovation with respect to mini-publics will be driven by civil society actors and democracy entrepreneurs – organisations like America Speaks, or National Issues Forums, for example – with principled motivations to structure public conversations in ways that compensate for anti-deliberative frames. It is clear from this very abbreviated list of systematic roles for deliberative mini-publics that, as yet, we lack theory that is closely articulated enough to form and guide researchable propositions.

Framing effects represent a deep challenge to deliberative democratic theory and practice. Frames challenge deliberative democracy on its own ground: talk-based politics. It is, after all, talk that carries frames. Whether used as political strategy or as part of how we conceptualise political issues, frames bring with them meanings, symbols and pre-reflective judgements that undermine deliberative forms of influence, which should operate through offering and redeeming validity claims (Habermas 1998) and making inferential structures of commitments explicit (Brandom 1998). Here we have sought to show that, however real and deep the challenge, it can nonetheless be theorised and practically addressed. From the perspective of theory, we have argued that it is not framing *in itself* that is anti-deliberative but a more limited set of problematic frame *types* – what we have called *dominant, polarising* and *group-based* frames. Once we theorise how each kind of frame works, we can also see that each admits of practical responses. Designed mini-publics represent the most advanced kind of response to date and their key features can be adjusted to the specific challenges presented by each kind of problematic frame. But it remains to be seen how mini-publics might function within broader deliberative systems. Addressing this problem will require us to further develop the concept of *deliberative systems*, within which mini-publics might have roles that would include mitigating the effects of anti-deliberative frames.

References

Barker, D. C. (2005) 'Values, frames and persuasion in presidential nomination campaigns', *Political Behavior* 27 (4): 375–94.

Benford, R. D. and Snow, D. A. (2000) 'Framing processes and social movements: an overview and assessment', *Annual Review of Sociology* 26: 611–39.

Bohman, J. (2006) 'Deliberative democracy and the epistemic benefits of diversity', *Episteme* 3: 175–91.

Brandom, R. (1998) *Making it Explicit: Reasoning, representing and discursive commitment*, Boston, MA: Harvard University Press.

Brewer, P. R. (2001) 'Value words and lizard brains: do citizens deliberate about appeals to their core values?', *Political Psychology* 22 (1): 45–64.

—— (2003) 'Value, political knowledge and public opinion about gay rights: a framing based account', *Public Opinion Quarterly* 67: 173–201.

Brewer, P. R. and Gross, K. (2005) 'Values, framing and citizens' thoughts about policy issues: effects of content and quantity', *Political Psychology* 26 (6): 929–48.

Chong, D. and Druckman, J. N. (2007a) 'Framing public opinion in competitive democracies', *American Political Science Review* 101 (4): 637–55.

—— (2007b) 'Framing theory', *Annual Review of Political Science* 10: 103–26.

—— (2010) 'Dynamic public opinion: communication effects over time', *American Political Science Review* 104 (4): 663–80.

Cutler, F. and Johnston, R., with Carty, K., Blais, A. and Fournier, P. (2008) 'Deliberation, information and trust: the British Columbia citizens' assembly as agenda setter', in M. E. Warren and H. Pearse (eds) *Designing Deliberative Democracy: The British Columbia Citizens' Assembly*, Cambridge: Cambridge University Press.

Druckman, J. N. (2001) 'On the limits of framing effects: who can frame?', *The Journal of Politics* 63 (4): 1041–66.

—— (2004) 'Political preference formation: competition, deliberation and the (ir)relevance of framing effects', *The American Political Science Review* 98 (4): 671–86.

Druckman, J. N. and Nelson, K. R. (2003) 'Framing and deliberation: how citizens' conversations limit elite influence', *American Journal of Political Science* 47 (4): 729–45.

Dryzek, J. and Niemeyer, S. (2008) 'Discursive representation', *American Political Science Review* 102 (4): 481–93.

Entman, R. M. (1993) 'Framing: toward clarification of a fractured paradigm', *Journal of Communication* 43 (3): 51–8.

Estlund, D. (1997) 'Beyond fairness and deliberation: the epistemic dimension of democratic authority', in J. Bohman and W. Rehg (eds), *Deliberative Democracy: Essays on reason and politics*, Cambridge, MA: MIT Press.

Gamson, W. A. and Modigliani, A. (1989) 'Media discourse and public opinion on nuclear power: a constructionist approach', *American Journal of Sociology* 95 (1): 1–37.

Goodin, R. (1980) *Manipulatory Politics*, New Haven, CT: Yale University Press.

Gross, K. and D'Ambrosio, L. (2004) 'Framing emotional response', *Political Psychology* 25: 1–29.

Habermas, J. (1984) *Theory of Communicative Action* (T. McCarthy, trans., vol. 1), Boston, MA: Beacon Press.

— (1998) *Between Facts and Norms. Contributions to a discourse theory of law and democracy*, Cambridge, MA: MIT Press.

Lang, A. and Warren, M. E. (2012) 'Supplementary democracy? Democratic deficits and citizens' assemblies', in P. Lenard and R. Simeon (eds), *Imperfect Democracies*, Vancouver: University of British Columbia Press.

Lau, R. R. and Schlesinger, M. (2005) 'Policy frames, metaphorical reasoning, and support for public policies, *Political Psychology* 26 (4): 77–114.

Macagno, F. and Walton, D. (2008) 'Persuasive definitions: values, meanings, and implicit disagreements, *Informal Logic* 28 (3): 203–28.

Mackenzie, M. and Warren, M. E. (2012) 'Two trust-based uses of minipublics in democratic systems', in J. Parkinson and J. Mansbridge (eds), *Deliberative Systems*, Cambridge: Cambridge University Press.

Mansbridge, J., Bohman, J., Chambers, S., Christiano, T., Fung, A., Parkinson, J., *et al.* (2012) 'A systemic approach to deliberative democracy', in J. Parkinson and J. Mansbridge (eds), *Deliberative Systems*, Cambridge: Cambridge University Press.

National Issues Forum (2000) *Racial and Ethnic Tensions: What should we do?* Dayton, OH: National Issues Forum Institute.

Nelson, T. E. and Kinder, D. R. (1996) 'Issue frames and group centrism in American public opinion', *The Journal of Politics* 58 (4): 1055–78.

Nelson, T. E. Oxley, Z. M. and Clawson, R. A. (1997) 'Toward a psychology of framing effects', *Political Behavior* 19 (3): 221–46.

Parkinson, J. and Mansbridge, J. (eds) (2012) *Deliberative Systems*, Cambridge: Cambridge University Press.

Rawls, J. (1993) *Political Liberalism*, New York: Columbia University Press.

Steiner, J., Bächtiger, A., Spörndli, M. and Steenbergen, M. R. (2004) *Deliberative Politics in Action: Analyzing parliamentary discourse*, Cambridge: Cambridge University Press.

Warren, M. E. (2006) 'What should and should not be said: deliberating sensitive issues', *Journal of Social Philosophy* 37 (2): 163–81.

— (2008) 'Citizen representatives', in M. E. Warren and H. Pearse (eds) *Designing Deliberative Democracy: The British Columbia Citizens' Assembly*, Cambridge: Cambridge University Press, 50–69.

— (2009) 'Governance-driven democratization', *Critical Policy Analysis* 3 (1): 3–13.

Warren, M. E. and Pearse, H. (eds) (2008) *Designing Deliberative Democracy: The British Columbia Citizens' Assembly*, Cambridge: Cambridge University Press.

Chapter Thirteen

Towards a New Era of Deliberative Mini-Publics

André Bächtiger, Maija Setälä and Kimmo Grönlund

Participedia, an open-access platform collecting details on democratic innovations worldwide, documents the spread of the use of mini-publics around the world. Mini-publics have been organised in Western and non-Western countries, in democratic and autocratic ones, as well as at the local, regional, national and transnational level. Overall, the experience with mini-publics worldwide and in unlikely places (such as China or divided societies such as Northern Ireland and Belgium) has been largely positive, indicating that mini-publics may work better than more sceptical opponents predicted (*see* Dryzek 2010). Though many political scientists and theorists embrace the implementation of mini-publics, however, they still confront a number of challenges. In this chapter, we address these challenges and try to come up with recommendations for how to avoid them. First, the academic debate in political science has so far been dominated by one specific design, namely the Deliberative Poll® (DP), which is undeniably an extraordinary scholarly and practical achievement (*see* Fishkin in Chapter Three of this volume). At the same time, the DP's dominance in mini-public practice and research might have held back other designs that may be equally or even better apt to achieving specific deliberative and democratic ideals. Rather than applying the same 'unified' design to all situations and policy questions, we think that a multitude of creative and carefully crafted designs is needed. By testing and comparing different models of mini-publics, the scholarly community could gain a better understanding of how to realise the various goals of deliberation.

Second, while we do know quite a lot about the input and output dimensions of mini-publics, that is, who participates and how opinions change, we know surprisingly little about their internal functioning. The 'standard story' behind the DP, for instance, is that it creates an optimal institutional setting for deliberation (Fishkin 2009). Thus, deliberation is virtually inscribed in the institutional setting, allowing scholars to dispense with closely and intensively studying the actual process of deliberation and opinion formation. But, as several contributions in this volume have underlined, it is still a rather open empirical question whether deliberation in mini-publics actually occurs as expected.

Third, and perhaps most importantly, the question of 'scaling up' looms large. By this we mean the problem of institutionalising mini-publics in order to make them an essential element in the policy-making process. To date, too few mini-publics have had a discernible impact on actual policy-making, frequently being relegated to the role of academic toys that delight rather than political devices that 'bite'. We need to better understand when mini-publics 'bite' and when they do not. And we need to think about novel ways of making them 'bite'.

Several of these challenges have already been highlighted and addressed by chapters in this volume; this chapter will try to give a concise overview of these challenges while simultaneously sketching some possible pathways of how to effectively deal with them in the next generation of mini-publics. We start with some considerations concerning the basic ideas of mini-publics and the methodologies applied in studying them, then turn to design choices and finally discuss the perennial problem of 'scaling up' mini-public deliberations.

Thinking about mini-publics

In his book, *When the People Speak: Deliberative democracy and public consultation*, Fishkin identifies 'the need for a social science research program assessing the merits and limitations of various institutional designs that might realize deliberative democracy' (Fishkin 2009: 98), where '[t]he idea is to assess the designs that best stand up to critical scrutiny so as to capture the promise of deliberation and avoid potential objections to it' (*Ibid.*: 157). To date, such a research programme is only in its infancy even though an increasing number of scholars are systematically assessing the conditions, processes and outcomes of mini-publics (*see*, for example, Sanders 2012; Esterling *et al.* 2011; Gerber *et al.* 2012). In the following, we provide some sketches of what such a social science research programme on mini-publics might look like.

We propose an approach that we think has the potential to integrate various ongoing research efforts around mini-publics. It is anchored in an expanded (Mansbridge *et al.* 2010) conceptualisation of deliberation, also called Type II deliberation (Bächtiger *et al.* 2010). Mansbridge and others (2010: 55) have defined deliberation as 'communication that induces reflection on preferences, values and interests in a non-coercive fashion'. Type II forms of deliberation therefore stress the desirable consequences of deliberation, whereas the classic, Type I, model of deliberation stresses the process of deliberation and its quality. As Warren (2007) has succinctly put it:

> [F]rom the point of view of democratic institutions and systems, we should be more interested in the outcomes of communication than communicative intent. If angry demonstration is necessary to persuade others that they should notice unpleasant facts, it is a contribution to deliberation, although the initial intentions may not be 'deliberative'.

The normatively desirable outcomes of deliberation are manifold, ranging from preference-change in common-good-oriented directions to desirable side-effects such as efficacy and trust (Grönlund *et al.* 2010). We think that by identifying essential goals of deliberation first, we are in a much better position to think about the various design choices that optimally realise these goals. Fung (2003) has long argued that different designs of mini-publics may help to realise different goals. Morrell (Chapter Ten in this volume) proposes a similar approach to cope with psychological biases in the process of deliberation. He writes: 'Once we understand what deliberative success means, it becomes easier to elucidate evidence on what might contribute to this success.'

Morrell (this volume) identifies three desirable outcomes of deliberation: a fully reflective public opinion; a democratically rational or reasonable decision; and an epistemically correct decision. This is a very useful starting point; however, since there is some overlap among the three outcomes, we simplify the issues and limit the goals of deliberation to two essential ones, namely epistemic fruitfulness and inclusion (*see also* Mansbridge 2010). Epistemic fruitfulness means that deliberation gets us to the 'correct' answer, or at least, to the best possible answer to a given problem or decision-task (Estlund 1997; Talisse 2009; Landemore 2013).

Following Young (2000), the idea of inclusion entails both internal and external inclusion. External inclusion is strongly based on the notion of political equality (O'Flynn and Sood in Chapter Four of this volume), which is a central concern of any democratic theory, emphasising the importance of including 'all affected' by the decision. Internal inclusion means that all participants contribute to deliberations and that their views are equally and fairly considered in the deliberative process. Inclusion may also mean finding common ground among diverse interests and promoting the ethical value of respect, that is, seeing the merit in other positions or having empathy for other persons or groups (Mansbridge 2010).

Epistemic fruitfulness and inclusion may go hand in hand but they may also be in tension. According to Landemore (2013), inclusion is a fundamental precondition of epistemic advancement: inclusion of the many maximises 'cognitive diversity', which, in turn, promotes epistemic fruitfulness. And the emergence of respect – especially seeing the merit in other positions – might be strongly tied to epistemic advancement and better understanding of other viewpoints. But there is also a prominent strand in democratic theory arguing that inclusion is an independent standard of democratic quality. Saffon and Urbinati (2013), for instance, claim that participation and inclusion of the many serves as a check against the undue influence of the powerful. On this account, the goal of democracy is not truth but equal liberty (Saffon and Urbinati 2013: 450).

From a deliberative perspective, finding common ground may sometimes mean compromising epistemic correctness. Therefore, it seems sensible to keep epistemic fruitfulness and inclusion as analytically separate goals. With regard to these two essential goals of deliberation, psychologists have long argued that the realisation of these two goals might entail a trade-off. In a laboratory study, Schweiger *et al.* (1986) found that contestatory formats in the form of 'dialectical inquiry' and 'devil's advocacy' were conducive to a higher level of critical evaluation of assumptions and better-quality recommendations than consensual formats, even though the latter were not geared towards finding easy consensus.

By contrast, when it comes to other deliberative aims, namely inclusion and finding common ground, consensual modes of communication may be better apt to achieve this goal. Indeed, Schweiger *et al.* (1986) found that subjects in the consensus groups expressed greater acceptance of their groups' decisions as well as a desire to continue to work with their groups compared to participants in dialectical inquiry or devil's advocacy groups. Even though these findings have not been replicated (at least not to our knowledge), they nonetheless suggest that we might need to carefully consider the appropriate communication formats and institutional designs to realise the two goals of deliberation, namely epistemic fruitfulness and inclusion.

Methodological choices

While the growth of mini-publics has been accompanied by systematic empirical research (for example, Luskin *et al.* 2002; Price and Capella 2002), the methodological rigidity of this research is sometimes questionable, at least when judged against classic experimental standards. As Setälä and Herne (Chapter Five in this volume) point out,

> mini-publics have typically also another purpose, that is, democratic innovation, and some experimental designs, although desirable from the scientific point of view, may not be compatible with this goal. The manipulation of certain aspects of the design of mini-publics, such as information, moderation or group composition, involves a risk of decreasing the quality of deliberations to the degree that a mini-public can no longer be regarded as a method of enhancing democratic participation.

The standard and quasi-experimental DP setup has obscured the full potential of the experimental approach. Setälä and Herne document the varieties and possibilities of experimental research for understanding the functioning of mini-publics.

In recent years, there have been some indications of increased methodological sophistication in the study of mini-publics. Farrar *et al.* (2010) have used data from a randomised field experiment within a Deliberative Poll® in order to explore the effects of deliberation on single-peakedness. Esterling *et al.* (2011) have disentangled the effects of information from the effects of small-group discussion (*see also* Bächtiger *et al.* 2011). Another issue is that most mini-publics (including DPs) do not qualify as true experiments since they either lack a true control group or create control groups out of those participants who are not interested in participating in the deliberative event. This, however, leads to comparisons among people with very different motivation profiles and does not allow the extraction of the true causal effect of deliberation. Setälä and Herne (in this volume) recommend 'that auxiliary hypotheses [such as information effects] related to the procedures of mini-publics would be studied through controlled experiments which use students as experimental subjects'. Finally, as Setälä and Herne argue, mini-public experiments should also be repeated with different subject pools, slightly different designs, different issues and in different political contexts. If similar results are always obtained, it is possible to conclude that that the finding is robust, despite variations in the experimental setting.

Another methodological challenge concerns what experimentalists call manipulation check. Much of the research on mini-publics remains primarily suggestive, focusing on the institutional conditions most likely to promote deliberation. There is a need for evidence that it actually emerges in practice. As Smith and Ryan (in Chapter Two of this volume) put it:

> A focus on preference and opinion change alone, however, tells us little about the deliberative quality of interactions within the mini-public. We should not take for granted that random sampling, balanced background information, facilitated small group discussion and plenary sessions in which experts are interrogated promotes deliberation.

Indeed, it is urgent to investigate what happens when people are supposed to deliberate.

Focusing on different communication modes, Bächtiger and Gerber (Chapter Eight in this volume) have made an attempt to investigate the amount of contestation and consensus in Europolis. Siu (2009), Himmelroos (2011) and Gerber *et al.* (2012) have applied the DQI to small-group discussion in mini-publics. Results show that ordinary citizens can achieve surprisingly high levels of deliberative quality, with some even qualifying as true 'deliberative personalities', scoring simultaneously high on complex reason-giving, common-good orientation, respect and empathy (*see* Gerber *et al.* 2012). At the same time, not everyone can deliberate at such high quality levels. Gerber *et al.* (2012) detected an important class-region bias in the ability of deliberating: compared to other participants, working-class participants from Eastern and Southern Europe had a much lower frequency of reaching the various standards of high-quality deliberation.

By the same token, we still do not really know what drives opinion changes in mini-publics. One of the major claims of deliberationists is that the communicative rationality of the discussion process is the driving force behind preference change, rather than other potential pathways, such as simple cue-taking, conformity pressures or strategic manipulation (*see* Bächtiger *et al.* 2010). Surely, the quantity of factual information absorbed plays a major intervening role (Luskin *et al.* 2002). But focusing on Europolis, a transnational Deliberative Poll®, Sanders (2012) presents a much more erratic picture. There is no consistent and robust effect of diverse mechanisms, that is, knowledge gains, deliberative quality, group pressure on opinion change. Much more research is needed to explore of what is really going on in mini-publics and what kinds of social and psychological mechanisms, exactly, are working when we are talking about deliberation.

Micro design choices

In the next two sections, we focus on the design of deliberative mini-publics. We first discuss the internal organisation of mini-publics (the micro design choices), and then turn to the question of the role of mini-publics in political systems (macro design choices), that is, the problem of scaling up. The micro and macro aspects of the design of mini-publics are to some extent interlinked. As this book documents, there is a great need to seriously consider various institutional and other design choices to realise the two essential goals of democratic deliberation, that is, epistemic fruitfulness and inclusion. We provide a non-exhaustive list of design choices that help to realise these two goals. We focus on recruitment, modes of discussion, facilitation, decision rules, group composition and framing.

Recruitment

Creating a representative sample or a 'microcosm' of the population (cf. Fishkin 1995) is the goal of most mini-publics. The goal follows the logic of survey research and aims at fulfilling the ideal of external inclusion. Typically, the organisers of mini-publics apply random selection in recruiting participants (Brown 2006). Yet, depending on the goals of deliberation, random sampling may not be a panacea. First of all, random sampling might lead to unrepresentative samples if the sample size is small. Contrary to Dahl's original idea of approximately 1000 participants, mini-publics are usually much smaller. Often, fewer than 100 participants gather for deliberations. When a small probability sample is drawn from a population of millions of people, sampling errors become huge and the randomly drawn mini-public might be anything but a 'microcosm' of the population.

Random sampling may, however, be conducive to achieving the epistemic goals of deliberation. As Mercier and Landemore (2012) argue, random sampling is a highly appropriate technique for obtaining sufficient cognitive diversity, which is crucial for epistemic fruitfulness. But when it comes to inclusionary goals, this may not be necessarily the case. There may be good reasons for over-sampling certain social groups to ensure their presence, sometimes in higher numbers than their proportion in the broader population. For example, a critical mass of participants from minority social groups may be needed to ensure their voices are recognised and heard (James 2008; Derenne 2012: 27). Or, as Smith and Ryan (Chapter Two in this volume) concur:

> There is error and bias in sampling for DPs and he fails to recognise the important role that stratification or quotas, as well as the crafting of recommendations, can play in legitimising designs. While the social scientist may desire probability sampling for good academic reasons, its virtues will not always be recognised in politically sensitive situations.

Recruitment to mini-publics should be done considering the pros and cons of probability sampling. First, probability sampling can be used if the sample size is large enough. If the mini-public is small, the issue of representativeness should be addressed separately. Second, attrition related to self-selection needs to be thought of. It may be difficult to attract people with low levels of political efficacy or with a lack of political interest. Therefore, stratification and over-sampling should be considered in order to guarantee external inclusion, especially when the sample size is small. Third, and directly related to the second issue, representation should not only cover different social groups but also different viewpoints (Dryzek and Niemeyer 2008). One of the reasons for this is that people will always belong to multiple statistical categories and it is impossible to know in advance how each individual ranks his or her various identities (Brown 2006: 218). A combination of (stratified) probability sampling and opinion-based recruitment might be an option. With opinion-based recruitment, we mean a process where a raw (probability) sample is first surveyed on the issue at hand. After this, the organiser can create strata based on opinions and apply a further recruitment method within the opinion strata.[1] At this stage, random selection can be applied anew.

Communication modes

The core of any deliberative mini-public is the discussion phase. Most mini-publics prime on what Fishkin calls systematic discussion.[2] Systematic discussion is a fairly generic format that may entail both contestatory and consensual forms of engagement (Bächtiger 2011). This generic format, however, may not optimally realise both epistemic fruitfulness and inclusion. As Bächtiger and Gerber (in Chapter Eight of this volume) empirically demonstrate, there was a surprisingly low level of contestation in Europolis, a pan-European Deliberative Poll®. As mentioned before, psychologists have provided empirical evidence that (properly organised) contestation may greatly benefit the epistemic dimension of deliberation. Surely, as widely documented by Fishkin and his associates, deliberative mini-publics are conducive to knowledge gains. So far, knowledge gains have usually been measured through quiz-type factual knowledge questions; thus, in order to advance the epistemic dimension of citizen deliberation, mini-public discussions might benefit from being enriched with debating-style elements. By the same token, the level of consensual forms of discussion was also quite low in the Europolis DP. Thus, if one wants to advance inclusiveness in citizen deliberation, a more dedicated focus on constructive and problem-solving engagement might be in order as well. Focusing on the Australian Citizens' Parliament, Curato and Niemeyer (2012) show how inclusiveness was 'produced' by a specific mediation technique deployed by facilitators, namely, 'appreciative inquiry', the goal of which is to emphasise strengths that people can build on.

---

1. Naturally, this method also has its limitations. Sometimes deliberative mini-publics are organised around scientifically complex issues on which people might not have clear pre-deliberation opinions.

2. Personal communication with James Fishkin.

Facilitation

Discussion modes are strongly intertwined with facilitator activity. As Landwehr (Chapter Six in this volume) details, facilitators have a panoply of options for realising the goals of deliberation. For instance, they can try to 'rationalise' communication by insisting on generalisable arguments and trying to keep emotions at bay. Or they can make special efforts to include disadvantaged participants. While the importance of facilitators in mini-publics is frequently discussed, research on the effects of facilitation is surprisingly scarce. DPs institutionalise one type of facilitation, namely, a relatively limited intervention that tries to bolster inclusion and civility. Despite the fact that Deliberative Polls® are constructed in such a way as to yield a uniform treatment of participants, facilitation styles might still vary in practice. Thus, researchers might profit from such variations to study the effects of different facilitation styles. Future research might also think of setting up facilitators with different tasks, ranging from mediator tasks to devil's advocates. Notice finally that some scholars (Bevir and Ansari 2012) have also suggested that we refrain from organising mini-publics with facilitation, since participants in deliberation are democratic subjects and not guinea-pigs in an experiment (*see* Landwehr, this volume).

Decision rules

Deliberative polls are based on the assumption that designs ending with a collective recommendation are worse than designs ending with individual judgements. In this regard, Fishkin is concerned that the goal of making a collective recommendation undermines political equality because social pressure can be put on individuals to bend to the collective will (Fishkin 2009: 132–3). But this may be deficient, for two reasons. First, there is strong current in deliberative theory that considers deliberation without decision as improper deliberation (*see* Thompson 2008). Second, there is an ongoing debate whether unanimity or majority better fulfils the epistemic goals of deliberation (Austen-Smith and Feddersen 2006; Mathis 2011). McGann (2006) makes a case against unanimous decision-making rules since these would provide actors with perverse incentives for deliberation. In his view, majoritarian decision-rules force actors to be more open-minded and deliberative, since they have no guarantee that their arguments and interests will be included at the end.

Psychologists have argued otherwise, namely that unanimity creates incentives for serious deliberation (*see* Mendelberg 2002). Mathis (2011), too, demonstrates formally that the unanimity decision-rule is superior in achieving full opinion-sharing and information revelation, under the (plausible) condition that individuals provide 'verifiable evidence' for their private information. As Caluwaerts and Kavadias (Chapter Nine in this volume) underline, not only do decision-rules strongly matter for the quality of deliberation in mini-publics, it is unanimity – and not majority – that is conducive to higher deliberative quality. A Finnish experiment tested whether (and how) majoritarian decision-rules (captured via groups making decisions through a secret ballot) and unanimity decision-rules (captured via groups asked to formulate a common statement) affect deliberative outcomes. While there were no systematic differences between the two decision modes in terms of opinion of changes, participants' knowledge increased more in the common statement groups (Setälä *et al.* 2010). Thus, appropriate decision-rules may help to advance specific goals of deliberation.

Group composition

Psychologists have long argued that group composition is a crucial factor affecting both process and outcomes of discussions (*see* Mendelberg and Karpowitz 2007). The DP set up builds on random assignment to groups in order to avoid homophily effects (that is, that similar people group together). As mentioned in the context of recruitment, random assignment is an appropriate device when we want to ensure (cognitive) diversity. But it may be less appropriate when considering inclusionary goals. While certain minorities may be well represented in some small groups, they may not be well represented in others. Consequently, in some cases they may lack the 'critical mass' and hence the confidence to voice their own concerns (James 2008: 120–3). It might even be worthwhile to consider the potential benefits of enclave deliberation, that is deliberation among like-minded, although the whole notion seems incompatible with the idea of a 'mini-public'. Combined with more inclusive forms of deliberation, however, enclave deliberation could be conducive for the articulation of interests, innovation and mobilisation among the disempowered (Karpowitz *et al.* 2009).

There are several findings suggesting that different social inequalities play a role in deliberative mini-publics, despite the fact that particular efforts have been made to facilitate inclusive deliberation. For example, women and people with less education tend to participate less actively in deliberations (Mendelberg and Karpowitz 2007; Setälä *et al.* 2010). In this regard, Karpowitz *et al.* (2012) have demonstrated that the combination of appropriate group composition and institutional rules (unanimity) helps to overcome such biases. Caluwaerts and Kavadias (Chapter Nine in this volume) obtain similar results: they identify a complex interaction effect of group composition with decision-making rules. Again, specific goals of deliberation might be advanced by the different design choices.

Framing

Another design element is 'framing'. As Calvert and Warren (Chapter Twelve in this volume) show, most scholars of deliberative democracy have discussed framing in opposition to deliberation. But frames – say Calvert and Warren – 'are not just an unfortunate part of political strategy; they are an essential and inevitable part of persuasion'. Following the framing literature (*see*, for example, Chong and Druckman 2007), one might consider confronting participants in deliberative mini-publics with specific frames in order to make them think about and discuss issues in different ways. Focusing on the extension of political rights to foreigners, Baccaro *et al.* (2013) have confronted citizens with different framings of the issue, namely, a 'democratic' frame emphasising the 'all-affected principle' and the right of foreigners to participate in local affairs versus a 'communitarian' frame emphasising the importance of becoming a citizen before one is entitled to political rights. Of course, inserting specific frames into deliberative mini-publics has a manipulative dimension, which some may not deem appropriate from a normative vantage.

This *problématique* notwithstanding, a key question is: which frames hinder or promote deliberation? Calvert and Warren identify three frames that potentially undermine deliberation: dominant, polarising and group frames. Polarising frames, for instance, 'create difficulties because actors speak past one another. But they may also create disincentives to speak at all by creating an environment of epistemic "discounting", in which any argument that appears to be grounded in a competing frame, regardless of its content, is given less weight'.

In this regard, Fishkin (Chapter Three in this volume) stresses argumentative balance, that is, 'the extent to which arguments offered by one side or from one perspective are answered by considerations offered by those who hold other perspectives'. As Calvert and Warren argue, balance may not always be an adequate solution. In the case of highly dominant frames, for instance,

> it may not be enough to expose people to competing frames by introducing alternative viewpoints to the conversation, either because these competing frames are not as strong, or because the dominant frame has become so embedded that nothing else resonates quite as well.

One possibility pointed out by Calvert and Warren is to disaggregate issues, 'which both reduces the cognitive demands on participants, and also focuses questions in ways that enable relevant forms of information to be brought to bear'.

Technology

A final design choice concerns the 'technical architecture' of mini-publics (Strandberg and Grönlund, Chapter Seven in this volume). According to Dahl's (1989) original idea, each mini-demos would consist of a randomly selected group of citizens which would deliberate for a year. The use of telecommunication technologies in mini-populi was suggested by Barber in 1984 and Dahl in 1989. However, most mini-publics to date have been face-to-face. Online mini-publics provide many interesting opportunities and also open up many important research questions. Given the promise of information and communication technology (ICT) to overcome barriers of space and time, there is real potential for extending the reach of mini-publics. This calls attention to another design issue, that is, whether mini-publics should be one-shot events or more permanent bodies. Normally, deliberative mini-publics require relatively short engagement from their participants. ICT-based deliberative bodies would allow asynchronic deliberation, which allows people to participate in discussions at the time most convenient for them. Therefore they could be regarded as one solution to the trade-offs between demands of engagement and participants' time limitations.

In the ICT context, there are also opportunities to set up conversations in ways which not only guarantee the full anonymity of participants, it may also help to wipe out a number of social and other cues that psychologists have shown to influence persuasion. In other words, online platforms can encourage participants to focus on the content of the message rather than on its context. With regard to epistemic fruitfulness, Mark Klein (2011) has designed an online deliberative forum called *Deliberatorium*. Klein and his team developed an algorithm that automatically evaluates argumentative quality. If argumentative quality turns out to be insufficient, the algorithm alerts the participants and provides them with additional and controversial insights on the topic. Conversely, there is a long line of research showing that face-to-face discussion is crucial when it comes to build up trust and commitment. Therefore anonymous and chat-style ICT may not necessarily be the best option when inclusiveness is regarded as the goal.

'Scaling up' mini-public deliberations: Macro design choices

Despite some very encouraging examples (for example, Warren and Pearse 2008; Gastil and Knobloch 2012), the experience of mini-publics may, in many respects, look rather disappointing, considering the great interest of political theorists and scientists in these practices. Some or the most influential practices, such as participatory budgeting in Porto Alegre, are not mini-publics within the meaning adopted in this book; and others are found in non-democratic contexts, such as Chinese cities (Fishkin *et al.* 2010). Goodin and Dryzek's (2006) article already suggested that the impact of mini-publics remains relatively limited. The tendency of analysts to focus on exemplary cases (for example, Smith 2009) can lead to over-estimatation of the impact of mini-publics. So, how could mini-publics best be organised in order to fulfil their potential for enhancing the quality of the deliberative system?

As we have argued before, one major challenge relates to the internal workings of mini-publics; another challenge relates to their broader effects. Mini-publics can be considered as practices that aim to bring about 'enlightened' or considered public opinion. The questions remain of what is the role of this kind of technique in the macro processes of public debate and policy-making and how it relates to those institutions where decisions are actually made. These questions can be approached from the perspective of both normative political theory and empirical political science. Normative theorists typically sketch situations in which the use of mini-publics would be desirable, especially by defining the types of political problems to be addressed by mini-publics.

It has been suggested that deliberative mini-publics should be used to overcome the problems of complexity of policy-making and the problems of democracy that follow from the increasing need for supra-national governance (Dahl 1989). Mini-publics have been suggested as a remedy for the problems of underdeveloped or polarised public opinion (Fishkin 2009; Luskin *et al.* 2014). Mini-publics and other forms of deliberative citizen participation have been called for on constitutional issues and other issues of great social importance (Ackerman and Fishkin 2002). Moreover, mini-publics have been considered as a possible remedy for public distrust in policy-makers. Mini-publics are especially needed when elected representatives have vested interests in the matter at hand, such as proposals for electoral reform (Thompson 2008).

There are some promising examples of mini-publics being used in situations described by democratic theorists. The Citizens' Assembly in British Columbia was a thoroughly studied and documented process during which a proposal for a new electoral system was drafted in a process of citizen deliberation. The proposal was then submitted to a referendum in which a clear majority of voters (57.7 per cent) accepted it. However, due to a special majority requirement in the referendum, the process did not lead to an electoral reform (Warren and Pearse 2008). More recently, Oregon has institutionalised the process of so-called Citizens' Initiative Review (CIR) in which citizen panels evaluate and provide voting recommendations on citizens' initiatives before they are submitted to a referendum (Gastil and Knobloch 2011).

The decision to organise a deliberative mini-public is usually made top-down, which means that policy-makers, typically civil servants and public officials or, in few cases, elected representatives, call for a mini-public on specific issue. There are a variety of motivations behind mini-publics and the actual practice of mini-publics often looks quite different from the vision of political theorists. It has been suggested that deliberative mini-publics are sometimes used for strategic reasons, such as strengthening the position of policy-makers or promoting their political agenda (Parkinson 2004). In this respect, the practice of mini-publics resembles government-initiated referendums (Setälä 2011).

Moreover, new forms of governance, especially at the transnational level, may further increase the need for new forms of representation and claims of democratic legitimacy. Carolyn Hendriks (2009) has described new forms of network governance as 'a democratic soup'. In the context of governance networks at the transnational and other levels, mini-publics can be regarded as a means of legitimising policy-making processes through claims of inclusiveness and representation. However, although mini-publics can enhance the inclusion of different social perspectives, they do not involve similar mechanisms of the accountability of representatives as traditional institutions of representative democracy.

Mini-publics may turn out to be convenient from the perspective of policy-makers because they do not necessarily limit their room for manoeuvreing. Mini-publics allow policy-makers to 'cherry-pick' those recommendations and ideas which best suit their own political agenda. It must be pointed out that this kind of 'cherry-picking' may not be a result of a conscious strategy but rather of ways in which people tend to process political information. As has Parkinson has pointed out (2004), those who actually make political decisions do not engage in deliberation in mini-publics. Therefore, they are not necessarily willing or able to follow the most important rationales which mini-public deliberations come up with. These kinds of issues emerge whenever the resolutions formulated by a mini-public are simply distributed among policy-makers, which was the case in the Danish practice of consensus conferences. The situation is likely to become somewhat better if policy-makers are, for example, expected to respond publicly to the recommendations of mini-publics.

Despite the aforementioned problems, there may also be too much cynicism about the use of mini-publics in policy-making. Deliberative mini-publics have sometimes been perceived as purely technocratic tools, 'stripping off' their emancipatory functions (*see* Bevir and Ansari 2012). But if recommendations for mini-publics are taken up into the design of policies and better align them with citizen preferences, technocratic intentions may actually serve democratic purposes. Moreover, political actors may also want make use of the 'cognitive diversity' of citizens and profit from the 'wisdom of crowds' (Landemore 2013).

There is some empirical evidence from Switzerland showing that political authorities in Swiss municipalities perceive that deliberative mini-publics have provided them with novel insights and new ideas. Stutz's (2013) study suggests that deliberative mini-publics are used either for obtaining better information about citizens' preferences (in the sense of a sophisticated feedback mechanism) or to approach the goals and agendas of political actors and citizens. Especially in the context of Swiss direct democracy, detailed knowledge of the reasoning and rationales of ordinary citizens may indeed be essential for designing policies in such a way that makes them winners in a direct democratic vote. More generally, in order to understand the impact of mini-publics, attention must be paid to the interaction of mini-publics with those institutions which actually make political decisions and with the public at large.

Dahl suggested some years ago that mini-demoi should be used in the preparation of laws in the context of representative institutions (1989: 340). There is a lot of 'division of labour' in legislative procedures and much of the deliberative work related to legislation is delegated to committees, which, in addition to elected representatives, may include representatives and stakeholders. Deliberative mini-publics could be seen as a stage in the process of preparing laws and they could be used in the same way as these preparatory committees. If mini-publics are to be used as a part of the legislative process, particular attention should be paid to the procedures applied in mini-publics as well as to the interaction between mini-publics and those actually legislating. In this scenario, mini-publics could be used as preparatory or consultative bodies in representative democracies. Later on, we consider the possibility of actually giving them powers to make decisions.

A central issue of the macro design of mini-publics pertains to how they are initiated and how their agenda is set. The current practice, in which mini-publics are used on an *ad hoc* basis on issues decided by policy-makers themselves, may be considered problematic in certain respects. Regardless of whether policy-makers are elected or not, they are likely to be reluctant to organise deliberative mini-publics if they suspect that the resolutions of mini-publics might challenge their own positions. There are some ways to escape this problem. One way would be to pre-define the types of issues on which mini-publics are required. Following the suggestions made by democratic theorists, these could include technically and morally complex issues, constitutional issues or issues involving the vested interests of representatives, such as electoral laws. Another way to remedy this problem would be to establish procedures that allow a certain number of citizens to demand the organisation of a deliberative mini-public on a particular issue. The third possibility, already suggested by Dahl (1989: 341), would be to establish a mini-public to define the issues to be discussed by other mini-publics.

A related question is whether mini-publics should concentrate only on one issue at the time or whether they should be allowed to deal with several issues. There is an, admittedly small, risk of log-rolling if a mini-public deals with more than one issue. For this reason, it might be recommendable to assign only one issue to each mini-public, apart from situations in which issues are clearly non-separable (Lacy and Niou 2000). Dahl (1989: 340) describes the organisation of mini-populi as follows: 'One mini-populus could decide on the agenda of issues, while another might concern itself with a major issue. Thus one mini-populus could exist for each major issue on the agenda'. The structure described by Dahl would address the above-mentioned problems of agenda-setting and the possibility of log-rolling when using deliberative mini-publics.

Cristina Lafont (2014) has recently pointed out the 'normative dilemma' that emerges when mini-publics are supposed to play a decisive role in public policy-making: the implementation of mini-publics' policy recommendations would either be superfluous or illegitimate. They are superfluous if mini-publics mainly close the knowledge gap between experts and citizens; then politicians could ask experts straight away to enhance the epistemic quality of public policies. Earlier we have shown that mini-publics can provide valuable insights into citizens' preferences for policy-makers, especially if they have institutional incentives to observe them.

This leaves us with the question whether swift uptake of mini-publics' recommendations would be illegitimate, as Lafont argues. In particular, Fishkin has characterised Deliberative Polls® as an instrument representing an 'enlightened' public opinion as opposed to the 'raw' opinions of the general public (Dahl 1989: 340; Fishkin 2003). This means that the large group of non-deliberating citizens may (or in Fishkin's interpretation, should) not have the same opinions as the small group of deliberating citizens after the deliberative event. The implementation of the 'enlightened' will of the people might thus be an illegitimate move in the democratic process.

To some extent, the legitimacy problem pointed out by Lafont is similar to the one that can emerge between citizens and elected representatives. Based on their better access to information and opportunities to deliberate, representatives may claim to have more 'enlightened' preferences than citizens. However, citizens' relationship to elected representatives is different from their relationship to 'citizen representatives' in mini-publics because the former can be held accountable at elections whereas the latter cannot. Indeed, the legitimacy problem pointed out by Lafont may be the main reason why it may not be possible to provide mini-publics with powers to make actual decisions in the context of representative democracies.

The outcomes of deliberative mini-publics may be in conflict not only with the opinions of the group of non-deliberating citizens but also with those of elected representatives. Mini-publics could thus potentially undermine the legitimacy of representative institutions if these two end up making completely different policy recommendations. However, disputes on the question of who gets it right may not be worthwhile because all processes of deliberation are necessarily path-dependent (Goodin 2009: 111–14). Instead, it would be more productive to develop patterns of communication between mini-publics and elected representatives. Following Goodin (2009: 118–19), the focus in these communications should be on the reasons given for and against different policy alternatives.

The role of mini-publics in the policy-making process could thus be strengthened by introducing transparent and public interaction and communication between mini-publics and policy-makers. Spokespersons of mini-publics could be publicly heard in elected representative bodies; or, alternatively, elected representatives could be publicly heard in mini-publics. This kind of interaction would encourage elected representatives and other policy-makers to make public their reasons to support particular policies. In fact, mini-publics could be considered as a stage of processes of 'reiterated' deliberations and as a means to enhance deliberative accountability (*cf.* Gutmann and Thompson 1996: 137–44). Different forms of transparent and public communication between mini-publics and policy-makers can be expected to enhance communicative rationality in processes of public decision-making.

An alternative way of understanding the impact of mini-publics is to consider their impact on public-opinion-formation more generally. Of course, one might asked whether this is necessary in the first place. If democratic deliberation is primarily thought as a process of making informed and reasonable public decisions, there is a need for a 'division of labour' in the democratic system and 'scaling up' in this sense may not even be considered necessary. However, from the systemic perspective, it seems that, in some situations, the public at large should not only trust in decision-making but should also reflect on the reasons justifying decisions or, in some cases, should actually get involved in public decision-making. From this perspective, it seems relevant to ask how, exactly, deliberative mini-publics could interact with the public at large. In most cases, deliberative mini-publics have not received much publicity at all – this seems to be the case especially in small-N mini-publics that are used as consultative bodies in policy-making.

It remains debatable how much of an impact mini-publics have had on people's opinions even in cases that have received much attention (*see*, for example, Goodin 2012). The first precondition for mini-publics to make an impact is public awareness of their existence. There is some evidence of public awareness of some high-profile Deliberative Polls® that were organised in conjunction with referendum campaigns (Fishkin 2003). Public awareness may be regarded as a necessary but by no means sufficient condition for mini-publics to make an impact, however. Most importantly, the basic idea of mini-publics, which emphasise reasoning processes, may be quite alien to the mass media; therefore the prospects of enhancing the impact of deliberative mini-publics through media coverage may be limited.

In this volume, Niemeyer criticised the idea that deliberative mini-publics should be regarded as trusted sources of information and he argues that people should not just trust but, at least to some extent, 'simulate' the processes of reasoning in mini-publics. Similar concerns have been raised by Lafont (2014), who argues that mere trust may not be good enough for non-deliberating citizens to defer to a mini-public recommendation. However, we argue that, from a more empirical perspective, the use of properly designed mini-publics as trusted sources of information is an important possibility.

It is well established in political psychology that political parties and other interest groups provide voters with cues and help them to approximate their more informed preferences (for example, Lupia and McCubbins 1998). In Switzerland, for instance, booklets containing information on parliamentary proceedings (distribution of votes) and relevant pro and con arguments are distributed to voters before popular votes. In the more contestatory contexts of majoritarian democracies, mini-publics could be used to articulate the relevant pro and con arguments related to a particular policy, without these arguments being automatically associated with certain parties or interest groups. A central idea in the case of the Citizens' Assembly in British Columbia was to use a deliberative mini-public as a 'trusted information proxy' in the referendum campaign (Warren and Pearse 2008). A similar rationale is followed in case of the Citizens' Initiative Review, used in Oregon, where reasoned voting recommendations on popular initiatives are formulated by a mini-public and distributed to voters (Gastil and Knobloch 2011).

In other words, we think that mini-publics could provide an important cue for decision-making for non-deliberating citizens. Deliberative mini-publics could counteract the effects of frames and motivated reasoning that people apply in the context of 'normal', partisan politics. This is pointed out by Calvert and Warren, who analyse in Chapter Twelve of this volume how mini-publics could counteract the harmful effects of framing. Moreover, studies on motivated reasoning show that citizens' political opinions are affected by their attitudes and affections towards partisan political actors (for example, Slothuus and de Vreese 2010). Mini-publics do not usually involve partisan shortcuts, which may encourage citizens to focus on political arguments. Therefore, it might be expected that mini-publics would help to stimulate more reflective attitudes towards political arguments, although this hypothesis requires empirical testing.

If mini-publics are expected to enhance not just 'trust-based' but also 'argument-based' approaches among citizens, the biggest issue pertains to how the reasoning processes of mini-publics are communicated to the wider public. In the case of the Citizens' Initiative Review in Oregon, as we have pointed out above, reasoned voting recommendations are distributed to the electorate (Gastil and Knobloch 2012). However, as in the parliamentary arena, this kind of a one-way communication may not be optimal because it is open to various biases in how people process and interpret political information. Another, yet more demanding, possibility would be the combination of mini-public deliberations and public hearings, an experiment that was tried in the Citizens' Assembly in British

Columbia (Warren and Pearse 2008). This kind of communication between a mini-public and public at large would naturally require deeper and more long-standing commitment by the members of a mini-public.

Another way in which mini-publics might influence the public sphere has to do with the 'side-effects' of mini-publics, that is, their capacity to enhance participants' civic skills. There is some empirical evidence on the capacity of deliberative mini-publics to enhance participants' political knowledge, capacity to understand different viewpoints and other skills needed in political participation (Andersen and Hansen 2007; Grönlund et al. 2010). However, improved capacities for processing political information and facing disagreement concern only that small fraction of the whole population that actually participates in deliberative mini-publics and, in this respect, the positive impact of mini-publics seems to be very limited. However, if mini-publics were made an established practice and larger parts of the population participated in them, they might have a stronger impact on civic culture.

The use of deliberative mini-publics cannot be, as such, an alternative to representative democracy. Quoting Dahl (1989: 340) we see 'the institution of the mini-populus [...] not as a substitute for legislative bodies but as a complement'. Even though electoral democracy will continue to form the basis of representative government, changes in character of political issues, forms of governance and citizens' political behaviour call for institutional reforms (cf. Warren 2003). In order to enhance the role of mini-publics in policy-making processes, we recommend institutionalisation of their use and the development of forms of public communication between mini-publics and elected representatives and other policy-makers. In the context of transnational governance, mini-publics could have an even larger role. The lacuna of representative democracy in transnational contexts calls for creative ideas for new forms of democracy. Carefully designed and implemented deliberative mini-publics with clearly defined roles in decision-making are, according to our view, an alternative worth pursuing.

In conclusion, the era of deliberative mini-publics is yet to begin. Deliberative mini-publics can enrich democratic governance only if appropriate (and scientifically tested) micro design choices align with a full consideration of the macro challenges in the democratic system.

References

Ackerman, B. and Fishkin, J. S. (2002) 'Deliberation day', *Journal of Political Philosophy* 10 (2): 129–52.

Andersen, V. N. and Hansen, K. M. (2007) 'How deliberation makes better citizens: the Danish Deliberative Poll on the Euro', *European Journal of Political Research* 46: 531–56.

Austen-Smith, D. and Feddersen, T. J. (2006) 'Deliberation, preference uncertainty, and voting rules', *American Political Science Review* 100 (2): 209–17.

Baccaro, L., Bächtiger A. and Deville, M. (2013) *Deliberating the Boundaries of the Demos: Evidence from two experiments with citizens*, mimeo.

Bächtiger, A. (2011) *Deliberation in Swiss Direct Democracy: A field experiment on the expulsion initiative*, report, Switzerland: National Centre of Competence in Research.

Bächtiger, A., Niemeyer, S., Neblo, M., Steenbergen, M. R. and Steiner, J. (2010) 'Disentangling diversity in deliberative democracy: competing theories, their empirical blind-spots, and complementarities', *Journal of Political Philosophy* 18 (1): 32–63.

Barber, B. (1984) *Strong Democracy: Participatory democracy for a new age,* Berkeley, CA: University of California Press.

Bevir, M. and Ansari N. (2012) 'Should deliberative democrats eschew modernist social science?', paper presented at the annual meeting of the Western Political Science Association, 22–24 March 2012, Portland, Oregon.

Brown, M. B. (2006) 'Survey article: citizen panels and the concept of representation', *Journal of Political Philosophy* 14: 203–25.

Chong, D. and Druckman, J. N. (2007) 'Framing theory', *Annual Review of Political Science* 10, 103–26.

Curato, N. and Niemeyer, S. J. 'Appreciative and contestatory inquiry in deliberative forums: can group hugs be dangerous?' paper presented at the conference Deliberative Democracy in Action, Åbo Akademi University, June 2012.

Curato, N., Niemeyer S., and Dryzek J. S. (2013) 'Appreciative and contestatory inquiry in deliberative forums: can groups hugs be dangerous?', *Critical Policy Studies* 7: 1–17.

Dahl, R. (1989) *Democracy and its Critics*, New Haven, CT: Yale University Press.

Derenne, B. (2012) *G1000 Final Report: Democratic innovation in practice*, Legal deposit D-2012–8490–09, Brussels: G1000 DOI: 10.1111/j.1467–9248.2012.01005.x.

Dryzek, J. S. (2010) *Foundations and Frontiers of Deliberative Governance*, Oxford: Oxford University Press.

Dryzek, J. and Niemeyer, S. (2008) 'Discursive representation', *American Political Science Review* 102 (4): 481–93.

Esterling, K. M., Neblo, M. A. and Lazer, D. M. J. (2011) 'Means, motive, and opportunity in becoming informed about politics: a deliberative field experiment with members of Congress and their constituents', *Public Opinion Quarterly* 75 (3): 483–503.

Estlund, D. (1997) 'Beyond fairness and deliberation: the epistemic dimension of democratic authority' in J. Bohman and W. Rehg (eds) *Deliberative Democracy*, Cambridge, MA: MIT Press.

Farrar, C., Fishkin, J., Green, D., List, C., Luskin, R. and Levy Paluck, E. (2010) 'Disaggregating deliberation's effects: an experiment within a deliberative political', *British Journal of Political Science* 40: 333–47.

Fishkin, J. S. (1995) *The Voice of the People: Public opinion and democracy*, New Haven, CT: Yale University Press.

—   (2003) 'Consulting the public through Deliberative Polling', *Journal of Policy Analysis and Management* 22: 128–33.

—   (2009) *When the People Speak: Deliberative democracy and public consultation*, Oxford: Oxford University Press.

Fishkin, J. S., He, B., Luskin, R. C. and Siu, A. (2010) 'Deliberative democracy in an unlikely place: deliberative polling in China', *British Journal of Political Science* 40 (1): 435–48.

Fung, A. (2003) 'Survey article: Recipes for public spheres: eight institutional design choices and their consequences', *Journal of Political Philosophy* II (3): 338–67.

Gastil, J. and Knobloch, K. (2013) *Evaluation report to the Oregon state legislature on the 2010 Oregon Citizens' Initiative Review*, Department of Communication, University of Washington.

Gerber, M., Bächtiger, A. and Shikano, S. (2012) Deliberative abilities of ordinary citizens. Evidence from a transnational Deliberative Poll (Europolis), Mimeo.

Göritz, A. S. (2004), 'Recruitment for online access panels', *International Journal of Market Research* 46: 411–25.

Goodin, R. E. (2009) *Innovating Democracy: Democratic theory and practice after the deliberative turn*, Oxford: Oxford University Press.

—   (2012) 'How can deliberative democracy get a grip?', *Political Quarterly* 83 (4): 806–11.

Goodin, R. E. and Dryzek, J. S. (2006) 'Deliberative impacts: the macro-political uptake of mini-publics', *Politics & Society* 34 (2): 219–44.

Grönlund, K., Setälä, M. and Herne, K. (2010) 'Deliberation and civic virtue: lessons from a citizen deliberation experiment', *European Political Science Review* 2 (1): 95–117.

Gutmann, A. and Thompson, D. (1996) *Democracy and Disagreement*, Harvard: Belknap Press.

Hendriks, C. (2006) 'When the forum meets interest politics: strategic uses of public deliberation, *Politics and Society*, 34 (4): 571–602.

—   (2009) 'The democratic soup: mixed meanings of political representation in governance networks', *Governance* 22 (4): 689–715.

Himmelroos, S. (2011) 'Democratically speaking – Can citizen deliberation be considered reasoned and inclusive?', paper presented at the ECPR Joint Sessions of Workshops, St. Gallen, April 2011.

James, M. R. (2008) 'Descriptive representation in citizen assemblies', in M. E.

Warren and H. Pearse (eds) *Designing Deliberative Democracy: The British Columbia Citizens' Assembly*, Cambridge: Cambridge University Press.

Karpowitz, C. F., Mendelberg, T. and Shaker, L. (2012) 'Gender inequality in deliberative participation', *American Political Science Review* 106 (3): 533–447.

Karpowitz, C. F., Raphael, C. and Hammond, A. S. (2009) 'Deliberative democracy and inequality: two cheers for enclave deliberation among the disempowered', *Politics & Society* 37: 576–615.

Klein, M. (2012) 'Enabling large-scale deliberation using attention-mediation metrics', *Computer Supported Cooperative Work* 21 (4–5): 449–73.

Lacy, D. and Niou, E. M. S. (2000) 'A problem with referendums', *Journal of Theoretical Politics* 12 (1): 5–31.

Lafont, C. (2014) 'Deliberation, participation and democratic legitimacy: should deliberative minipublics shape public policy?', forthcoming, *Journal of Political Philosophy.*

Landemore, H. (2013) 'Deliberation, cognitive diversity, and democratic inclusiveness: an epistemic argument for the random selection of representatives', *Synthese* 190 (7): 1209–1231.

List, C., Luskin, R. C., Fishkin, J. S. and McLean, I. (2013) 'Deliberation, single-peakedness, and the possibility of meaningful democracy: evidence from deliberative polls', *Journal of Politics* 75 (1): 80–95.

Lupia, A. and McCubbins, M. D. (1998) *The Democratic Dilemma: Can citizens learn what they need to know?*, Cambridge: Cambridge University Press.

Luskin, R. C., Fishkin, J. S. and Jowell, R. (2002) 'Considered opinions: deliberative polling in Britain', *British Journal of Political Science* 32 (3): 455–87.

Luskin, R. C., O'Flynn, I., Fishkin, J. S. and Russell, D. (2014) 'Deliberating across deep divides', *Political Studies* 62 (1).

Mansbridge, J. 'The deliberative system disaggregated', paper presented at the Annual Meeting of the American Political Science Association, Washington DC, September 2010.

Mansbridge, J., Bohman, J., Chambers, S., Estlund, D., Føllesdal, A., Fung, A., Lafont, C., Manin, B. and Martí, J. L. (2010) 'The place of self-interest and the role of power in deliberative democracy', *Journal of Political Philosophy* 18 (1): 64–100.

Mathis, J. (2011) 'Deliberation with evidence', *American Political Science Review* 105 (3): 516–29.

McGann, A. (2006) *The Logic of Democracy: Reconciling equality, deliberation, and minority protection*, Ann Arbor: University of Michigan Press.

Mendelberg, T. (2002) 'The deliberative citizen: theory and evidence', *Political Decision Making, Deliberation and Participation* 6: 151–93.

Mendelberg, T. and Karpowitz, C. (2007) 'How people deliberate about justice: groups, gender, and decision rules', in S. Rosenberg (ed.) *Deliberation, Participation and Democracy*, Palgrave: Basingstoke.

Mercier, H. and Landemore, H. (2012) 'Reasoning is for arguing: understanding the successes and failures of deliberation', *Political Psychology* 33 (2): 243–58.

Parkinson, J. (2004) 'Why deliberate? The encounter between deliberation and new public managers', *Public Administration* 82 (2) 377–95.

Price, V. and Capella, J. N. (2002) 'Online deliberation and its influence: the electronic dialogue project in campaign 2000', *IT & Society* 1 (1): 303–2.

Saffon, M. P. and Urbinati, N. (2013) 'Procedural democracy, the bulwark of equal liberty', *Political Theory* 41 (3): 441–81.

Sanders, D. (2012) 'The effects of deliberative polling in an EU-wide experiment: five mechanisms in search of an explanation', *British Journal of Political Science* 4 2(3): 617–640.

Schweiger, D. M., Sandberg, W. R. and Ragan, J. W. (1986) 'Group approaches for improving strategic decision making: a comparative analysis of dialectical inquiry, devil's advocacy, and consensus', *Academy of Management Journal* 29 (1): 51–7.

Setälä, M. (2011) 'The role of deliberative mini-publics in democratic systems: lessons from the experience of referendums', *Representation* 47 (2): 201–13.

Setälä, M., Grönlund, K. and Herne, K. (2010) 'Citizen deliberation on nuclear power: a comparison of two decision-making methods', *Political Studies* 4: 688–714.

Siu, A. (2009) *Look Who's Talking: Examining social influence, opinion change, and argument quality in deliberation*, PhD dissertation, Stanford University.

Slothuus, R. and de Vreese, C. H. (2010) 'Political parties, motivated reasoning, and issue framing effects', *Journal of Politics* 72 (3): 630–45.

Smith, G. (2009) *Democratic Innovations: Designing institutions for citizen participation*, Cambridge: Cambridge University Press.

Stutz, M. (2013) *Deliberationsverfahren in Schweizer Gemeinden: Gründe und Auswirkungen. Eine Analyse des Kantons Aargau*, BA Thesis, University of Lucerne.

Thompson, D. F. (2008) 'Deliberative democratic theory and empirical political science', *Annual Review of Political Science* 11: 497–520.

Warren, M. E. (2003) 'A second transformation of democracy?', in B. E. Cain, R. J. Dalton and S. E. Scarrow (eds) *Democracy Transformed? Expanding political opportunities in advanced industrial democracies*, Oxford: Oxford University Press, pp. 223–49.

— (2007) 'Institutionalizing deliberative democracy', in S. Rosenberg (ed.) *Deliberation, Participation and Democracy: Can the people govern?*, London: Palgrave-Macmillan.

Warren, M. E. and Pearse, H. (2008) *Designing Deliberative Democracy: The British Columbia Citizens' Assembly*, Cambridge: Cambridge University Press.

Young, I. M. (2000) *Inclusion and Democracy*, Oxford: Oxford University Press.

Index

CPSIA information can be obtained
at www.ICGtesting.com
Printed in the USA
LVHW051621301221
707553LV00004B/100